MARKETING RESEARCH:
A MANAGEMENT OVERVIEW

CONTRIBUTORS

Louis J. Babic, Jr.
Joseph C. Bevis
Louis Cohen
Emanuel Demby
George W. Dick
Stephens Dietz
Thomas A. Ehrhart
George Gallup
Norton Garfinkle
Peter Langhoff
Alcuin W. Lehman
Walter P. Margulies
Arthur C. Nielsen, Jr.
Alfred Politz
Herbert W. Robinson
Horace S. Schwerin
Daniel Starch
Russell S. Tate, Jr.
Elmo C. Wilson

EDITORS

Evelyn Konrad
Rod Erickson

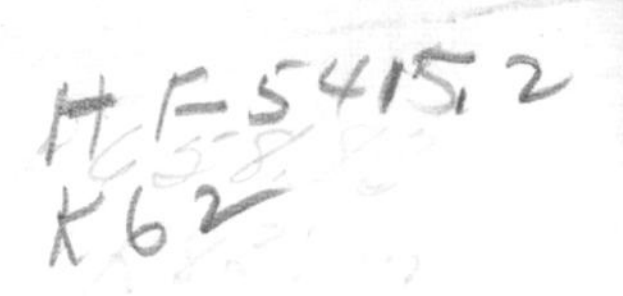

MARKETING RESEARCH: A MANAGEMENT OVERVIEW

AMERICAN MANAGEMENT ASSOCIATION

NEW YORK

This book has been distributed without charge to AMA members enrolled in the Marketing Division. Those members who are enrolled in other divisions, or who wish extra copies, may order the book in a hardcover edition at $6 per copy. Price to nonmembers, $9.

Library of Congress catalog card number: 66-27859

PREFACE

- WHAT PRODUCTS will consumers want to buy from us two or three years from now?
- How much investment capital should we allocate to restyling and retooling?
- What do our customers and the consumers think of our products and our company, and what policies will favorably precondition our marketplace?
- Will a diversification merger that we are considering strengthen us in the financial community, or may it raise doubts about our top management's competence in the new area?
- How much advertising support should we give to our various brands, and what kind of sales appeal should be stressed in each case?
- Which combination of media will give us the maximum exposure with the specific target audience in the right context?

These questions are merely a handful of the hundreds of questions facing corporate management in the normal course of conducting business. Their sole common denominator: diverse forms of marketing research can help to provide the rationale for sound decision making in each of these many areas.

When management is aware of the far-reaching impact that these decisions have upon the corporation, it becomes obvious that responsibility for the decision-making tools cannot be blithely delegated to research specialists, regardless of these researchers' professional competence. It is not only that the stakes are large—and the long-range effects of the decisions nearly immeasurable. The need for management sophistication about marketing research, as a decision-making tool, also reflects this truism: sound decisions can only result when all the component parts of the decision-making process are fully understood and can be evaluated by the decision maker in the proper perspective.

Does this truism imply that management should become research specialists? Obviously, this would be an unrealistic recommendation. It does mean, however, that management today must have sufficient awareness of the developments and possibilities in marketing research in order to anticipate the role of marketing research in specific management decision problems, to evaluate alternatives, to appraise recommendations, and to interpret research results correctly.

Fundamentally, management sophistication about marketing research is a factor of experience. However, such firsthand experience can be so costly—not in terms of the direct research costs, but because of the effect that management's interpretation of the findings may have upon key decisions—that the attempt to precede or supplement direct experience with exposure to marketing research thinking and case histories may be low-cost insurance against glaring errors of commission and omission alike.

It is in this spirit that American Research Bureau in cooperation with the American Management Association initiated the compilation of this up-to-date study of marketing research. This book does not offer a critical evaluation of research methodologies, nor is it intended to provide professional researchers with a map to the labyrinth of research experimentations. For these professionals in the research community this book may be a compact source of current and up-to-date thinking by leading figures in a diversity of marketing research areas; it may also serve as an indication of innovations in these differing research specialties that may be just around the corner.

However, basically this book has been compiled for top and middle corporate management, regardless of previous exposure to marketing research techniques and methodologies, in order to touch upon the multitude of decision-making tools that they can draw on in a broad variety of everyday business problems.

As a member of the marketing research industry, American Research Bureau feels that all sound informational projects designed to lift the mystique from all currently accepted aspects of marketing research should be encouraged and supported by the varying segments of the business community that ultimately have a stake in valid and useful decision-making tools. To date the information gap between the marketing research community and corporate management is still but partially bridged, and the dialogue initiated in this book is a modest beginning when contrasted with the mutual problems of misunderstanding.

The vested interest that management has in cutting across technical jargon and in learning the true function, limitations, and potential of marketing research can hardly be sufficiently stressed. Wrong marketing decisions cited as examples of either faulty research or misuse of correct findings have become clichés in both open and behind-the-door discussions of corporate management and researchers alike.

It may serve little purpose to seek scapegoats in either discredited research approaches or in faulty management interpretations or, for that matter, in management refusal to use marketing research prior to making certain decisions when the findings might or might not have contributed to sounder judgment. There is no doubt, however, that genuine familiarity on the part of all levels of corporate management with the important decision-making tools in the diverse marketing research specialties will inevitably lead to clearer understanding of the functions of marketing research and better use of these tools.

PETER LANGHOFF

EDITORS' NOTE

IN ORDER TO UNDERSTAND FULLY the meaning and importance of marketing research, the management executive who reads and studies this book may wish, first of all, to keep in mind an essential marketing concept which motivates the marketing executive who is the prime user of the data described in this volume. The concept can best be phrased this way: The modern management executive must be consumer- or customer-oriented rather than factory-oriented. He must be aware of the needs, reactions, and motivations of his corporation's marketplace if he is to contribute to the fullest in the long-range maximizing of corporate profits.

This book has been designed to fulfill that specific management objective. It is intended to summarize the best thinking available among the leading professional marketing researchers, whether these executives be in management of specialized research firms, in related businesses such as package design or advertising agency activities, or, indeed, in manufacturers' management.

In developing the contents of this book, the editors have had valuable guidelines about the information needs and interests of the American Management Association's broad, diversified membership from the AMA editorial department, particularly from Jerome W. Blood, editor of membership books. In line with his suggestion, we have avoided a textbook approach, and we have used instead the following definition of our prime area of interest: this book is directly concerned only with the many and varied areas of marketing research entailed in reporting to management on consumer activities, opinions, interests, and motivations.

Of course, this area in itself is probably one of the most diverse aspects of marketing research, since it must reflect probing into the consumer's reaction to the parent company manufacturing a product, the consumer's need for a product, and his exposure to advertising messages concerning this product. Indeed, our goal has been the tracing of the many elements of specialized marketing research which can and should be applied to understanding the development of a salable product or service from the time of the product's inception or birth through its actual consumption cycle.

There are other areas of marketing research we have excluded from this book. These marketing research activities would not fit into this cradle-to-maturity product concept only because their focus is upon the development of management information not as directly relevant to consumer behavior as the areas we have selected. For example, product pricing, while deeply affected by marketing research, must also take into account such individual-firm economic concepts as marginal costs and marginal revenue, which may either balance or outweigh the marketing research findings. Another aspect of marketing research—sales forecasting—also has ramifications beyond consumer behavior, such as the weighing of investment capital expenditures for future production capacity (plant expansion and the acquisition of machinery and personnel), so that its relevance to the consumer is indirect and long-range.

What are the logical areas of marketing research as we have defined it? We include *opinion research* intended to play back to management attitudes in the corporation's marketplace about any aspect of the corporate entity or corporate activities that may have a direct impact on the sale of the firm's products or services.

Product concept research to determine the real or imagined need for a new product is a vital part of consumer research, useful in guiding the corporation's R&D effort.

Once the product has been produced or is scheduled for production, a crucial information need is satisfied by diverse *packaging research* techniques.

As the product reaches the market, the manufacturer buys a diversity of *flow-of-goods measurements* to answer his questions about consumer buying cycles and his brand's competitive share of the market.

Since virtually all consumer products today are sold under individual brand names, advertising is a crucial component of the marketing mix. *Media research* answers the advertiser's questions about the audience to his sales message via the diverse advertising media. These include, of course, national media, from magazines to network TV and network radio, and basically local media, ranging from newspapers and outdoor to spot TV and spot radio as distinguished from network.

Perhaps the most complex aspect of marketing research is *advertising-effectiveness research*. Here the advertiser and his agency try to find out not merely how many people may have been potentially exposed to the sales message in the diverse media, but also how persuasively this message may have penetrated the consumer's mind and how effectively it may be motivating this consumer to buy his product or services.

In brief, we have taken our own definition of the marketing man's motto as our guideline. This definition of marketing research is exclusively confined to those areas of information gathering which weigh consumer attitudes or behavior.

Ultimately this book has been designed to report the status today of the marketing research industry as defined and to open up the dialogue between this industry and the corporate management of the future.

Now that we have completed our task, we both want to express our special gratitude to Ann Zeleny of Evelyn Konrad Public Relations, who gave to this project not only many hours of work and thought, but also her infinite patience.

EVELYN KONRAD
ROD ERICKSON

CONTENTS

MARKETING RESEARCH:
A MANAGEMENT OVERVIEW

SECTION I

THE BROADER VIEW OF MARKETING RESEARCH •

IN THE MID-SIXTIES marketing research has accounted for expenditures ranging from a low estimate of $200 million to a high of $450 million a year. The most recent available data seem to indicate that the high figure may be a conservative estimate for planned marketing research volume and expenditures in 1967. Current trends in corporate management philosophy as well as in the research industry itself seem to indicate that the half-billion dollar volume predicted for 1967 may merely herald the modest beginnings of the most research-conscious era in American management history.

Certainly in sheer dollar volume alone, marketing research has been one of the fastest growing sectors of service industry in this decade. But despite the obvious and undisputed growth of marketing research, these rapidly spiraling annual volumes do not come into focus without a parallel appraisal of related management activities. The figures may well reflect the vigor and continuously increasing importance of this infant industry with its modest origin in the twenties and thirties and its real growth in the postwar economy. Yet they cannot be evaluated with any perspective until they are viewed in their dollar relationship to other factors in the marketing mix.

For example, even a half-billion dollars begins to look meager in relationship to the more than $16 billion advertising expenditures forecast for 1967. When the $500 million marketing research volume is split into the multiplicity of diverse research and information activities that the totality of marketing research comprises today, the figures don't look nearly so large. Actually, a surprising percentage of the total dollar volume in marketing research comes from activities that are not directly related to advertising at all and which, therefore, make less meaningful the contrast in annual volume that management puts into marketing research as compared with the dollars spent on advertising.

However, this game of management arithmetic can lead to some interesting findings:

- Management spends less than $.035 on marketing research for every dollar put into advertising.
- When advertising research is broken out of the total marketing research volume, this ratio is reduced to something less than $.01 spent in this area of research for every dollar spent in advertising.
- Lastly, when this small ratio of research to a key component of the marketing mix is contrasted with other management costs, such as the cost of pensions or annuities, it becomes apparent that dollar volume may not be the most meaningful measure of the importance of marketing research in the economy today.

The question of the corporate image. All marketing research starts with a basic question from top management: "Will this new product be profitable?" In the past the question was answered by experienced and intuitive marketing executives. In the present, the question is answered by intensive depth research, a fund of knowledge accumulated over the past years, and computers which have been programmed to anticipate such management questions.

Most managements think of research as pertaining to frequently purchased consumer items in the food or drug field. This is an unnecessary limitation. Research today can supply the answers to any questions, starting with those concerning the corporate image. The impact of the corporate image affects the profit-and-loss statement of every executive in management, the sale of stock, and the confidence the company inspires in customer and stockholder alike. The corporate image inevitably relates to the sales effort of the company. An introduction of a new product is almost always supported by the corporate image.

Before going into any detailed examination of research, the corporation must first understand itself. Management should list a number of basic questions. In order to formulate these questions, management must fully understand the impression made by corporate identity design and research and must formulate a policy that suits the corporate goals and reflects responsiveness to the firm's specific needs to communicate with the diversity of its publics.

It is important to realize, first of all, the basic fact that every company organized to do business, whether in a manufacturing or service industry, has a corporate image from the day it opens its doors for doing business throughout its existence and frequently lingering long past the time when it may finally liquidate its assets or even merge into another or larger corporate entity. This image is the sum total of impressions that all the firm's varying publics have of the corporation, and these publics include not only the customers of the firm or consumers of its products, not only its stockholders and employees, but also the general public which may come in contact with the corporate name through the signage of the firm's delivery trucks or of its plants. In brief, a corporation cannot avoid making an impression; it can, however, help shape the impression that will be formed.

The term "corporate identity," which claims many originators, may well have been coined within the industrial design industry, since it refers to all the visual contact which a corporation has with the public. This visual contact may begin with the corporate name and include the factory signage previously mentioned, but it extends as well to letterheads, employee uniforms, company literature, brand naming, package design, and advertising.

It is in the latter three components of the marketing mix that corporations, particularly among the top 100 advertisers, sometimes disagree on the components of the most effective policy. We are referring here to corporate endorsement of product lines.

On the one extreme, historically, there is the school which holds with the Campbell Soup Company's strong endorsement policy, where company and brand name are identical. This policy at Campbell's was modified to some extent as a result of the diversification mergers which added to the corporate product line such nonsoup brands as the Pepperidge Farm and Franco-American lines, among others. However, the basic philosophy can be summed up this way: the addition of the corporation name to the individual brand package lends a strong corporate endorsement intended to build consumer confidence and capitalize upon the strength of the familiar name. By the same token, say the proponents of this marketing school, each successful brand carrying the corporate name further strengthens the name and impact and reputation of the parent company.

On the opposite pole in this marketing dichotomy is the General Motors and Procter & Gamble school which in effect considers individual brands autonomous in the marketing sense, expecting each to justify its life cycle through its profit-and-loss performance and, indeed, encouraging competition between their own brands. While P&G was once considered a classic example along with General Motors of this "nonendorsement" school, the fierce competition for shelf space and consumer attention and the spiraling costs of media combined to modify this traditional view. Today even P&G lends a form of corporate endorsement to any new brand launched by this soap giant, at least during a six-month introductory period.

Between the extremes of these opposing philosophies lie the multitude of U.S. companies in diverse industries which practice corporate endorsement of some products and services while allowing others—perhaps those more remote from the accepted competence of the parent company—to stand alone on their own name and identification.

Prior to formulating and establishing an overall policy, corporate management is well advised to research the state of its corporate identity and reputation to find out whether the impression or image that its diverse publics have of the corporation—its size, its diverse activities, its characteristics, personality, and impact upon the community—are a reflection of the way management views the corporation or would like to see it understood. No image is static. Indeed, sophisticated corporations engage research specialists who do periodic "image audits" to gauge whether the combined corporate policies—in financial, marketing, industrial relations, and other areas of corporate interest—are producing the desired effects.

The genesis of all research lies in the corporation itself. If the corporation is strong and has a clear image, the odds are that the products the corporation plans will be successful, all things being equal. Without a clear corporate image that is accepted by the consumer as a symbol of quality, no corporation can be successful.

The importance of the package. Obviously a key factor in reinforcing the company's identity in the mind of the consumer is the package. Incredible though it may seem to those in modern marketing, for many years one of the most primitive areas of marketing research was package design. Even today, some companies employ a staff artist or use local artists who pay no regard to the psychological impact of color, lettering, brand name, appealing illustration, and other factors which, in a self-service supermarket, result in an instant impulse purchase. Add to these factors the necessity of complying with increasing Government regulations, legal restrictions, and warnings, the need for notations of weight and ingredients, and in some cases the need to add major advertising claims, and the complexity of the research job becomes evident. The advertiser certainly faces difficulties which cannot be handled by an amateur, even though the amateur may be a talented artist as such.

Because of the complexities of Government regulations and other factors in package design a new segment of the marketing research industry has grown up within package design firms. Originally, the firm of Raymond Loewy, for example, was noted for its ability to develop a new approach to package design. The purpose of each new design was to call consumers' attention to the whole product line. Later in the evolutionary development of such design companies, psychologists were added to their staffs and experiments were begun with color, type face, and reproduction of photographs on boxes; differing weight and quality of boxes under various marketing conditions; reaction of boxes to moisture, heat, cold, and shipment over long distances; shelf life and kitchen life; and may other factors that today are taken for granted.

Design firms now examine and analyze product problems from concept to consumption and present solutions. Nor are these solutions limited to the packaging of products. Design firms now offer an entity of design in a corporate cradle-to-grave sense. It includes the logo, the stationery, the stock certificates, the symbols on the trucks, and advertising and packaging symbols, to the extent that a proper design has continuity far and beyond the original marketing concept. In other words, corporate identity reaches out to the consumer through all phases of the company's life.

The purpose of all this exercise is to force the selection of the product in a self-service supermarket, discount house, or drug store—in all of the emporiums where self-help is a way of life. Needless to point out, self-service accounts for the bulk of consumer purchases today and is a growing custom in American marketing. For these reasons, no knowledgeable marketer today will introduce a new product, or tolerate senility of design in an older product, without engaging the attention of experts.

There are many design companies available to advertisers today. Many are schisms of larger companies; many have been started by bright young artists coming out of colleges and universities who have taken courses in subjects pertinent to the total design. One noteworthy design company is Lippincott & Margulies. Others include Sandgren & Murtha, Walter Dorwin Teague Associates, and Raymond Loewy-William Snaith, to mention just a few.

It is essential that any corporate executive looking for a design house examine not only the large ones but many of the younger ones. Lists of these are easily obtained by referral, through advertising agencies or the Industrial Design Institute. Incentives to search in depth for the right man and the right product are the high cost of design and the higher cost of errors. A large design house can represent an extremely large investment in out-of-pocket cost. Smaller design houses, however, have done satisfactory work for a fraction of the cost.

In addition to the industrial design companies, there are advertising agencies that also have a total package design service available to their clients and sometimes to nonclients. There is no question that this is a growing field, and more sophisticated methods are only beginning to be employed.

* * *

This section therefore sets the stage for later, more detailed discussions of particular marketing research problems by considering management's need for research and the uses that are being found, increasingly, for its findings.

A look at the extent, nature, and growing potential of the industry is followed by a sampling of some of the basic questions facing manufacturers to which marketing research is providing satisfactory answers. One company which specializes in answering such basic questions is the Opinion Research Corporation, of Princeton, New Jersey. Its experience encompasses all types of corporations and all types of corporate questions. A number of examples are reported here by its chairman of the board. (While some corporations have their own research departments, most supplement staff research by buying specially tailored research from ORC or from a number of other marketing and opinion research firms, including Social Research, Incorporated, Daniel Yankelovich, Incorporated, and John F. Kraft, Incorporated, among others.)

Package research of course has the answer to many of management's questions—including the strengthening of an established brand, the launching of a new one, or even the introduction of a completely new product. For this reason we conclude with a survey, by a competent authority, of the very special role of package research in the overall context of marketing—or consumer—research.

Marketing Research and Management Decision Making •

EVELYN KONRAD

In terms of its reach and impact upon both U.S. industry as a whole and on the American consumer, marketing research is unquestionably and without qualification the single most influential service activity—well beyond what the dollar measurement suggests. How does marketing research affect the American consumer in his everyday life? It is essential to analyze this influence if one is to understand the marketing research function today.

Let us briefly summarize all the levels of decision making which affect the consumer and which are today based on some form or another of marketing research. They include the very concept of a new product or service (whether there is a consumer demand or need for such a product or service); the form and shape that this product or service should take; the patterns of distribution that will be most effective for reaching its market. Marketing research is also a factor in the product or service pricing structure. It is used to determine the name of the product as well as its packaging; and this consumer research approach to "packaging" applies to the selling of service as well—for example, the service that a bank, insurance company, or brokerage house may offer. In brief, there is a vast amount of marketing research that is conducted during the period when corporate management decides that it might like to add to its line of products and services and the time when R&D puts the thoughts on the drawing board—long before the product actually reaches the consumer.

The function of marketing research in bringing the product or service to the consumer through advertising is a more familiar one. It encompasses all forms of test marketing and advertising-effectiveness research, including copy platform and media schedules (readership and radio-TV audience measurements), shelf counts, and other audits seeking to establish the flow of goods from the manufacturer to a buyer or consumer.

In the corporate structure marketing research has become a management decision-making tool that involves not only the marketing research technicians and professionals in the corporation. Because of the vast dollar expenditures based upon marketing research findings, it is today a function that must be understood by both middle management, ranging from product managers to marketing and advertising directors, and top management, including president, executive committee, and financial men—in brief, all those members of top corporate management who are directly responsible for the profitability of the corporation. To illustrate this point, let us simply realize that even decisions on mergers and acquisitions more often than not take into account such marketing-researched questions as the following:

- Does the company's image in the consumer's mind encompass the new products to be acquired through acquisition or merger?
- Can new products or services to be acquired through merger or acquisition be distributed through the company's existing channels of distribution?
- Will the new lines to be acquired through purchase or merger strengthen or dilute the corporate image for the existing lines?
- Should all lines produced by the merged entity be marketed under a single corporate umbrella or under the concept of marketing competing brands?
- Can the costs of marketing additional lines be amortized through a unified advertising approach? (This is a serious consideration in this era of staggering media costs.)

Is marketing research answering management's information needs today? A look at the diversity of services and techniques available would seem to indicate that it is. However, a deeper probing into the structure of this segment of service industry and into the management philosophy and organizational problems which prevail today raises some questions.

Like other segments of the service field, marketing research is more responsive than creative. This seeming indictment of service business in general and marketing research in particular refers not to the substance of the marketing research product but to the marketing research industry's appraisal and definition of management's information needs. This appraisal and definition is a reflection of organizational patterns within the corporations that are the key buyers of marketing research data rather than an attempt to initiate trends by anticipating the changes which may become inevitable in these management organizations as the information explosion gathers momentum.

This dichotomy becomes apparent in the split between varying corporate staff functions and corporate line functions. For example, even in those corporations whose activities are entirely based on manufacturing and marketing mass consumer products, the marketing responsibility is rarely represented at the top corporate level. Furthermore, by tradition and in response to obsolete needs, the marketing and financial-accounting functions are separated.

The marketing research industry is therefore structured to address itself to highly specialized problems within the marketing mix rather than taking the more progressive view that it is part of a total information service which, in order fully to answer the staggering information needs of top corporate management, must leave behind some of its parochialism and learn to transcend the jargon-ridden world of the technician in exchange for a more management-geared orientation.

These observations may seem esoteric until their practical implications are put under scrutiny. By taking a parochial and, perhaps on some scores, an inevitably specialized view of their research function, the variety of independent marketing research companies are continually selling to specialized counterparts in the corporate structure. Also, they are vying with each other, competing for a share of a total and sometimes somewhat arbitrary corporate or brand marketing research budget. In brief, a specialist in packaging research may find himself fighting for dollars that had been assigned to a motivational study of consumer attitudes; the firm offering a valuable research postanalysis of an advertiser's spot TV campaign may be bucking a research dollar shortage due to previous spontaneous allocation of budgets to pre-planning research. While competition is, of course, recognized as a basic stimulus to the economy and to industry, it seems in marketing research to be an obstacle to the development of comprehensive marketing research planning and programs.

It's hard to say who is to blame for this fratricidal competition—corporate management or the research firms' management. But as management of mass-distributed products in particular becomes more conscious of marketing research—a trend reflected by the vast increases in marketing research staffing among the leaders of the top 100 advertisers—it seems inevitable that budgets will reflect the need for a greater diversity of research activities. The question which will then face the independent research firm will be this basic problem: whether to build growth on an ever increasing share of the budget for more and more specialized services or whether to view their previous area of specialized expertise as part of a broader information complex more representative of marketing management information needs.

Some indications that the latter view may be the pattern of the future are only beginning to loom on this industry's horizon. While it was once possible for a brilliant young research expert with a new wrinkle or insight to open up shop in a phone booth with a good list of free-lance field staffs, the era of the computer may be writing an end to this frontier of individual enterprise. Not that the door is totally shut on inventiveness. Indeed, one researcher did switch in this decade from being an advertising agency research director to owning a syndicated research service with a growing agency client list. His success might seem to indicate that the opportunities are better than ever, but such a conclusion would be misleading.

The era of the small new enterprise financed on a shoestring is more a symptom of the past than such isolated recent successes might indicate. Indeed, the current pattern of mergers between long-established research companies and computer service firms is far more indicative of the pressures of these times upon the marketing research industry.

The first such merger occurred in 1961 when C-E-I-R acquired the American Research Bureau, a leading TV-ratings supplier. This year alone, however, two other comparable computer firm-research firm mergers have taken place so far: Computer Sciences Corporation bought Alfred Politz Research, Incorporated, and Computer Applications, Incorporated, bought W. R. Simmons & Associates. Audits and Surveys Company, a post-World War II challenger of the Nielsen Food & Drug Index, made a mid-1966 deal with Time Incorporated for its computerized warehouse tape information retrieval system—another proof that marketing research companies must plunge knee-deep into the computer age if they are to prosper and indeed survive.

For the computer service companies themselves, the apparent advantages of buying or merging with marketing research firms are twofold. When these mergers involve major syndicated research firms, the computer company is, in effect, buying a key customer. Furthermore, in a business where the software is often expensive to develop, difficult to understand, and harder to sell without considerable lead time, such mergers are providing the computer firm with a tangible, visible, and easier-to-understand end product.

The computer itself is having a twofold impact within the marketing research industry. By its ability to digest marketing research findings at the interpretive stage with a previously unheard-of speed, it inevitably whets the appetite of marketing and top corporate management for risk-lessening data. At the same time, the "computer to computer" psychology which was inevitable is creating pressure upon most segments of the marketing research industry to add computer capacity and facilities to their basic research methodology. This computer fever has not yet become rampant among those marketing research firms whose activities are basically in the area of specially designed and tailor-made studies. However, it is a truth of the marketing research industry, as it is of product manufacturing, that the assembly-line data producers will inherit the world. Even today, it is the firm with the syndicated research service—the philosophic counterpart of the assembly-line manufacturer—which accounts for the bulk of the research volume in terms of revenue.

One such pressure is the fact that research sophistication within major corporations is becoming more the truth than a mere catchword. The professionals, both on corporate staffs and within agencies, are no longer impressed with new concepts and techniques. The vast dollar stakes implicit not only in the high cost of the marketing research services themselves but, even more so, in the high cost of wrong decisions force expensive validations of research techniques and methodology. In a business whose conclusions are based on statistics and sampling processes, such validations frequently require elaborate cross-checks of different sample populations and expensive attempts to duplicate near-laboratory conditions which, in the behavioral sciences, are, of course, more an objective than a feasible reality.

Various trends within the corporate structure will affect the marketing research industry within this decade. Several key patterns have emerged in the early sixties which differ more in their manifestations than in their cause. The cause is management's realization that marketing research has a direct and often startling impact on the corporate profit and loss statement. To cite an obvious example, few companies could afford to live through repeated Edsel failures.

This fact—the direct relationship, certainly within mass consumer product manufacturing companies, between marketing decisions and corporate profits—has not yet produced the inevitable integration between marketing and financial functions on the corporation level. It has, however, been a key reason why major consumer goods manufacturers have wrested away marketing decisions from advertising agencies—where they had been briefly and uncomfortably lodged in the late fifties—and brought them closer and closer to the corporate management decision level.

The by-product of this change in management philosophy has been an almost desperate staffing of marketing research departments within such corporations. Indeed, many major advertising agencies that added expensive overhead in the late fifties in order to offer this then popular research counseling capacity are beginning to feel the pinch. While the advertisers' own talent search in this specialized area has siphoned off a number of executives previously in agency ranks, there is nonetheless a growing gap between the amount of overhead agencies still carry in this function and the amount of billing and activities they can attribute to it.

The marketing research director of one of the top five advertising agencies in worldwide billing puts it this way:

> Advertisers have taken on marketing and marketing research responsibilities that they should never have passed along to the agencies in the first place. From that viewpoint, the present trend among clients to staff up for the sake of developing their own marketing plans on sound research bases is a salutary plan.
>
> However, the inevitable by-product is a lack of assignments in agency research departments which is just about the liveliest topic of concern among agency marketing research directors today.

This man's observations are echoed by his counterparts in the majority of leading advertising agencies, some of which justify their department budgets by making a valid but costly point: an agency must be closely involved with the advertiser's marketing and research planning activities in order to plan the advertising function in the proper context.

However, for agency management with its profit and loss responsibilities, the depth of agency involvement in marketing must eventually be proportionate to revenue. If the commission system of agency compensation begins to give way to fees, it may become more difficult for agencies to justify marketing research staffing unless the salaries of these executives are charged directly to the client rather than being considered as the cost of a service arm to account management. On the other hand, the struggle for client compensation for marketing and marketing research activities is an old one in agency history, preceding the changes in compensation patterns. It is reported, for example, that heavy-spending advertisers such as Colgate, Procter & Gamble, and Lever always demanded substantial marketing research services as part of a complete agency service without paying additional research fees. This was balanced in their thinking by the substantial agency commission on network TV packages which required only nominal supervision.

The advertising agencies' lessened marketing research and marketing planning responsibilities will have a longer-range effect on client-agency relations than the immediate dollar income, however. It has long been understood by advertising agency management that the closer it could bring the agency into the market planning function, the tighter its hold on the advertising account. This hold is being weakened today, not only by the advertisers' increasing assumption of those marketing planning and marketing research functions which most agency research directors acknowledge to be part of the client's corporate responsibilities, but also through advertiser encroachment on an area that has previously been a stronghold of agency research strength—advertising research.

A survey of leading advertisers and advertising agencies revealed conflicting viewpoints. "This is a function which we must control and which properly belongs within the agency," agency research directors agree. And advertisers' research men are equally adamant on the other side of the argument: "It is absurd to think that the agency should through this function be the judge of its own performance. In effect, advertising research is a policing function that properly belongs in the advertiser's hands."

While the theoretical argument continues, the facts certainly indicate that advertisers are moving deeper and deeper into the area of advertising effectiveness research and, indeed, into a position of greater influence upon media research decisions with all the inevitable implications for media control.

Since both advertisers and agencies are currently buyers of marketing research, this struggle for control of the function is not going unnoticed by the marketing research industry. To some extent, the effect is healthy in that the broadened interest in the research function as a whole has definitely increased the size of the market for such service. One obvious result, for example, has been an increase in research underwritten by the leaders among the diverse media. A negative by-product, strangely enough, is a greater concentration of research decisions among a smaller number of men, as preferences within the marketing research units of a handful of advertisers determine the media and advertising research services to be used by a large number of these advertisers' multiple agencies.

As to the final outcome of the power struggle on the advertiser's side—certainly among the top 100 largest-spending companies—the remainder of this decade will see a continuation of the trend toward deeper involvement in both marketing and advertising research. Since management has seen and understood the tremendous dollar implications of marketing research findings and decisions, it is unlikely that management will soon delegate responsibility for this function in its entirety to any outside source, whether it be the advertising agency, management consultants, computer service organizations with programming strength, or, for that matter, the independent research services themselves. Rather, it is likely that many of the marketing research services will soon find their trained and professional counterparts on the staffs of the leading U.S. corporations with a stake in the mass market.

However, the influence of marketing research upon marketing, advertising, and management decisions makes it unlikely that advertising agencies will forgo the availability of staff marketing research completely. Even if the advertiser dictates the choice of the service to be used or is involved in this choice, certainly no major intermediaries such as advertising agencies, marketing consultants, or package designers can afford to be without their own experts in these areas—if only in answer to a peculiarly American management syndrome of professionals requiring their counterparts to speak to in all problem areas.

For the marketing research industry itself, this trend, if properly understood, may open up some new areas of opportunity. Despite the growing specialization of marketing research services, advertisers' interest in the diversity of these functions may open the door to more generalists—more marketing research services with answers to a greater diversity of research problems. After all, on the advertiser's side, the man who has the final say on the research criteria to be used for media decisions may be the same man who determines the budget and selects the store audit service at one end of the spectrum and the packaging research at the other end.

Unfortunately, the marketing research companies are not structured to take advantage of these changing patterns in management thinking and the changing research needs of the era. The problem, not surprisingly, is to a large extent one of money. To a lesser but equally meaningful degree, the obstacle facing marketing research firms as new needs arise is firmly entrenched in their own management thinking.

To a surprising extent the marketing research industry is still a first-generation business. This means that the same men who may have had a creative insight into the marketing process and a certain research technology are for the most part still the same ones with the managerial responsibilities in the majority of the research firms, and they are therefore wedded to concepts developed one or more decades ago. On the whole, the marketing research business has not yet outgrown the prima donna and the personality cult—equating this segment of service industry with creatively dominated businesses such as advertising agencies, architectural firms, and industrial design firms rather than with established, organization-oriented segments of service industry such as insurance and banking. In brief, professional management concepts have not yet made major inroads within the marketing research companies.

Since marketing research straddles an uncomfortable fence between art form and science, and since the marketplace itself has more thirst for innovation than discipline about sound criteria, multimillion-dollar stakes in research billing can shift from one competitor to another on the basis of minute improvements in archaic technology rather than on the basis of a new overall concept.

This indictment may sound severe unless it is probed in some depth. A review of the area of marketing research that produces the highest revenue will give some indication of the peculiar inertia within the marketing research business where truly new thinking is concerned. This relatively unchanged area is, of course, the entire field of reporting on the movement of mass consumer goods from the factory to the buyer. The greatest need in this area is for a predictive rather than a historic research service that would not only provide the manufacturer with raw purchasing data but would combine it with "reason why" information which would make it possible for the manufacturer to alter his marketing strategy in immediate response to the findings. Such data are unavailable today. What advertisers buy in its place is a diversity of accurate, historic records based on store audits. Without denying the importance of such point-of-sale-based information, the question arises of why the basic technology in this area has remained substantially unchanged since it was pioneered by the A. C. Nielsen Company in the early thirties. True, a diversity of expansions, refinements, and reporting improvements, as well as interpretations and depth analyses, have been added to the basic data, partly in response to a true marketing need and partly, of course, in response to competition from new services ranging from established companies such as Market Research Corporation of America and Audits & Surveys to relative newcomers like Ehrhart-Babic. But will a truly revolutionary new concept addressing itself to the needs of today's marketing in this particular area come from these expert sources?

It would be unfair to make a negative prediction, but unrealistic to assume any such new concept. A look at the economics of the marketing research business will provide an answer. Take for example the Nielsen Company, the undisputed giant in this reporting area with its Food & Drug Index, which has a $30 million-plus annual stake in the existing service. It may be unfair to single out this company from its colleagues in marketing research, but the point that must be made can be illustrated by citing the typical problem facing this research company management as it does the management of other research firms with their varying specialties: to discard an existing and profit-making research service with a good record in an established market for a speculative new service that may well undermine the established money maker is akin to expecting Detroit to retool for drastically new models on a year-to-year basis. The capital investment required by the marketing research companies for such drastic remodeling is considerable. The market demand may be there, but who is willing to finance it?

This problem, however, is basic not only to the future prosperity of the marketing research companies but to the potential validity and importance of marketing research as a management decision tool. It is responsible for the vicious cycle of research fads which prevails today and which, unfortunately, siphons off and absorbs the time of potentially creative researchers with an interest in management and marketing decision needs.

The awareness of the need for broader-scope marketing research thinking is neither new nor original. Indeed, some thought-provoking comments on this subject were made at the Fiftieth American Marketing Association Conference in New York in June 1965 by A. S. C. Ehrenberg, director of Aske Research, Ltd. in London, who said:

> Research companies do not know how to charge for general research, and thus continue in their narrow fact-gathering or survey-mongering ways, or at best try to provide direct "solutions" (however pseudo) to isolated "problems."
>
> Advertising agencies are still largely devoid of advertising research techniques of known validity or usefulness and seem therefore mostly to have recourse to research as a gimmick.
>
> Manufacturers' marketing and research personnel tend to side defensively with their agencies and research companies, instead of saying to their own managements: "We don't know anything, our agencies and research companies know less—let us have some funds for basic research. Here are some examples of how basic research works and pays off in the marketing field.

If it is the minutiae of research technology—indeed, the gimmickry of it—which dominates the activity and thinking of research management today, the blame must be shared by those who either buy the multitude of services or affect the buying decision. These buyers, even in the recent past, have rarely been sufficiently knowledgeable in this art-science form themselves to make their judgments purely on the basis of the problem-solving merits of the service, but rather have made them on the basis of the fashionable, safe choice. Again, ultimate responsibility comes to roost with top corporate management, which all too often assumes that a Ph.D. degree is a guarantee of objective insights without necessarily trying to determine in what field of specialization the degree was earned and what background and knowledge it might indicate. Unfortunately, there is no consumer's guide to help management in its choices of research service, and the stress is therefore upon judgment. But judgment can be exercised only when it is based on fact, and it is a peculiar truth of marketing research today that the facts about the validity and value of individual research services are nearly as confusing and controversial among the research professionals as they must seem to the management executives who have the ultimate responsibility for making wise choices.

What is the solution to this quandary, if any? And what may be the answers to this problem in the remainder of this decade? Greater familiarity with marketing research in its present state is essential on all levels of management, whether the individual executive is directly involved with marketing research decisions or not. It is essential that fact be substituted for mystique if better planning and thinking are to lift this budding young industry to a new maturity.

In this age of conflicting pressures upon management philosophies, a greater awareness of the broad-scope uses for marketing research may add fuel to a controversy about management organization that could come to a head in the near future. This controversy is based upon the now mutually exclusive needs for greater specialization at even higher decision levels, on the one hand, contrasted with the growing need for sophisticated top-echelon generalists on the other hand. Put more simply, this is the current problem: Can a financial officer satisfactorily fulfill his responsibilities without an understanding of marketing and its tools in this competitive era? Can a marketing man fulfill his corporate responsibilities without a full grasp of the profit and financial results implicit in his activities?

This cross-fertilization concept has the broadest implications for marketing research, which—despite the present segmentation and specialization of the business—so obviously bridges both functions in terms of the decisions which it influences. It can therefore never be stressed too much that the management executive who is strongly motivated to insure his own continued progress must be alert to the present state of marketing research, not only in order to understand a basic and growing decision tool, but also in order to understand the drastically new patterns likely to develop in this area during the crucial remainder of this decade.

Some recent comments by marketing research directors of major advertisers and of top advertising agencies help to give perspective and dimension to the views about marketing research that prevail within the marketing and advertising community today. The leading advertisers—particularly in the food and soap fields which dominate the mass consumer markets—are assuming increasing control of data gathering to the point of designing and interpreting much of their own research and frequently commissioning the field work rather than the creative aspects of marketing research. The director of marketing research for one of the large food companies puts it this way: "Research is so complex that interpretation from the research people themselves is necessary for its proper use. We tend to buy the data-collecting process from the outside."

The associate manager of marketing research for a soap giant points out that the company's own research staff gathers answers directly from the consumer. While the firm does buy answers "partially" from outside research sources, he adds, "our research department is responsible for accurate data gathering and presentation. Statistical interpretation is also done by the research department, but the creative interpretation is done by the operating brand group."

Out of 26 leaders among the top 120 advertisers who were recently polled by the American Research Bureau to determine their corporate research philosophies, 25 answered that they both conduct and interpret their own research, while 16 of these 25 added that they also buy answers from outside research services but interpret them for management. In defining the function of the marketing and research department, 13 of the 26 respondents answered that going out and getting answers directly from the consumers was part of their responsibility.

The philosophic premises for the assignment of responsibility to the corporate marketing research departments are not as established as the premises for corporate advertising departments, and therefore, there are greater variations in the interpretation of department responsibilities. However, there are a significant number of marketing research directors in major companies who take much the same view of their department's function as most corporate advertising directors. In brief, they see themselves as having not so much a "go out and do" mandate but the job of setting policy and creative guidelines. One of these men, the director of consumer research for a major proprietary drug advertiser, sums up his department philosophy this way:

> Each [research] job is billed directly to a brand; we feel this helps get better involvement from the product managers and means most findings are definitely used. By having outside research firms do all our work, we im-

prove problem definition and get more objective analyses and recommendations.

This view, of course, parallels the way most sophisticated advertisers today work with their advertising agencies—ideally in harmony rather than conflict with staff advertising departments, and with the intent of getting maximum contributions from the outsiders. The corporate planning and research director of a household paper product company echoes this way of thinking: "We buy available service data and interpret internally; for projects we use research firms, audit objectives and procedures, and participate in the interpretation of findings."

While this seems to be the prevailing interpretation of the corporate research department function, and while it may well be the philosophy that will eventually dominate among the majority of major advertisers, the continuing tendency to grasp as much control as possible internally may be attributable in part to the newness of full-fledged marketing research departments in so many major companies. It may also be a reflection of the specialized approaches sold by outside services and the lack of interdisciplinary informal exchanges between them. It is the latter that may be leading the corporate marketing research director into the temptation of designing his own approach to answer specific needs.

In its depth interviews with selected marketing research leaders among advertisers and agencies, American Research Bureau also sought to find out what current developments in consumer research seemed to be considered most significant by this professional community in helping to market products. The following cross section of commentary may shed a little light on the priorities in marketing research thinking today:

> "Increasing ability to segment consumer markets, identify and understand needs of consumers for existing brands and new products."—*Director of marketing research for a major tobacco company*

> "Increase in capacity and versatility of computers, permitting a greater quantity of analyses and the use of more sophisticated analytical techniques."—*Marketing research executive of a leading soap company*

> "Appraising potential of new products—both our own and competitors'."—*President of a large food company*

> "First, subscription to syndicated surveys of advertising awareness and brand attitudes. Second, improved quality and reliability of field interviewing procedures, i.e., 'control interviewing' techniques."—*Marketing research manager of a pharmaceutical products advertiser*

> "First, simplified techniques for behavioral measures of initial and longer-

term product acceptance. Second, realization that the DAGMAR approach to advertising research can be effective despite concern over its truth value." —*Director of marketing research for a food products advertiser*

"First, concept generation and testing techniques; secondly, pretesting of advertising quality on a routine basis."—*Corporate planning executive for a paper products manufacturing company*

"Brand attitude, awareness and experience studies in connection with market testing new brands."—*Manager of marketing research for another tobacco leader*

"Creative groups working with focus sessions ('preresearch research') in idea and concept screening. Not new—but new to us."—*Director of marketing for a cosmetics firm*

"The development of consistent research programs for brands. The gradual improvement of advertising research methods and their application."—*Marketing vice president of a competitive drug and cosmetics firm*

"The use of switching brand behavior to help determine consumer target groups more precisely."—*Director of marketing research services of a paper products leader*

"First, studies conducted by our staff in the areas of promotions and product use. Second, specific media advertisement impact studies and our overall company image and ad impact study contracted to research firms. Third, continuing work in distribution studies of specific markets and our facilities within these markets."—*Corporate planning executive of a major rubber and tire company*

"The continuing development of computer technology which permits analyses of voluminous data and simulation of marketing behavior."—*Manager of marketing and consumer research for an oil giant*

Among the advertising agency marketing research directors interviewed for this study the predominant concern was with individual advertiser, agency, and research company attempts to measure the effectiveness of advertising. This emphasis is, of course, not surprising since the role of advertising agencies has never before been studied, reviewed, and scrutinized as thoroughly by agency clients as it has during this decade. Indeed, advertising effectiveness research, in the view of outspoken leaders on both the agency and the advertiser side, will continue to be the battleground for research control between these differing segments of the research industry. As might be expected, corporate marketing research directors consider this an essential policing function of the advertiser over his agency, while agency research directors consider it the *sine qua non* of their own operation. Upon deeper probing, both sides in this controversy agree that the other has an irrefutable stake in this relatively untested research area.

The view of the majority of agency marketing research executives may well be summarized in these answers from the research vice president of one of the largest advertising agencies, frequently in the limelight for its creativity. Asked, "What are the most difficult problems, in your view, in advertising research and/or marketing research today?" he answered:

> First, pretesting of advertising for effectiveness. None of the current techniques get at the real heart of the problem: persuasibility of advertising under cumulative impact of advertising or actual sales effectiveness of the advertisement or campaign.
>
> Second, how much advertising—in terms of frequency of exposures, or quality of exposures—is sufficient for a unit of effectiveness (however one defines it).

The basic conclusions emerging from interviews and discussions with marketing research leaders point out once again the growing importance of marketing research in the management decision-making process today. Key trends that management will have to contend with in the balance of this decade are the following:

- An increasing avalanche of statistical data will become available to decision makers.
- Increased and greatly diversified computer usage will add to the pressure for more information, but will also help to sift out and make meaningful combinations without the preponderance of facts and figures.
- The complexion of outside marketing research services available as sources of data may change more drastically during the remainder of this decade than during any comparable previous time as pressures for new combinations of data and spiraling costs of developing and computerizing this information make an impact on the present competitive scene.
- Above all, as the diverse management disciplines and sciences continue to take hold in U.S. corporate life, it is likely to become imperative rather than optional for the management executive of tomorrow to be conversant and knowledgeable about the research techniques available to him in his decision-making process.

Supplying Research Answers to Management's Questions •

JOSEPH C. BEVIS

THE RAPID ADVANCE of marketing research in the corporate scheme is often tallied in statistics of size—the number of newly established marketing research departments and the swelling membership of the professional societies.

Such massiveness is impressive but is no more significant, in my opinion, than the rising level of management expectations. Policy-making executives are tossing their toughest questions at marketing research and asking for reliable intelligence to help them gauge the probable effects of their decisions.

Many of these assignments have an obvious here-and-now urgency: Should we launch the new product in test markets? Will we feature theme *A* or theme *B* in the fall campaign? What special incentives for salesmen will spark the best effort? But the planning pointed two, three, or five years ahead can take on equal urgency in management's eyes. For with the accelerated pace of change, the decisions on what markets to go into and whether to manufacture or buy must be ironed out now in order for the future target dates to be met.

The following examples illustrate the variety of problems that executives present to market researchers and some approaches and techniques that have proved useful in Opinion Research Corporation's experience.

Is our image among our industrial customers pulling its weight? The major purpose of one corporate reputation study, undertaken by a leading manufacturer of glass specialties, was to point ways for improving its basic marketing strategy, with the focus on customer service.

Personal interviews with executives and purchasing agents of major industrial customers disclosed that the company's products enjoyed an unsurpassed reputation for quality. At the same time, not many customers were familiar with the entire product line, and a number voiced resentment over what they regarded as company indifference to their service requests.

On the basis of the research findings, the company (1) changed the corporate advertising program to feature its wide product line, (2) enlarged and revamped its selling and servicing procedures for major accounts, (3) expanded the role of its technical support staff, and (4) strengthened account handling procedures for the sales territories that showed up weakest.

Is our new product ready for launching into test markets? The costliest way to make new product mistakes is by trial and error within distribution channels. Well-planned pretests not only can reduce financial risks but, on the positive side, will sometimes save a potentially profitable product from premature death because of consumer refusal to buy.

The following is a case example. The research laboratories of a major food producer came up with a radically new product based on a revolutionary freezing process. A consumer in-use test was decided upon. Samples were placed in homes to obtain consumers' reactions to the packaging, preparation in the kitchen, and flavor. The result was a quite unexpected reaction. The package was approved and the flavor liked, but the appearance of the product as it was taken from the package was revolting (some said it looked like dog food). Subsequently, the appearance problem was solved. Tests showed that consumer acceptance of the product as a main dish meal was high, at a competitive price level. In the end, what prevented market introduction was prohibitive manufacturing cost.

Pretests, of course, are not infallible. The question inevitably arises, what would happen if a company put a product on the market despite negative pretest results? No one can predict with certainty, but in two cases at least practical experience is sobering. In one instance, a table radio was housed in a distinctive type of cabinet which, in our pretests, consumers rejected as clumsy and nonutilitarian. It was introduced anyway. When the distribution channels had been filled, sales stopped, and the remaining inventory was sold off at a loss.

In the second case, a low-priced vacuum cleaner met with small enthusiasm in the research soundings because it offered nothing different from competing models then on retail counters. Nevertheless, the company put the cleaner on the market. It did not sell and had to be withdrawn.

Should we make or buy? Traditionally this has been answered in terms of supply costs—for manufacturing, shipping, and warehousing. At times, however, an equally important factor is market position at the distribution end.

As a case example, a petroleum company was faced with a decision as to whether it should continue manufacturing tires in a limited number of grades for sale in its service stations or purchase from tire manufacturers in order to supply a full line of grades. A personal interview study was conducted among tire dealers, consumer users of the company's tires, and nonusers. After weighing the marked advantages of offering a full line at the point of sale, the company decided to discontinue manufacturing and market a full line covering all grades offered by major tire companies except their lowest grade.

How can we translate attitudes into consumer behavior? "Too many people vote dry and drink wet." This old saw stands as a constant warning against naive interpretation of attitudinal data. It is never safe to assume that because people subscribe to a broad principle they will apply it in the concrete instance. Our research case book on political behavior is loaded with examples.

Familiar to observers of consumer behavior is the tug-of-war between the ideal of saving money and the temptation to spend. This conflict was illustrated by a study made on behalf of a state association of savings banks.

The association sought guidance for deciding what services should be offered to customers and for advertising and promotion strategy. Depth research among adult residents of metropolitan and suburban areas was conducted by personnel especially trained in depth interviewing techniques, the interviews lasting from one to two hours each. The topic guide was prepared, and the results were analyzed and interpreted by ORC staff psychologists.

Among the key findings were that people extol the virtue of saving and believe thrift should be inculcated in their children at an early age but that a sizable number of adults will not discipline themselves to save just for a rainy day. People need a strong stimulus to save. As a rule, adults derive the most pleasure from, and in practice save most regularly for, the spending of sums saved up for a specific purpose.

The findings were applied in product planning and promotion. New types of "forced" savings accounts, modeled on the Christmas Club, were introduced for summer vacations, travel, down payment on a house, education, and a host of other spending goals.

Is our trademark right? Trademarks convey emotional messages by virtue of their design. In Exhibits 1, 2, and 3 are some of the types shown

MODERN OR ABSTRACT VS. TRADITIONAL OR HERALDIC

Notable Impressions Conveyed	*Modern*	*Traditional*	*Difference*
Modern	80%	13%	67%
Scientific and research-minded	76	16	60
Youthful	73	14	59
Forward looking	74	18	56
Long tradition of reliability	10	85	75
Stable	16	73	57

EXHIBIT 1

SUGGESTED MOTION VS. STATIC OR SYMMETRICAL

Notable Impressions Conveyed	*Suggested Motion*	*Static or Symmetrical*	*Difference*
Exciting	63%	22%	41%
Active	63	27	36
Forward looking	61	27	34
Progressive	60	28	32
Stable	23	63	40
Large company	26	62	36

EXHIBIT 2

to have strong symbolic meaning in our basic study *The Language of Corporate Trademarks and Symbols.*

What the trademark says to consumers may be sharply at odds with what management or the designers intend it to say. Research often provides the only reliable evidence on meaning, especially when the mark must serve to cover a diverse product line.

The following is a case example. Research for a company marketing a broad line of food products disclosed that its existing trademark suggested friendly partnership between the company and the homemaker but in its

FEMININE

Notable Impressions Conveyed	*Masculine*	*Feminine*	*Difference*
Strong or powerful	81%	12%	69%
Men customers	74	14	60
Scientific and research-minded	64	23	41
Warm and friendly	12	78	66
Relaxed and informal	15	72	57
Consumer products	20	69	49
Beautiful or attractive	21	67	46

EXHIBIT 3

associations was too narrowly focused on certain of the company's products and tended to exclude others. A second test among housewives experimented with modifications of the design elements. Definite changes were produced in the connotations (some suggesting products the company did not sell), but still the product coverage was narrow-gauge.

Hence, in search of a mark that would be suited to a broad line of food products and also to nonfood items sold in grocery stores, the research turned to three semiabstract designs, tested in color and black and white with different logotypes. All three projected a broad and positive product image, at the same time registering strong company name identification. One of these designs was adopted and is now actively promoted in the company's TV and print advertising.

Is our sales message getting through to our prospects? Answers to this question, of the substantive sort that can be translated into sales strategy and tactics, frequently require more than measuring the register of key points in the sales message. More fundamentally, are the appeals we use geared to the customer's hopes and expectations? Why do some customers buy and other prospects, who receive the same message, fail to buy? A communication may arouse interest and create emotional tension yet fail of its objective if it does not also provide a comfortable and reassuring way out. This holds particularly true in direct selling.

For example, a manufacturer of do-it-yourself hi-fi assembly kits, sold through direct mail, was interested in increasing the effectiveness of his flyers and catalogs. The company was receiving plenty of inquiries but a disappointing percentage of orders.

The basic scheme of the study made for this company was a comparison of catalog requesters who bought with those who did not. Personal interviews were conducted in eight cities from New England to California, divided equally between buyers and nonbuyers. The inquiry covered anticipated satisfactions from using the product, self-confidence in using it, technical knowledge of the product field, ownership of related product items, and reactions to printed communications. The findings pointed a finger at the culprit: overtechnical descriptions and language. This was no barrier to fans with special technical knowledge, but it scared off the unsophisticated, who criticized the catalogs as hard to read.

On the basis of the research findings new promotional literature was prepared. Technical data were included for those interested, but the copy made it plain that no special knowledge or skill was required for following instructions and completing the job successfully.

To what product users should we point our advertising? Cadillac boasts of high owner loyalty and repeat purchase. However, most sellers in the consumer market must contend with fickle and changeable customers and, hence, maintain an unflagging effort to replace the switchers with new buyers.

A producer of cleaning and polishing products wanted to analyze the user market to reveal what kinds of customers were sticking with their brands and what kinds were deserting to competing brands, for what cleaning tasks.

The survey data were gathered through one of our subsidiaries, ORC Caravan Surveys, which fields a national probability sample quarterly. The study described consumer usage patterns for 18 generic product types, measured brand awareness for the leading sellers in the client's and competitors' lines, and ascertained for the two most recent purchases the buying switches from brand to brand. Accurate identification of the brands was facilitated by exhibiting large photographs of the 31 product packages.

The precision of a national probability sample with call-backs offers special advantages when the researcher needs to measure seasonal changes in usage; changes in consumer favor from year to year and which brands are gaining at the expense of which others; or the effects of specific promotional campaigns, both the client's and competitors'.

Can a distinctive user image help sell our product? In consumer markets particularly, many large-volume brands are virtually indistinguishable so far as the average person can tell by physical examination, taste tests, and the like. Cigarettes are an example.

The market strategist therefore considers the possibility: can we carve out a niche in the market by building a distinctive character for our product in terms of the type of people the public thinks use the product? In other words, can we build a user image that will help sell the product?

What have well-known cigarette brands accomplished going this route? This was the focus of a study commissioned by an advertising agency. The study was made by means of group discussions followed by self-administered questionnaires, involving 500 smokers. Table 1 gives the results for

CIGARETTE BRAND USER IMAGES

A Good Cigarette for:	*Percentage of Identification* *Brand X*	*Brand Y*
Laborers	64	5
Taxi drivers	62	7
Truck drivers	61	7
People who really enjoy smoking	58	20
Poor people	53	18
Lumbermen	52	8
People who never finished grammar school	49	19
Men	46	9
Hard-driving people	46	12
People who get a big kick out of life	44	15
Coal miners	44	16
Prize fighters	43	18
Unmarried people	42	25
People who are powerful	41	18
Cautious people	13	63
Women	28	57
Sissies	13	55
Light smokers	22	55
Doctors	15	52
Socially correct people	19	48
Wealthy people	16	46
Socially respected people	19	46
Religious people	22	46
Old people	23	46
Social climbers	14	44
Intellectuals	13	43

TABLE 1

two brands very much alike—both filter tips and regular (nonmentholated) tobacco. Note that brand *X* is masculine—associated with brawny types in lower class occupations. Brand *Y* is considered feminine—also upper class and older.

These two brands, each in its own segment, have been stand-out marketing successes. There is, however, another side to the story.

The maker of a third cigarette brand (apart from *X* and *Y* above) set out through TV and print advertising to personify its cigarette by creating a distinctive personality—the intelligent, discriminating man who makes up his own mind. A series of checks had shown unusual awareness of the advertising, but sales response was not in keeping.

We were asked to make a full appraisal. Did the audience relate to the featured personality? What was the brand image for this and competing brands? What effect did the advertising have on purchase of the sponsor's cigarettes?

The research disclosed that the projected personality was favorable—a man who planned his life carefully, took things seriously, would be a good neighbor, would be attractive to women. Moreover, the character was seen as a real smoker—who inhaled deeply and had never tried to stop smoking.

Where the advertising apparently missed connection was in establishing a linkage between the personality and the particular brand. People who identified with the personality did not extend this identification to smoking preference for the brand. Among other things, the campaign did not help the smoker resolve the conflict over whether to smoke or not in the face of possible consequences to his health. The campaign subsequently was dropped.

Is our corporate image working hard to support our selling efforts? A strong and favorable reputation can be a real help in many of the company's dealings with government agencies, employees and new recruits, dealers and distributors, and, of course, customers.

Marketing executives are of several minds as to the importance of house reputation in backing product acceptance and how much energy and money should be devoted to building it. There is no longer much question, however, that a favorable image promotes word-of-mouth advertising. The data charted in Exhibit 4 are from our study *The Corporate Image,* based on a national probability sample of 3,629 interviews. Shown are the aggregate results for 12 companies that market consumer goods.

Note that among people who have the least favorable image of the company, only 13 percent have recommended the company's products; among those who have the most favorable image, 54 percent have recom-

CORPORATE IMAGE AND PRODUCT ACCEPTANCE

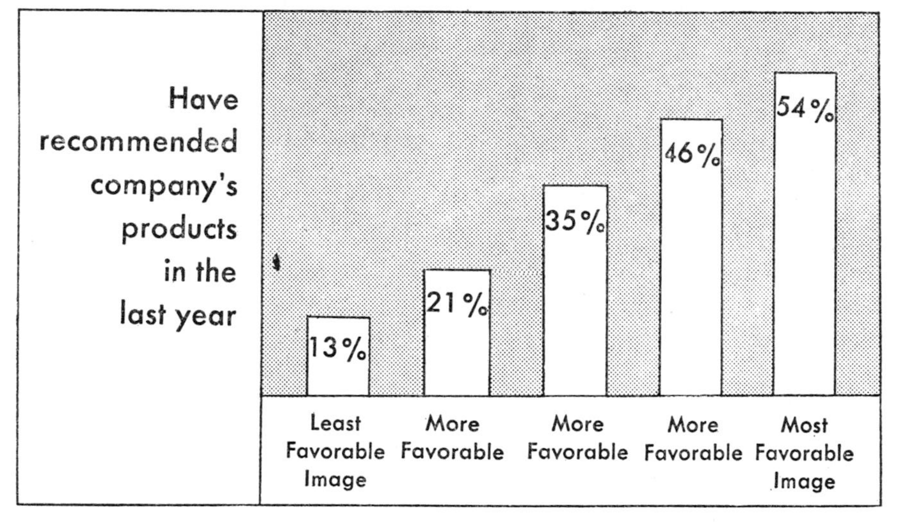

EXHIBIT 4

mended the products. The testimony is from people familiar with the 12 companies.

Some critics look on image building as hocus-pocus, an attempt to create a false front. But as the social scientist defines it, the image we have of something is simply the mental screen through which we filter those aspects important to us—subjective, yes, but the reality to which we react.

Realistic image measurement therefore fastens on what people *think,* not on what someone *wants* them to think. It proceeds on the assumption that the individual alone is competent to say what it is about a company that influences him, for good or ill. Our basic tool is a 50-item image profile derived from exploratory research which dug into how people judge companies, their experiences with them, and their sources of ideas. The item list distilled from the testimony is composed of four sections: the Producer-Distributor Image, the Management-Investment Image, the Corporate Citizen Image, and the Employer Image. The standard 50-item profile offers the user the advantage of ready comparison with other companies in the same industry, with average ratings as norms, and provides a systematic means to measure change at regular intervals, all at the savings effected by joint-operation shared cost. On the other hand, where image determinants are unique for certain industries, as for instance insurance compaines and banks, customized image measurement systems are developed and put to work.

Two generalized findings may be worth noting:

1. Sheer size is no guarantee of a strong public image. Some huge companies are not well known, and some others are known only in a few aspects.
2. A company does not have to be number one in its industry to be recognized. Some medium-sized companies have made their mark in the public's esteem in a relatively short time through aggressive use of mass communications.

What new products are compatible with our present product image? Among the many outspoken advocates of the marketing concept, Theodore Levitt will be remembered for his vigorous attack on managements which lock their thinking into production facilities and refuse to wake up to the challenge of broadening market opportunities.[1] Well and good; the rub for many companies comes in selecting, from among the most promising growth fields, those product lines that best capitalize on the company's existing consumer franchise. Here marketing research comes to the fore as an aid to sound judgment.

As a case example, a manufacturer of shaving products was considering a dozen different new product groups for its next marketing move. From the management's point of view, one of these was clearly superior because of its natural fit with the company's manufacturing skills.

The research was conducted in two phases. Phase one was developmental: hypotheses were formulated and the research instruments and questionnaires were tested. Phase two was quantitative, using probability sampling methods to provide findings projectable to the total American male and female populations.

The findings showed that the product best suited to existing manufacturing skills was not well accepted by consumers as a logical extension of the product family. Some other product types rated much higher in compatibility. Consumers tended to group products according to their end use, not according to the processes involved in manufacturing them.

The client decided on a new product in a high-rated group. The product was introduced and promoted and now is one of the top sellers in its field.

[1] "Marketing Myopia," *Harvard Business Review*, July-August 1960, pp. 45-56.

The Contribution of Package Research •

WALTER P. MARGULIES

THE PROBLEMS WHICH PACKAGE RESEARCH is called upon to solve center about increasing the sales of an established brand, the initiation into the market of a new brand, or, more rarely, the initiation of a new product. In each of these situations package research is used as a marketing technique —usually as an adjunct to package design—a diagnostician of marketing problems to the extent that they involve packaging, an indicator of routes to marketing solutions, but not as a selector of solutions. It is an aid to the reaching of management marketing decisions.

Package research will not insure a brand's success, because packaging by itself cannot offer such insurance. A well-conceived, well-researched, well-executed package will by itself only increase the probability of success. Packaging and its adjunct, package research, can comprise only two segments of a brand's total marketing strategy. They can only work successfully in combination with a clearly conceived goal for the brand, consistent, clearly conceived advertising and promotion, and a pervasively consistent, hard-driving brand management.

USES OF PACKAGE RESEARCH

Package research is most commonly used in four ways: (1) predesign, at the outset of a packaging program; (2) interim design during the design program; (3) postdesign, to test the effectiveness of final candidate designs; and (4) research evaluation of package designs currently operating in the market. It involves far more than merely the testing of current or proposed package designs.

When a new program to increase sales of an established brand is undertaken, it often involves redesign of the existing package. This can be either complete redesign or the refinement of specific components of the present design. The introduction of a new brand, a new product, or a new brand of an existing product always, of course, necessitates the creation of a new design.

The degree to which package research is involved and the types of techniques utilized vary with the type of product, the complexity of the specific problem, and budget availability. In each case the purpose of package research is to aid the designer—not to tell him what he wants to hear, but to help him hear and see factors of which he must be aware if he is to produce the optimum design solution for the problem involved.

Predesign research. Predesign research is becoming an increasingly important factor in marketing strategy. The enormous time- and money-saving advantages of predesign research as an indicator of areas for design exploration are more than evident. It is no longer feared by designers. Their claims that it hampers creativity are becoming less and less audible. It has proved to be no more awesome or stultifying to the designer than the study of consumer motivations has proved inhibiting to the copywriter. It is now evident to the designer that it helps him do faster and far more effectively what he had been attempting to do on his own all along—know his market so that he can effectively communicate with it.

Predesign research broadens the designer's scope of understanding of his audience and brings to this understanding a far greater degree of objectivity. It fills in whatever gaps exist in the information necessary to him if he is effectively to reach his audience. It investigates his audience to a greater degree both in number and in depth than he has either the time or the skill to do. It takes an extensive look into the consumer's motives, attitudes, opinions, beliefs, and biases. It evaluates more of the competition more thoroughly, thereby giving the designer a broader and more insightful idea of the strengths and weaknesses of the competition with which his design will have to contend. It can more thoroughly indicate those product or brand attributes currently conveyed by the brand's present packaging which the new design must aid in eradicating, and those which it should be geared to enhance.

It provides the designer with new insights and with reasons for shifting or retaining his initial ones. But it never designs his package for him. Within a clearly defined marketing context it does, however, free him to be creative.

Interim design research. Some designers also utilize interim design research. Conducted after preliminary design work has been completed, interim design research can be invaluable in correctly deciding the make-up of final candidate designs. It can test the degree to which various design elements contemplated for inclusion are capable of meeting the almost universal criteria of high visibility and high memorability. It can also be used to test the associated imagery of isolated design elements; for example, it can indicate which one of a number of colors or which combination of color and symbol will most effectively project an optimal combination of product-brand attributes.

Postdesign research. After design work has been completed, the leading candidate designs are further evaluated against previously established criteria for the design which will be optimum in terms of the marketing problem involved. Two or three candidates are usually selected as the most promising, and these usually represent varying interpretations of the design criteria. These candidates are subjected to postdesign research, whose task it is to determine the strengths and weaknesses of each, weigh these against each other, and provide valid indications as to which one design possesses the best market potential.

Design re-evaluation. A brand's package is a relatively static identifier designed for long-term use. It must operate, however, in a constantly shifting market. Re-evaluation is employed as a periodic assessment of the efficiency with which a package design is meeting the gradually shifting needs of the market. Based on the results of re-evaluation, small but significant refinements of the design are usually made. This type of research is commonly employed in two market situations: (1) where the product category is saturated with brands and where loyalty to a specific brand or product variety is relatively weak and usually transient, as in the case of cold cereals, detergents, and household cleaners; and (2) where the actually perceivable differences between the individual brands are slight, thus causing its image to be each brand's prime sales determiner, as in the case of cake mixes, instant coffee, beer, and, again, detergents and household cleaners.

TECHNIQUES USED IN PACKAGE RESEARCH

Each package research study is tailored to the specific problem it must diagnose. The research techniques employed for any specific study are selected from a group of basic techniques, and the application of each is based on the principle of expediency. The techniques involved fall into two general groups, those which test physiological responses and those which investigate the psychological.

Physiological techniques. Most of the physiological techniques have been adapted from the laboratories of experimental psychology and transmuted for use in simulated marketing situations. None is completely satisfactory for this purpose, since each is used to gather data concerning isolated reactions to a real object in an artificial situation. Their use is limited to obtaining answers to the following types of questions: Does the package meet the visibility and legibility standards of its environment—for example, in the case of a food product, how well does the package operate on the supermarket shelf? Are the package components which have the greatest visibility the same ones which have been designed for use as prime identifiers? How well does the package communicate the unique characteristics of its contents, as well as any prime functional advantages which it, itself, may possess?

Physiological techniques include numerous mechanical methods for measuring the speed and distance at which recognition and correct identification take place and for discerning the dominant image components and the order in which they dominate when presented in varying combinations. Primary mechanical methods include the tachistoscope, the distance meter, eye dominance meters, the eye movement cameras, and the filmstrip.

Since any error in the packaging of a brand can be very costly, machines originally tended to play an important role in package research. The latest thinking in the field, however, is to recognize that the results they produce are best utilized as supplements to those of psychological and survey research. For instance, while it may be of value to obtain a tachistoscopic measurement of the speed with which a package is recognized, such a measurement is not going to be much help to the brand's marketer if the package happens to be esthetically mediocre, connotes "poor quality" or "poor value for the money" to the consumer, or if the constellation of age, sex, and socioeconomic usage to which the package is keyed by the consumer happens to be the one which is "wrong" in terms of marketing for its product category.

Psychological techniques. The psychological techniques which are utilized in package research are adaptations of clinical psychology and psychiatry. They are the same techniques used in general consumer motivational research, the only difference being that the specifics involve aspects of packaging.

In research investigations of packaging problems, these techniques are generally utilized most extensively in the predesign phase. The most commonly used are the better known projective techniques, focused group and depth interviews. They are utilized in order to obtain information as to the consumer's psychological needs which the package should meet, those which the product it contains must meet, and the degree to which the package implies the desired product attributes. The reasons behind use patterns are investigated by these techniques. Corporate and brand-line imagery may also be investigated. If the brand for which the package is designed is one considered for endorsement by the corporation producing it, the degree to which the endorsement is desirable may be investigated, as well as the degree to which the package makes proper use of the corporate image values and the degree to which the package in turn enhances the brand and corporate image.

The projective techniques include attitude scales, sentence completion, variations of the semantic differential, and cartoons depicting pertinent situations for which the respondent is asked to fill in the "balloons" with what he or she feels might be being said by the people or "people surrogates" (usually animals) involved. They are used to obtain information which respondents cannot readily express directly, the often disguised reasons behind overt behavior. They are especially valuable in obtaining data concerning the underlying fears, apprehensions, and need fulfillment associated with the use of specific products, and the concomitant appeals of competitive brands and their packaging. They are also used to discern the personality types to which specific designs will appeal and the specific needs of these personality types as they are pertinent to the product for which brand packaging is to be designed. They are especially valuable where the product is a "personal" one (deodorants, "feminine hygiene" products, bathroom tissue), where the product is used either to control or to express some facet of the user's "personality" (girdles and cosmetics), or where the product is associated with the fulfillment or avoidance of neurotic needs (music, pet foods, low calorie or dietetic foods).

Their drawback is that their interpretation is highly subjective. In each case they are adaptations of standard tests geared to produce results of value in solving the specific packaging problem at hand. Unlike the basic projective tests from which they have been adapted they have not been validated by use with large numbers of carefully controlled respondents.

Projective test results are generally used as indicators rather than as valid findings. The use of this technique is usually incorporated into depth interviewing.

The types of individual depth and group interviews utilized most commonly by package research are themselves, to an extent, projective techniques. They are structured, in that respondents are given specific topics to discuss, but the respondents are allowed to discuss the topics in any manner and as freely as they desire. When put to competent use, this technique is invaluable as a tool for establishing directions for design exploration. Its value depends heavily upon the subtlety and acuity of the research analyst's interpretation of the results; its danger is subjectivity of interpretation. Its use is commonly criticized by those who do not understand the technique in terms of the "danger" or "invalidity" of the use of small samples.

The most widely utilized package research technique is that of predesign qualitative or depth interviewing combined with postdesign, random or stratified sample, quantitative or "survey" interviewing. Quantitative research here is to discern validly the degree to which in the estimation of consumers (the sample often being broken by heavy and light usage and nonusage of the product involved) each new design overcomes the vulnerabilities of the competition, of the current package, if there is one, and of the product itself.

The primary problem of package research is one to which none of these techniques can, of itself, supply a solution. That problem is how to obtain valid analyses of total packages (not just of the specific identifiers and key colors contained on the covering of the product and of the imagery which they evoke) within the market situation where they are encountered by the consumer. Each of the previously described research techniques can supply a piece of the total picture; it still takes an astute marketer to select the pertinent findings, draw the pertinent inferences, and implement the correct marketing strategy from the data supplied by the techniques in current use. It takes work, but it definitely can be done.

There is no presently developed research technique which is completely satisfactory; none which is completely reliable, completely sophisticated, or all encompassing. We are aware of the shortcomings of each of the major techniques; but we do not support the desire of some research practitioners, marketers, and managers to eschew all or nearly all of them in favor of "marketing intuition" or unsupported managerial know-how.

THE EFFECT OF PACKAGE RESEARCH ON THE CONSUMER

Package researchers like to say that their work affects the consumer by influencing her purchasing habits through its influence upon design, and that their work results in packages which persuade the consumer to purchase products and, within any specific product group, to purchase the brand whose package both physically and psychologically is the most pleasantly convenient. Physically, this is the package which is the most pleasant to pick up, to handle, to store, and to use. Psychologically, it is the one which, in all phases of consumer contact with it, evokes such pleasant anticipations and positive associations as to insure long-term repurchase.

But the actual extent to which a specific package influences the purchase decision, at any specific time or in terms of any specific combination of consumer experience and brand and package age, is not known—regardless of whether the package is the result of research. Research has not been able to come up with a method by which to measure accurately, or even to ascertain, all of the factors operating in any one specific purchase decision, or to measure the degree of influence which known factors have upon each other. These are next to impossible tasks. Even if, at a specific point in time, enough new brands in enough new packages could be assembled to provide a valid setting for experimentation, there would still be the problem of assembling "new" consumers who were uncontaminated by previous exposure to advertising, competitive brands, and so forth. To qualify for testing, in terms of possessing no brand prejudices, no product preconceptions whatsoever, a "new" consumer would have to be no more than about three years of age; therefore, her judgments would probably be somewhat less sophisticated than those of her mother.

THE CONSUMER'S EFFECT UPON MARKETING

A more fruitful angle from which to view the situation is to consider what the consumer has done. In terms of package research, she can be seen as very actively working for both good and ill. Her apparent inconsistencies have caused package research to sharpen its techniques, to set to work reading under and around her words rather than merely taking them at face value, and to attempt to establish models for determining such factors as the degree to which familiarity determines brand choice. All that is to the good.

What is downright dangerous is the fear which the consumer inadvertently instills in too many of those who interpret her wishes—including not only package researchers but other key figures in the conception and execution of brand strategy. The majority of these interpreters still seem afraid not to take her at her word. Such attentive listening will never let any of them go too far wrong, since literal interpretations of her choices and her limited, usually poorly verbalized, associations will prevent them from introducing anything which is a real departure from what she is used to. However, in terms of the package, not only will it prevent introduction of one which from her viewpoint is too gauche or too ineffectual but, by the same token, will prevent the introduction of the unique and the esthetically handsome. Although it ultimately would be far more pleasing to her, such a design is too often passed over in favor of something safer, some minor variation of the current package—the one which, if asked what she wants in an "ideal" package, she invariably sets about describing.

Just as they yearn for infallible machines, the impatient and the unsophisticated yearn for the consumer's hand to guide them. The tragedy is that it is usually in the final stages of market strategy planning that the consumer's influence becomes dominant. The fault does not lie with the consumer. It lies, rather, with the expert in whatever field who is afraid to make adventurous judgments and with the expert who, having done so, is inept at persuading management that his judgments are the logically correct ones to follow. In the final analysis, the consumer has neither choice nor voice. She chooses what she has been best trained to choose, and says what she has been best trained to say.

* * *

It should be understood by the potential user of package design research that each of the techniques enumerated is valuable independently of the others, and that time and budgetary limitations often preclude using all techniques on each new package. Determination of where to use research, and to what degree, ultimately depends on the same good business judgment which is the foundation of all marketing activities.

Examples of new packages which were developed using some or all of the described techniques include American Tobacco's "Tareyton," Coca-Cola's "Sprite," and the Betty Crocker cake-mix line for General Mills. Specifics of each research program are, however, closely guarded marketing secrets and the property of clients.

SECTION II

MEASURING THE MOVEMENT OF GOODS AT THE RETAIL LEVEL •

ONE OF THE OLDEST FORMS of marketing research is the reporting of the movement of goods from retail outlets to the consumer. All companies, of course, have sales records, and these sales records indicate the success or failure of the product. However, the sales records are necessarily intra-company. There is no evidence in a sales record as to where the business went other than to the brand being sold; the share of the market of that brand, the fluctuation of that product, and the rise or fall of other brands cannot be surmised from a company's own sales records.

Prior to the 1930's this competitive information was supplied by corporate espionage, best guesses, and primitive intelligence. Today the measurement of the movement of goods is quite refined and rapidly approaching the speed of the computer age. The largest supplier of this information, and the oldest, is the A. C. Nielsen Company. Through an arrangement with a cross section of retail outlets in the United States and various other countries, the Nielsen Company supplies advertisers with information on share-of-market trends; competitive data; information on shelf facings and out-of-stock position; and movement of sizes by brands, territories, and regions of the United States. Over a period of more than a generation, valuable information on trends and historic changes in brand strength and weakness has been charted. This information has minimized the risk in an advertiser's decision to introduce a new product or withdraw an old product from the market. The weakness in the data is only that they come several months after the fact and decisions involving deals, premiums, or other merchandising aids must be made after the fact.

Because of the financial success of the Nielsen Company, other companies entered into competition with it, offering more specialized services. The Nielsen Company is a syndicated service measuring food and drug products, basically, with occasional special services. The competitors selected a broader base. Audits & Surveys, which is the second largest marketing research company, accepts categories on assignment and measures an unlimited number of categories, not only in the food and drug fields but in hard and soft goods as well. The technique used is similar to Nielsen's.

Ehrhart-Babic also offers specialized services in store audits. The basic difference in the approach of this company is that there is a more specialized testing of goals which have been pre-established, particularly in test markets. For example, premiums can be tested in a retail panel of stores. These controlled store tests enable an advertiser to establish a national pattern through limited experimentation.

Another approach to measuring consumer purchases is the method of the Market Research Corporation of America. This company uses a panel of consumers reporting weekly on purchases of various products. A complete list of food and drug items are reported by approximately 7,500 households. By using a diary, the consumers report in considerable detail all pertinent data about their purchases, including price-off, coupon, in-pack premium, sizes, brand, type, flavor, and so forth. These diaries are processed weekly, and a voluminous amount of information is provided to subscribers to the service.

In this section Nielsen, Ehrhart-Babic, and Market Research Corporation of America report on their techniques and present case histories which illustrate the methods of using their reports.

Major companies subscribe to all three of these services on the theory that the services differ from each other and the sum total of the information in the composite represents sound marketing research from which multimillion-dollar decisions can be made.

There is, however, a development in this field which may make all present methods obsolete because of the current time lag in reporting the data. Most supermarkets are now studying plans to make their warehouse computer tapes available to one or all of these research companies. At the present time, Kroger has an arrangement with Market Research Corporation of America to process these data for major manufacturers of food and drugs. Other companies, such as Time Incorporated, are currently reporting regionally as marketing agents for a large number of supermarkets in the dissemination of this type of information.

Warehouse tapes simply report the movement of warehouse shipments to the retail outlets of a chain. They are on computer tape, and their basic purpose is to allow inventories to be kept at a constant level as well as to tell the managements of the billion-dollar supermarket chains the daily financial status of each district and retail store.

Since this information already exists in tape form, it is merely a matter of programming a second computer to extract an adequate national sample from representative chains throughout the United States to supply instant information about product movement. While it is true that inventory movement from the warehouses does not always reflect simultaneous movement in retail outlets, in this modern day of marketing most items move off the shelf in less than ten days. Only a few infrequently used items have a longer shelf life. Therefore, most marketing men agree that warehouse movement is equal to retail outlet movement for frequently purchased products.

The speed of reporting these data via computer tapes may more than make up for the minor deficiency in the accuracy of this information. It is possible to predict, therefore, that while consumer panels may continue to reflect consumer attitudes, measurements of the movement of goods in the future may no longer necessitate a physical count from store to store to check the inventory of each item in each category. The modern age will condense all this activity into the brain of the computer.

Flow-of-Goods Measurement •

LOUIS J. BABIC, JR.
and
THOMAS A. EHRHART

EXECUTIVES DON'T REACH THE TOP through sheer blind chance. The groundwork for any gain in position must be prepared carefully; steps must be planned in advance, and possibilities researched. This principle also applies to manufacturers and advertising agencies that want to get ahead.

Ehrhart-Babic Associates, Incorporated, specializes in conducting in-store research in test areas. This research is usually conducted in food and drug stores, but department stores, variety stores, discount houses, and other types of outlets may also be checked. The work is conducted in one or more of four ways: through store audits, controlled store tests, distribution studies, or dealer interviews.

Store audits, which are a continuous check of movement of a product in relation to competition, can be used in a number of ways. By the use of multiple test markets it is possible to test such variables as product name, price, advertising theme, and level of advertising support.

One of the most common uses of store audits is the test marketing of new products. With the high incidence of failure of new products (some estimates indicate that as many as nine out of every ten new products fail) it is necessary to obtain a measure of sales before introducing a new product nationally. There are research techniques that will measure a consumer's reaction to a product as compared with her reaction to competing products. However, a test market with store audits determines how well one product will *sell* in relationship to competition.

Usually two to eight test markets are chosen, depending on the number of variables to be tested. A test market can be the size of a city, a metropolitan area, a TV-coverage area, or a sales district. In this area, the test product is introduced just as if it were being introduced on a broader scale. It receives the normal sales support and advertising at the same level as if it were being introduced nationally.

We recommend that sales be checked for a two-month base period (before introduction) and then for a minimum test period of six months, so that the sales level of the new product can be found. For instance, in the first phases of introduction a new product may be able to claim 20 percent of the total market for that product class. But this figure is relatively unimportant; the key figure is the share at which sales level off. Obviously, different decisions might be made regarding the expansion of introduction of the new product, depending on whether the product has a 15 percent share of the market at the end of six months or a 5 percent share.

Another important use of store audits is in the field of advertising research. There are many times when a company would want to test-market a decision to be made regarding questions of the following type:

1. Am I advertising at the proper level? What effect would it have on sales if I increased the level of advertising? (By testing the results of an increased advertising theme in one market and comparing the results to another market where the advertising level remains the same, the company can obtain a measure of the effect of the increased advertising.)
2. Which of the several advertising themes being considered is the most effective? (By using separate test markets for each of the themes, the company can determine which theme produced the best results.)
3. Which medium or combination of media should be used? (By using

separate test markets and varying the media mix, the company can determine which is the most effective for the same expenditure of money.)

Another type of question that can be answered effectively through the use of store audits is in the field of sales promotion. A few such questions would be:

1. Which is the most effective premium?
2. Which is the most effective deal?
3. Which is the most effective package?

For instance, frozen orange juice in a rectangular container is currently in test markets. This is the type of radical change a manufacturer wouldn't want to risk without first thoroughly researching its possibilities.

The effect of price changes can also be measured through store audits. By changing the price in one area and maintaining the same price in another area, we can determine the effect of the change.

The mechanics of a store audit are fairly simple. First, an opening inventory is made of the product class to be audited. At the end of a predetermined period of time another inventory is made, and invoices are checked to determine the store purchases. Sales are computed on the following formula: Sales = Opening Inventory + Store Purchases — Closing Inventory.

The following is a hypothetical example: An auditor goes into a store and makes a count of the product class being checked. Let's assume the auditor counts 22 units of product *Y*. Four weeks later, the auditor returns and makes another count and finds that there are now 27 units on hand. Invoices are reviewed, and it is found that 24 units were delivered.

We then have:

Opening inventory	22
Plus retailer purchases	+24
Total available for sale	46
Less current inventory	—27
Total sales	19

Although the mechanics are quite simple, it requires an experienced store audit firm to conduct a test market properly because of some common pitfalls. Stores must be thoroughly checked to see that inventories are correct. Not only must shelves and stockrooms be inventoried completely, and any places where stock may be hidden, but stores must be checked for merchandise on display, for merchandise in windows or on conveyor belts, and for full cases of merchandise being used as bases for displays. This is the only way to maintain inventory accuracy. Also, invoice information must be complete. Primarily, regular deliveries must be checked for complete records, but all drop shipment records must also be available. In addition, credit memos on returned product must be obtained. And these are not the only important factors; the store audit agency must be alert to see that the proper sample is selected and that atypical store situations are properly reported to clients.

There are various types of panels that can be set up. Basically, these fall into two main types, the projectable and the high-volume-trend panel. In a projectable panel, the test is set up to include all sizes of stores in the test area. The results, in terms of both sales and share of market, are projected to the entire test area.

In a high-volume-trend panel, only high-volume stores are used. When the concentration of business is in high-volume stores, quite often a panel of these larger stores will provide the answer. Sales figures are not projected to the universe, but are representative only of the high-volume stores on the panel.

The second type of in-store research is *controlled store tests,* which are similar to store audits in test marketing, except that the test activity is restricted to panel stores. In introducing a new product in a test-market program, the product is made available to all stores in the test area. But in running a test to determine the effect of another size of a product, for example, we can test it only in stores which are on the panel. Naturally, in this case the test item cannot be promoted except in the panel stores themselves.

In the case of controlled store tests, the market research firm does much more than merely set up a panel. It usually makes arrangements for selling the test merchandise, delivery, maintaining test conditions as far as possible, and even billing of stores for merchandise received.

These tests are most useful when the factors being tested fall into the following categories: (1) new package sizes, (2) shelf arrangement, (3) new package design, (4) effectiveness of displays, (5) premiums, (6) location of the product in the store, and (7) price change. Such things as competitive deals cannot be controlled, but they can be measured.

The controlled store tests fit into three different types: the Latin square, matched panel, and side-by-side tests.

In a Latin square test each test variable is exposed in a different panel and over a period of time. Hypothetically, let's suppose we want to determine which is the better premium in a box of detergent: a steak knife or a small flashlight. We would also like to find out how much sales are increased by the addition of the premium. We would then set up three separate panels of food stores approximately equal in volume.

In the first panel we would set up test condition *A*, the steak knife premium. In the second panel we would set up test condition *B*, which is the flashlight premium. In panel three we would set up test condition *C*, which would be checking the normal movement of sales without either premium. At the end of the first test period the promotions would be switched, and the first panel would have the flashlight, the second panel would have the condition *C*, and the third would have the steak knife. After a second test period there would be another switch in the stocking arrangements, so that in three test periods each of the panels would be exposed to each of the test conditions. A diagram of the test conditions during the test is as follows:

	Panel 1	*Panel 2*	*Panel 3*
First test period	(A) Steak knife	(B) Flashlight	(C) Normal stock
Second test period	(B) Flashlight	(C) Normal stock	(A) Steak knife
Third test period	(C) Normal stock	(A) Steak knife	(B) Flashlight

In a matched panel, panels of equal volume are set up and results compared after different variables are introduced. Suppose one is going to change a package design and wishes to know what the effect will be. The suggested approach would be to set up a panel of stores twice the size of the subpanels desired. Sales are measured under normal conditions in all stores. On the basis of the data obtained, the panel is split into two panels of equal volume according to sales, inventory of the test product, and all-commodity volume of the stores. In the first panel we would put in the new package design and in the second panel maintain the old package design. Results could then be compared between the two designs.

In the third type of controlled store test, the side-by-side technique, two or more variables are placed side by side in a store and the customer is given a choice between them. For instance, in the example cited of the flashlight and steak knife premiums, store displays can be set up which would have an equal amount of merchandise with a flashlight and with a steak knife. Sales figures are obtained and the results compared for the two premiums. This method is somewhat artificial, however, as customers normally do not see merchandise displayed in this manner.

Each of the above methods has its modifications, strengths, and weaknesses, and the choice of the type of test to be used is predicated on the purpose of the test.

The third general method of research mentioned above was that of *distribution studies.* Distribution studies are a check of a representative group of stores to see how many carry a given product. Often distribution of competitive items is reported. In addition to distribution, shelf facings, prices, in-store locations, and other facts can be determined in the same store visit. Distribution on both a store-count basis and an all-commodity-volume basis can be secured. That is, a product may be in 50 percent of the stores on a store-count basis in a test area, but these stores may represent 75 percent of the all-commodity volume of the area.

Distribution studies can be done rapidly and preliminary figures submitted almost overnight. This allows for educated decision making with the advantage of really current data as a guide.

Effective use of these distribution studies can be made in planning advertising on new products. Just before advertising is scheduled to break, a distribution study can be conducted. If distribution is below a specified level, the advertising can be postponed until distribution is improved.

Another modified use of distribution studies is to study product aging. This entails visiting a representative group of stores and securing the code numbers listed on the packages. By decoding these code dates, the age of the product in the store can be determined.

At times it may be desirable to obtain the dealers' opinions on some marketing problem through *dealer interviews.* These interviews represent a fourth research technique and may be conducted individually or in conjunction with any of the other in-store methods being used.

In conclusion, it is necessary to note that in any test market situation there are certain rules that should be followed. First of all, remember that the test market activity is a miniature model of what will be done on a national scale if the test is successful. One should not advertise at a $10 million national rate in test markets if only $2 million would actually be available if the product were introduced nationally.

Second, be sure that the product has been properly researched before test marketing. There is no point in test marketing a product before product usage and performance tests have been completed. And if the consumer tests don't show the product to have consumer acceptance at least equal to that of the brand leader, the chances are that the product will be unsuccessful.

Third, establish goals for the tests and use a well-thought-out marketing plan. Don't wait until store audit results are in to decide how to use the store audits, but include them in the marketing plan. Define goals for the product in terms of share of market or in terms of sales. But, if possible, avoid depending completely on either one; the chances are that both will be needed. And plan to do some additional consumer test work.

In the fourth place, keep interference out of test-market operations. The whole secret of a successful test is that the product is given normal treatment. Tests have been ruined by the salesmen's putting extra effort into the test situation. In some cases they have gotten a list of panel stores and have obtained from these stores abnormal attention, such as extra displays. When this happens, the results of the test will be much more favorable than will ever be attained when the product is introduced nationally. It is difficult for a salesman to realize that this is a test of the product, not of his ability as a salesman.

Fifth, test long enough to be sure of meaningful results. A general rule of thumb is that a market test should run at least six months. In the case of fast-moving items such as cigarettes, this period may be shortened; in the case of slow-moving items it may be desirable to test for a period of a year.

Finally, give careful consideration to the selection of the test markets. These should be isolated enough from other areas to keep the results clean; and they should have adequate TV, radio, and newspaper coverage if this is to be an important factor in the test. Select cities where the leading chains will cooperate in these tests. A market in which a noncooperating chain group dominates may not be a good test market. And don't select the product's best markets for a market test; the results will be much more favorable than can be obtained on a national level.

Measuring Consumer Purchases •

RUSSELL S. TATE, JR.

CONSUMER PURCHASES REPRESENT the final score on all marketing effort. Purchases, or the lack of them, are the consumer's way of voting on how well the marketer has done his job—has developed a product that satisfies consumer needs, provided adequate distribution for convenient availability, communicated the merits of the product to consumers, and promoted and priced the product appropriately.

In today's specialized economy marketers usually do not deal directly with consumers. In most instances marketers sell to distributing organizations who in turn make the products available to consumers. Direct contact between producer and consumer is missing and must be developed through additional channels of communication.

Measurement of consumer purchases is one important way of keeping score in the marketplace. As part of this process, the Market Research Corporation of America has maintained over the past 25 years a National Consumer Panel of households reporting weekly on purchases of various products. In recent years similar consumer panels have been established to measure consumer purchases in test markets. Information and analyses from panel data have led into further questions requiring development of facilities to measure in-store conditions and to survey consumers on the "reasons why" affecting purchases.

Continuing purchase information from consumers has been used by marketers in a variety of ways—both as continuing progress reports on their own and competitive strategies and to evaluate the impact of specific marketing tactics.

Continuous information on consumer purchases obviously permits progress reports on sales trends of a particular product and the various brand shares of that product. Is the product class showing a healthy growth trend, leveling off, or going into a decline? Is the brand keeping pace with competitors' brands? This type of progress review is only the prelude to more detailed analyses designed to determine opportunities for improvement in sales.

Total sales of any product during a given time period are equal to the number of consumers purchasing times the frequency of purchase times the average purchase size. All marketing efforts are designed to influence one or more of these elements in order to increase total sales.

Consumer purchase data enable marketers to follow trends in each of these factors in order to evaluate past efforts to influence them or to develop new marketing efforts. For example, a marketer might discover that his brand is falling behind competitive brands in number of purchasers, thus requiring additional advertising to attract more buyers. He might discover that the average purchase size is smaller than for competitive brands, thus suggesting a review of his package sizes or consideration of multiple-pricing offers to "trade up" average purchase size. In his advertising, he might stress alternative uses to increase frequency of purchase.

Continuous measurement of consumer purchases from the National Consumer Panel enables marketers to separate purchases into those by new buyers and by repeat buyers. It answers such questions as: Have our marketing plans provided desired penetration of the market, or do we need additional effort to increase the number of tryers? Is the product sufficiently acceptable so that it is building a solid franchise of repeat buyers, or are the purchases heavily one-time novelty purchases?

Since the shelf price of many products is a decision controlled by distributors and can change from day to day, particularly on weekends, marketers often do not know how this important element is affecting sales of their product. Knowing the price paid for each consumer purchase permits an analysis of the actual effect of prices on consumer purchases and of what portion of the purchases occurred at various prices. It also permits measurement of the degree to which retailers pass on to the consumer various allowances made by the manufacturer.

Information also is obtained on special prices paid by consumers, including coupons and off-label price deals. This type of information enables marketers to evaluate the effect of promotional tactics: are they attracting new customers or loading up existing buyers?

In general, measurement of consumer purchases and identification of the purchasers provide opportunities to understand the nature of the marketing or sales output from several points of view. For example, they permit an evaluation of market concentration, indicating what parts of total sales are accounted for by heavy, medium, and light buyers, and how a given brand compares with competitive brands in this respect. They show whether business comes from a few heavy buyers or from a great many light buyers. Depending on these factors, a marketing plan to increase total sales can take quite different directions.

Identification of purchasers permits development of detailed customer profiles. These describe the people who are buying the brand—by age, income, education, family size, and many other characteristics. This has implications for product concept, media selection, copy theme, and many other elements of the total marketing effort.

In today's affluent society market segmentation is becoming increasingly important. That is, it is sometimes profitable to develop products appealing to specific segments of the consumer market. Because of this it is increasingly important to know how well a product is doing in the part of the market for which it was designed.

In addition to the usefulness of knowing the nature of the market currently existing for a product, as indicated above, a continuous record of consumer purchases provides unique opportunities for evaluating the interaction of competitive efforts. In a variety of ways, marketers can evaluate the dynamics of brand switching to determine where customers are coming from and to whom customers are being lost, and under what circumstances. This is essential in a marketer's evaluation of his own efforts as well as in evaluating the impact of competitive efforts on his own franchise.

Many of the above applications of continuing consumer-purchase data are even more useful in evaluating new product introductions. During the early stages of a new product it is particularly important to determine whom the product is appealing to in evaluating the success of the product concept and the promotional strategy involved. It is even more important to determine whether a new product is building a solid core of repeat buyers to insure continuing sales volume.

Because of the complexity of the marketing process, no single type of information is sufficient for all marketing decisions. Detailed information on the nature of the market for a product often suggests hypotheses regarding possible problems or opportunities which require additional information. This might include a check on the adequacy of distribution or the attitudes and opinions of consumers toward a particular product. Because of this, MRCA has found it necessary to develop capabilities for checking in-store conditions and for extracting information from consumers on reasons why.

Consumer-purchase measurements are obtained by means of the National Consumer Panel, a sample of 7,500 households which stays relatively stable over time. In essence, it is a miniature United States, including all types of families, living in cities of all sizes, in every part of the nation (except Hawaii and Alaska).

Within those bounds imposed by the statistical limitations of the sample, the Panel reflects purchasing behavior of the total population or that of specific geographical regions.

Members of the Panel use a preprinted diary to write down significant details about their purchases of grocery and beauty-aid products: the brand, type, flavor, or variety purchased; the quantities bought; the price paid; the store where purchased, including all types and organizations; whether a special inducement (price-off, coupon, in-pack premium, and so forth) was received; and other such details of value to marketers. They are compensated monthly for doing this.

Each week Panel families send their diaries to MRCA's data-processing center. Here the information is extracted and processed through computers to provide types of analyses desired by marketers.

To provide additional information regarding in-store conditions, product or advertising awareness, or "reasons why" research, MRCA maintains a field department providing survey capabilities in a cross section of the United States. For example, MRCA has field representation in 92 of the 100 largest markets and in approximately 200 markets in total, permitting development of needed information on custom studies tailored to a client's particular problem. This type of research is directed by specialized project directors and executed with the help of extensive data-processing facilities.

The gathering of consumer-purchase information benefits the consumer. One important aspect of our system of social organization is freedom of choice by consumers. Each consumer purchase represents a favorable vote for that particular product. Measurement of these purchases is a way of tallying the votes to assist marketers in providing consumers with what they want most.

An interesting example of this process occurred several years ago. An imaginative marketer had developed an intriguing food supplement product with considerable appeal to children. The market for which this product was intended suggested the use of TV during children's programs as the ideal communication part of the marketing effort.

Sales started off with a bang. Limited production facilities were hard pressed to meet the demand for filling trade channels. Consumer purchases indicated an extremely high rate of trial. Everything looked great except for one disturbing factor: within three or four months it became obvious that while a high percentage of consumers would be likely to try this product once and some would make a second purchase of a flavor variation, very few would purchase more than a second time.

Very early in the game it was easy to conclude that the product would eventually run out of new buyers and would have no future. This type of information helped to prevent an unfortunate investment in additional factory capacity to provide a product that consumers didn't really want. The product is no longer available.

While this example may be a little extreme, it is not completely unique. Undoubtedly, product testing in the early developmental stage indicated some enthusiasm for this product. Unfortunately, whatever testing was done did not properly evaluate whether the product would wear well in terms of repeat purchasing. While this illustration represents a clear-cut decision not to invest in factory capacity for a product that consumers don't want, the more usual application involves decisions on whether to invest in plant capacity to produce sufficient products to meet the demand for a 5 percent brand share versus a 15 to 20 percent brand share.

Wise decisions by marketers based on what consumers really want are an important part of the process of allocating resources in the direction indicated by freedom of choice.

The following is a case history on the use of consumer-purchase information. A short time ago, one of our clients was interested in developing a new concept in pet food. This new concept incorporated the element of convenience along with nutritional and taste considerations.

Because of the very nature of the new product, the convenience concept came through strong in developing the marketing program. Product tests also indicated that pets were enthusiastic about the taste of the new product. Consequently, the product concept developed in the total marketing program came through as a convenience for owners and a treat for the pets.

During the early stages of marketing, initial trial was high, repeat purchases were quite good, and total sales were encouraging. After a few months, however, total sales were not living up to expectations. What had gone wrong? Was the product itself a failure? Did pets get tired of this particular product?

One clue to the problem was indicated in the measurements on frequency of purchase. Purchase frequency was somewhat less than for other pet foods. This aspect of product performance was similar to the pattern of products enjoying a specialty market.

To get at the answers, additional research was indicated. A survey was conducted to determine some of the reasons why this particular purchase pattern had developed. Results of this survey indicated that pet owners viewed the product as an occasional treat for their pets rather than as a continuous steady diet. A review of the product concept that had evolved in the overall marketing effort indicated that this was the point of view that had been presented. As a result, the marketing concept was changed substantially. Greater emphasis was given to the theme of nutritional quality on a continuing basis.

After this change in marketing strategy, this story had a happy ending. Frequency of purchase increased substantially. Total sales increased to satisfactory levels. The product now represents one of the real success stories in marketing.

Marketing Research in the Marketplace: An Accurate Measurement of Consumer Sales •

ARTHUR C. NIELSEN, JR.

TO BE SUCCESSFUL TODAY, a manufacturer has to be a jump ahead of changing consumer demands. He must evaluate and improve his product constantly, offer quality and convenience, use attractive packaging, have an efficient distribution system, and culminate the process with an effective advertising and promotion effort. It's no wonder that billions of dollars are spent in the distribution and marketing of consumer goods. Further, the complexity of the process and today's keen competitive conditions emphasize the fact that efficiency is more essential than ever before.

The result is an obvious need for an evaluation of the manufacturer's progress and how it compares with that of his competitors within the total market. Since a great share of any marketing budget is directed to consumers, the best and most logical place to obtain such information is in the marketplace.

The manufacturer cannot depend on his factory sales to indicate promptly or accurately the effect of changing marketing tactics on consumer sales. Continual fluctuations in wholesale and retail inventories create a factory sales curve which often has little immediate relationship to the consumer sales curve. Exhibit 1 gives an example of the usual conflicting factory and consumer sales figures for a manufacturer over a period of one year.

Obviously, the manufacturer knows there is a lag between factory and consumer sales. The problem, however, is that the lag can be either positive or negative, depending on the type of promotion, the season of the year, the nature of competitors' activities, and many other factors. Furthermore, the manufacturer requires marketing information for each important competing brand.

A continuing audit which measures the consumer sales of the entire product category and that of each important brand, together with its share of the total market, is one accurate and practical way to evaluate consumer response to marketing expenditures. This procedure provides a dynamic picture of the changing marketplace.

The concept of systematically measuring consumer sales was introduced by A. C. Nielsen Company in 1933. In addition to being offered in the United States, the Nielsen Retail Index Services are offered in 12 European countries and Australia, New Zealand, and Canada. Worldwide, the company employs some 6,500 full-time people. Nielsen also measures local and national television audiences, provides a consumer promotion service, processes coupons for retailers and manufacturers, maintains magazine circulation lists and reader inquiry services for publishers, and investigates marketing problems through a special research service.

Retail Index Services provide prompt reports of consumer sales measured at the stores when the sales take place. A client can use this information to key his marketing and production to trends in consumer preference. If necessary, products can be changed to conform with changes in the marketplace. Complete data on competitive products are also provided. Share changes are reported as products are improved, promotional appropriations are altered, and new marketing approaches are instituted by competitors or by the client company. The manufacturer obtains knowledge of many different techniques and situations and is thus able to visualize the complete picture and the alternative moves. Such overall knowledge

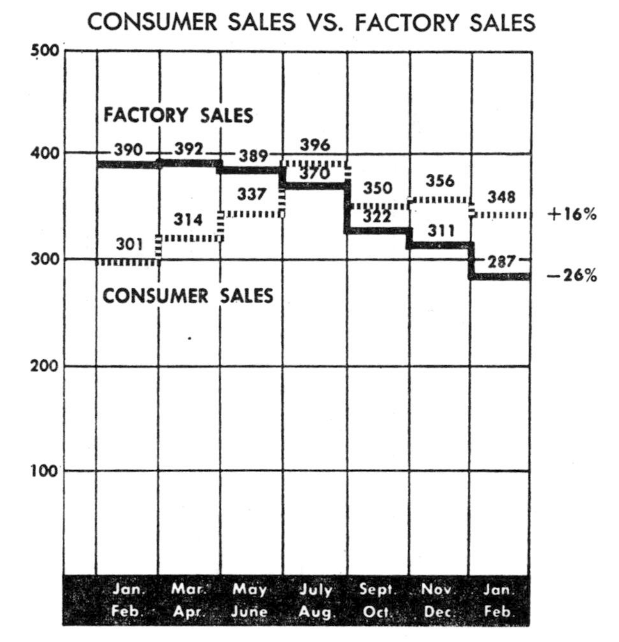

EXHIBIT 1

is unavailable without an accurate, continuous measurement of the entire market.

Equally important, consumer sales figures are available by region, client sales area, county type, and store type, as well as nationally. This permits the measurement of such things as the effectiveness of regional promotions, changes in advertising appeal, and acceptability of new products in test areas. Consumer sales data also can be matched to sales areas.

Another essential segment of information is the reporting of consumer sales by sizes and types of stores. With important store types identified, the manufacturer can concentrate his sales and merchandising efforts where they will achieve optimum results.

A list of the basic information contained in the bimonthly reports is given in Exhibit 2. In addition to food sales, Retail Index Services are also available in the drug, camera, and pharmaceutical fields in the United States. These, and other product categories, are available overseas. Information for the manufacturer's product and each important competing product is given separately. Trends are shown by repeating all work every two months.

Besides the basic information, special studies are available regarding:

COMPLETE LIST OF DATA SECURED EVERY 60 DAYS IN FOOD STORES*

1. Sales to consumers
2. Purchases by retailers
3. Retail inventories
4. Days' supply
5. Store count distribution
6. All-commodity distribution
7. Out-of-stock
8. Prices (wholesale and retail)
9. Special factory packs
10. Dealer support (displays, local adv., coupon redempt.)
11. Special observations (order size, reorder, directs vs. whlse.)
12. Total food store sales (all commodities)
13. Major media advertising (from other sources)

BROKEN DOWN BY:

BRANDS		TERRITORIES	YOUR OWN TERR.		COUNTIES POP. RANGE	STORES	PKG. SIZE	PROD. TYPE
YOURS		New Eng.	1	10	Metro. New York	Chain	Small	X
Competitors	A	Metro. New York	2	11	Metro. Chicago			
	B	Mid. Atlantic	3	12	Other Metro. 19 next largest mkts.	Independent:	Medium	
	C	East Central	4	13				
	D	Metro. Chicago	5	14	B counties Metro. areas over 100,000	Super		Y
	All others	West Central	6	15		Large	Large	
		Southwest	7	16	C counties 30,000-100,000	Medium		
		Pacific	8	17		Small	Giant	Z
Total		Southeast	9	18	Rural Others Under 30,000			

*Substantially the same kinds of data are collected in all types of stores audited.

EXHIBIT 2

FOOD STORE REPRESENTATION*

(Based on U.S. census of distribution and our own continuing studies)

3,000,000 CONSUMERS

(over 875,000 family units)

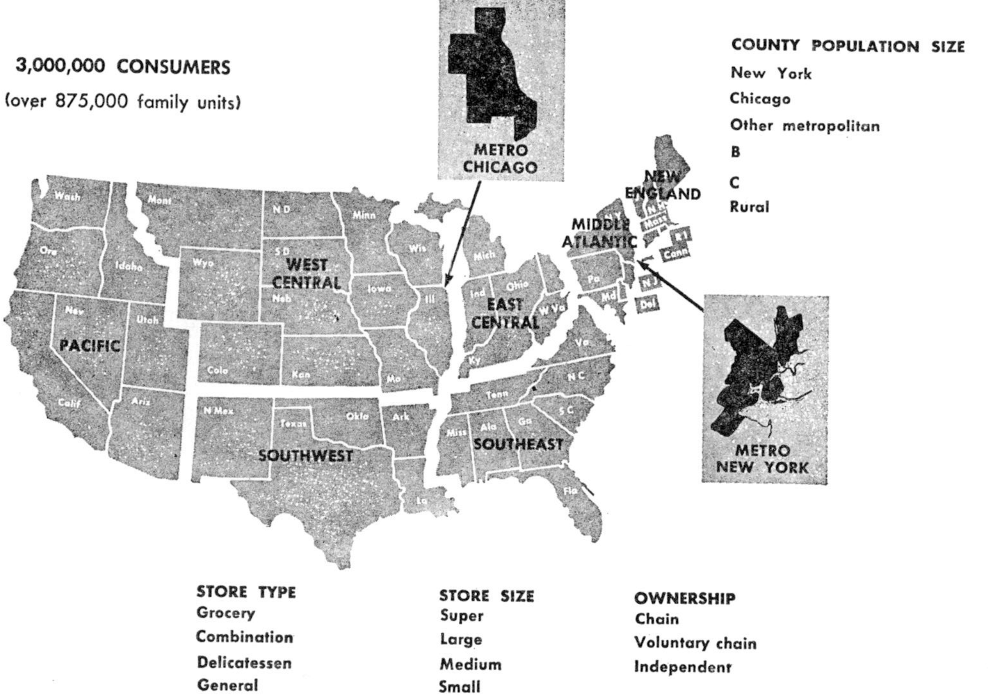

COUNTY POPULATION SIZE
New York
Chicago
Other metropolitan
B
C
Rural

STORE TYPE
Grocery
Combination
Delicatessen
General

STORE SIZE
Super
Large
Medium
Small

OWNERSHIP
Chain
Voluntary chain
Independent

*The selection of all types of stores audited follows a similar pattern.

EXHIBIT 3

PRINCIPLES OF NIELSEN
RETAIL INDEX AUDITING

"Alpha" brand of cake mix (39¢ size)
in Super X Market

INVENTORY:	FOR JUNE-JULY PKGS.	VALUE
July 9	114 Pkgs.	
Sept. 10	93 Pkgs.	
Change	21	
PURCHASES		
From manufacturer (1 order)	12	$ 3.72
From wholesalers (4 orders)	48	15.00
Total	60	$18.72
CONSUMER SALES		
Packages	81	
Price, per pkg.		$ .39
Dollars, total		$31.59

STORE PROMOTION	YES	NO
Inside goods display	☒	☐
Other goods display	☐	☒
Local advertising	☒	☐
Premium offers	☒	☐
Coupon Redemption	☒	☐
Special Price	$	.33

EXHIBIT 4

1. Relationships between inventory and sales shares.
2. Comparisons of the movement of goods in stores charging various prices for the product.
3. Sales in stores that display the product versus those that do not.
4. The effect on sales of stock location, shelf position, and shelf facings.

These data help manufacturers solve some extremely difficult marketing problems.

The Nielsen Retail Index obtains its information from a sample of stores. Many technical factors enter into the selection of this sample, and thousands of skilled man-hours are spent each year selecting and maintaining a cross section of retail outlets whereby each territory, each county size, and each store size and type is represented. The sample stores, located in 597 counties, are in shopping centers, small towns, rural areas, and other areas.

Over 22,000 chain and independent stores are used in producing worldwide Nielsen Retail Index Services, and retail sales are audited at least once every 60 days in each store. The basic selection of food stores in the United States is shown in Exhibit 3. Contracts made with the sample stores permit auditors to take inventories and audit the invoices or warehouse withdrawal records for all goods coming into the store. Exhibit 4 is an example of how each item is audited and the supporting data recorded.

Nielsen store audits do not rely on memory or opinions. The retailer agrees to make invoices available and permit the inventory. As such, a retailer must provide records of all merchandise received, regardless of source, as well as an accounting of all merchandise returned or sold to another retailer. Simple in principle, the audit is complex in practice. The auditors must be familiar with all methods of buying and selling, plus the invoicing of thousands of products. All of the many package

CONSUMER SALES—ALL BRANDS

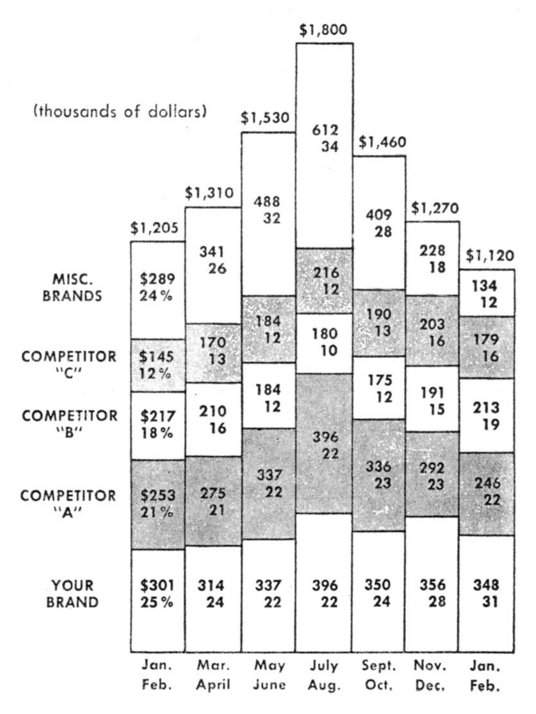

EXHIBIT 5

COMPETITIVE POSITION BY MARKET—AND IMPORTANCE OF MARKET TO TOTAL

Consumer Sales—Commodity No. 73

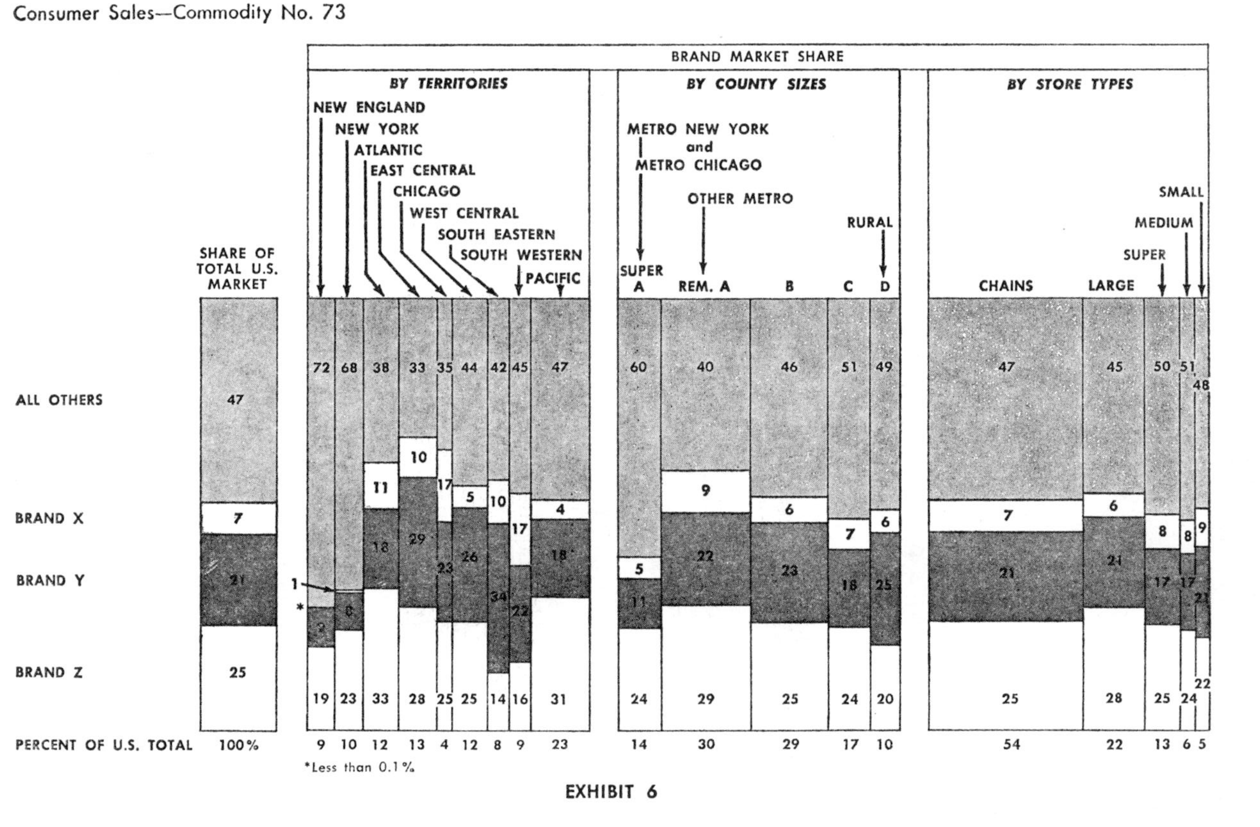

EXHIBIT 6

sizes and every one of the thousands of brands found must be properly identified and classified.

The accurate auditing of a retail store is a complex task requiring full-time specialists. In addition to being college trained, Nielsen auditors have six months of special training and are under close supervision at all times. All the data gathered in the field are systematically checked at production headquarters for possible error. Then they are fed into a complex of computers and processed according to the specialized needs of the clients. Reports are prepared and reproduced in the production department.

Experienced client service executives analyze, interpret, and relate the facts in terms of the subscriber's individual requirements. The salient factors are translated into charts and presented at regular bimonthly meetings. Miniature reproductions of the presentation and detailed summaries of the results are reproduced for client use. Of course, these reports are treated in the strictest confidence.

Information on competitive progress is especially important to the manufacturer. One index of the effectiveness of current marketing tactics is provided by the product's market share, a brand's percentage of the total market. The market-share trends for a product group are illustrated in Exhibit 5. Actual reports, of course, identify brands.

A territorial breakdown of national Retail Index data provides a sound basis for realistic distribution of the total marketing effort. For example, the chart in Exhibit 6 shows that brand *Z* is weakest in the South, in rural areas, and in small stores. If the manufacturer relied only on his sales records, he could underestimate the potential of these outlets or markets. Retail Index data show the actual situation in each sales territory by share of consumer sales, by county sizes, and by types of stores. As a result, the manufacturer can see individual market characteristics in perspective.

The use of factory production figures can be very misleading in determining seasonal markets and scheduling promotions. Exhibit 7 illustrates how an advertising effort based on factory sales missed the important buying season revealed by a consumer sales audit. The following year the advertising was correctly timed to "lead" consumer sales, which resulted in a substantial sales increase.

In another situation, a manufacturer changed his advertising and found that his factory sales fell 19 percent. Although it appeared that his approach was a mistake, Exhibit 8 reveals the actual situation—that his new advertising program was improving his competitive position. Note that all retail inventories are down 15 percent and retail sales on all brands

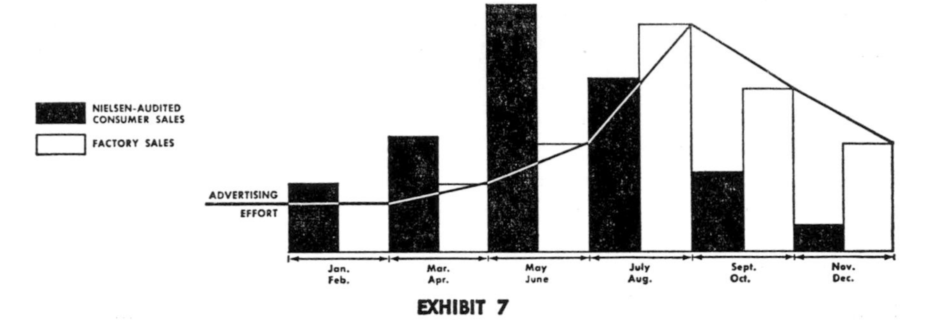

EXHIBIT 7

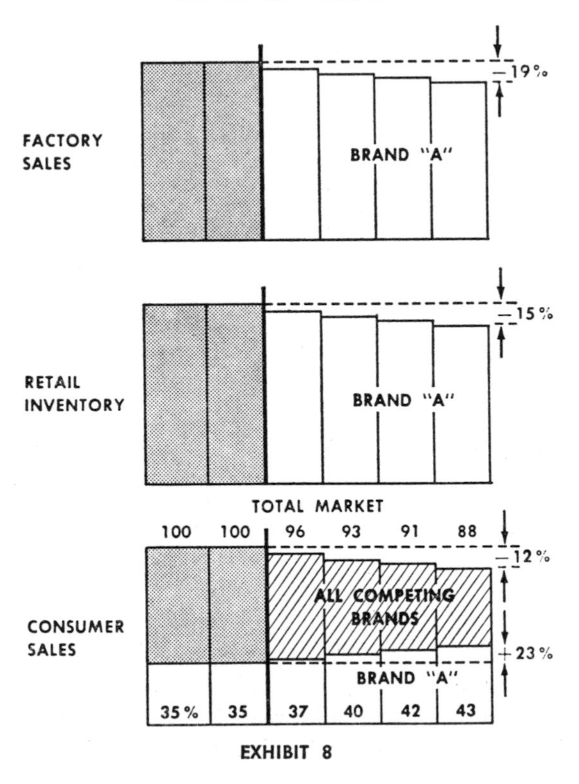

EXHIBIT 8

down 12 percent. Yet this manufacturer's share of the total market actually went up 23 percent. Of course, the reverse could have been true: a gain in factory sales could occur after an advertising change even though the share of market actually dropped. The point is that an accurate report of consumer sales is the only accurate method of measuring sales progress.

Most promotions can cause a temporary increase in the share of the market, but the real test comes after the promotion period when the product user is ready to purchase under normal conditions. The Retail Index data can be used in evaluating the overall results of any special marketing effort. It can also serve as a useful guide in planning future promotions.

The results of a very successful one-cent promotion are shown in Exhibit 9. Note that six months after the promotion, sales went up 32 percent over normal levels. Of course, it is just as important to know if a promotion fails to obtain its objective. For instance, Exhibit 10 illustrates a negative situation which was not alleviated by a one-cent sale. True, there was a momentary sales increase, but the product resumed its decline at the end of the promotion.

Also important in research is the reporting of data on retail distribution and out-of-stock conditions in terms of number of stores, as well as store importance in terms of sales volume. The value of this information is illustrated in Exhibit 11. The brand in the example is distributed in only 65 percent of the available retail outlets. However, placement is in the important stores which account for 92 percent of the volume. With this information, the manufacturer realized it might not be worthwhile to direct his sales effort toward the smaller stores which accounted for only 8 percent of the volume. Especially important was the fact that 5 percent of the out-of-stock stores were responsible for 11 percent of the total volume. Logically, the manufacturer concentrated on correcting this situation in the larger stores.

A vital area of advertiser and manufacturer concern is test marketing. After a product innovation receives initial approval, the usual procedure is to test it on a small scale. In general, Nielsen favors area testing wherever possible, because the base is broader and more representative than in city testing; this results in greater accuracy. In test marketing, the regular Retail Index stores are supplemented by additional stores to insure a satisfactory level of accuracy. The procedures for processing the test data are the same as those used in the national audits, as described above. The Nielsen Test Marketing service measures new or improved products,

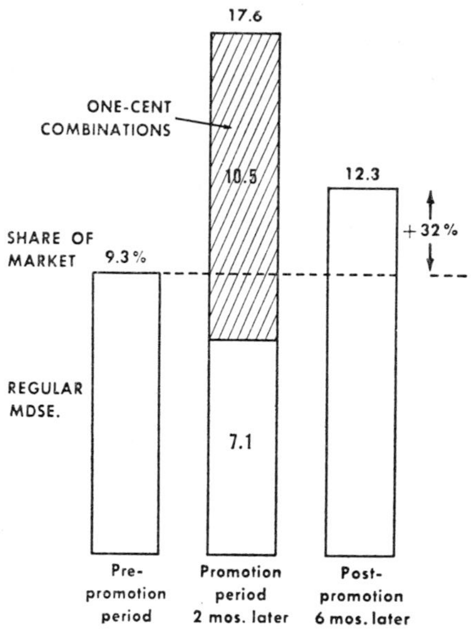

EXHIBIT 9

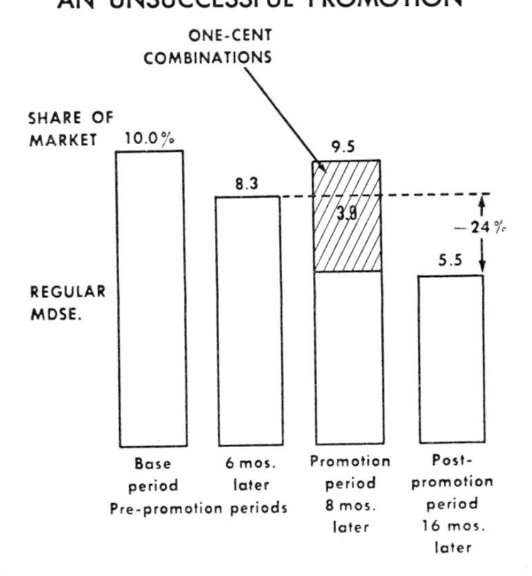

EXHIBIT 10

EVALUATING DISTRIBUTION

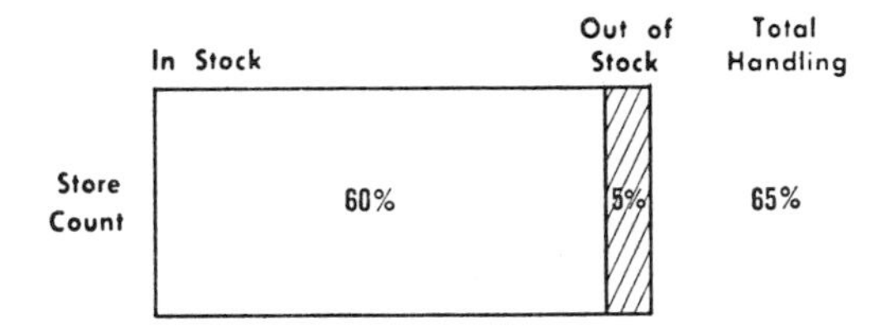

The information above is useful—but taken alone it can be misleading. Note that distribution is actually very good, as expressed below in terms of *volume.*

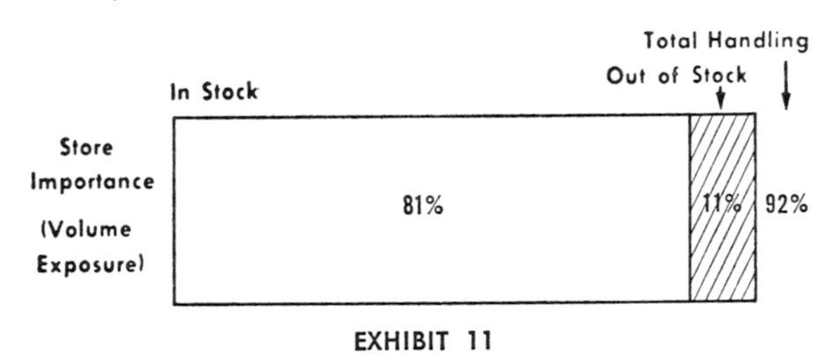

EXHIBIT 11

price changes, advertising media, package changes, and promotions—to name a few areas of application.

Manufacturers introducing new products should obtain complete information in many fields. Size of market, trends, seasonal characteristics, most popular prices, retail gross profits, and most effective advertising methods are some of the areas in which research information is available.

In the final analysis, each manufacturer's product and marketing effort are judged by the public in the highly competitive atmosphere of the retail store. It is here, at the point of sale, that each manufacturer should be accurate and objective in evaluating his performance in comparison to that of his competition.

In order to make valid marketing decisions, management must have actionable facts at its disposal—facts that are timely, precise, clear, and dependable. For these reasons, research on consumer sales is used today on a continuous basis by leading manufacturers in the food, drug, pharmaceutical, toiletries, cosmetic, confectionery, tobacco, photographic, and other product fields, both in the United States and overseas.

SECTION III

MEDIA RESEARCH •

MEDIA RESEARCH, or the qualitative measurement of the availability of a consumer to receive an advertising message, is quite scientific today and shows promise—thanks to computers and competition among services—of becoming more refined in the future.

The magazine and newspaper research with the measurement of print circulation, via the Audit Bureau of Circulations, provides an exact base figure. From information on multiple readership, length of time the magazine is exposed in the home, pass-on circulation, combinations of magazines in the home, and so forth the advertiser has data supplementary to the basic audit. Politz and Starch are active in measuring this kind of bonus circulation.

In general, advertisers accept the basic audit as a minimum potential exposure and all pass-along circulation as a bonus. Advertisers are, of course, interested in the maximum reach and frequency of a campaign of ads in a given magazine or in a combination of magazines, and they accept the information available as adequate.

Panels, personal interviews, and telephone interviews are used to validate this type of bonus information. Certainly, there is some question about the reliability of data other than audit figures, but there is enough evidence from the composite data over the past decade to indicate that this information is viable.

The great skepticism on the part of advertisers, the FTC, FCC, and Congressional investigating committees is reserved for the measurement of television. There are few corporate executives today who do not have serious doubts that 1,000 homes can correctly measure 54 million television homes, despite all the investigations, auditing, and probing. Yet the scientific fact remains that it is indeed possible for 1,000 homes properly to reflect a national viewing audience within acceptable statistical standards. Qualified mathematicians, working on behalf of advertisers, colleges, and government bodies, have unequivocally endorsed the sampling techniques used by the Nielsen Company to measure national television audiences, accepting the statistical limitations clearly set down by mathematical formula in the reports themselves.

It is equally true that the measurements of local TV ratings by ARB and the local Nielsen TV Index—using the diary method—are equally reliable, given the same restrictions on interpretation. A substantial part of this book is devoted to an explanation of methods of sampling and editing of the diary method, which is the principal form of measuring local TV and radio audiences. The extent of demographics—that is, age, education, sex, economic status, and other fundamental descriptions of the home audience—is also fully discussed and examined, including usage of the data by the advertiser.

While Nielsen and the American Research Bureau are the largest companies in this field, it must be noted that there are other important ones offering such services. C. E. Hooper does a substantial number of telephone interviews to measure broadcast media audiences. Trendex also does telephone interviews, some on a national basis; Pulse uses a personal interview technique and measures radio homes throughout the United States; Mediastat has a diary which measures both radio and TV patterns; Simmons and Politz do some work in this field.

A new research company which offers another dimension has entered the field—Brand Rating Research Corporation. Largely by the use of a fixed panel answering an extensive questionnaire, this BRI service relates the media audience with buying habits. This information enables an advertiser to select his media buy in direct relationship to the potential consumer of his product. In a relatively short time this service has been used extensively by advertising agencies for media planning. As with all services, there are limitations. The factor of recall in obtaining TV information on the BRI questionnaire tends to inflate TV viewing, since the respondent is aided in his recall. But, in general, the information is reliable enough to cause many advertisers to use it as a principal media-planning tool. A description of the method and several case histories are included in the following chapter.

It is recommended that executives of corporations expending large amounts of money on TV and other media set aside enough time to satisfy themselves that the reports of circulation are satisfactory to them. Network or station executives or independent research companies are available to explain in detail what can only be summarized in this book. It is also possible to read the Madow Report of the Government committee that investigated the ratings and to learn their conclusions and recommendations. Furthermore, there is a Broadcast Rating Council which now acts as a watchdog over all radio and television research companies. This committee conducts a special audit by established auditing firms in all phases of broadcast in media research. The purpose of the audit is to assure the advertiser that the rating service does what it says it does. The advertiser must also be informed as to why the rating service does what it does and on its relative reliability.

The prognostication on the future evaluation of media audiences appears to be favorable. The present methods are acceptable within statistical error. While the meter, the diary, the personal interview, and the telephone interview all have limitations, in general the information supplied, when properly used, is thoroughly valid. Furthermore, the composite information tends to validate each service. And each year brings refinements: there is increased use of computers and increasingly rapid reporting of the data, making it possible for advertisers to take action on the basis of this information.

On Media Function and Its Measurement •

ALFRED POLITZ

THE PURPOSE OF THE BEST-KNOWN and most widely used media research is to aid advertisers and their agencies in the selection of media for advertising specific products. The selection is guided, of course, by an attempt to obtain the maximum contribution to sales for each dollar.

It is nearly impossible to discover the sales contribution by means of experiments in which one newspaper is compared with another, one magazine with another, or one TV show with another. And it is, for most practical purposes, too expensive.

Even more difficult is the problem of making sales-contribution comparisons between media. If a TV program as a medium is compared with a given magazine, it is very hard to document that a given commercial accompanying the TV program provides as good a measure for the program as a given ad for the same product provides for the magazine. The influence of copy is an interfering factor in measurement, since the total contribution of advertising to sales actually rests on both media and copy. Variation of copy, even within the same medium, leads to a variation of sales contribution.

The term "sales contribution" is deliberately used rather than the term "sales," since sales in the end are the result not only of medium and copy but also of distribution, pricing, product performance, and merchandising, as well as many other factors. Discrimination between sales and sales contribution is the only way to avoid a certain confusion. Inasmuch as sales are influenced by multiple factors, sales success per se cannot be used as a measure of advertising.

It should be mentioned that research companies have made numerous experiments in which the contributions to sales by forces other than advertising were kept sufficiently constant so that the residual differences observed could be very safely attributed to advertising. But the fields in which such experiments can be carried out are limited, and the experiments are too costly for most advertisers to engage in.

This explains why the greatest portion of advertising research in general and media research in particular reduces its ambition and uses criteria assumed to be "correlated" with sales contribution. The situation is somewhat analogous to an attempt to estimate comparatively the amounts of money which two men have in their respective bank accounts. If there is no firsthand evidence, it is possible to look at their houses and at their clothes. If *A*'s house and clothes look prosperous, the chances are that his bank account is greater than *B*'s, whose house and clothes appear shabby.

The estimating procedure is useful if it is constantly recalled that the evidence deals with probabilities and not with certainties. There are some eccentrics who live in shabby houses and have substantial bank accounts, and there are prosperous men who live in elegant houses and have all their money invested in securities rather than in bank accounts. The procedure is justifiable if the most direct approach—that is, getting the information from banks—is not possible.

Before discussing criteria and operational problems, it seems worthwhile to emphasize the fact that this chapter deals only with media research which is not conducted as confidential research for an individual advertiser. The distinction is important—exemplified by the fact that much confidential information provided for advertiser clients contains more measurements of television than of radio, magazines, newspapers, or outdoor. This is simply the reflection of the amount of money being spent by those particular clients in these various media. It is perhaps unfortunate that the search for adequate criteria is strongly conditioned by operational costs and by so-called salability.

Certain criteria cannot be ascertained by mail interviews, but they can be by personal interviews. Yet there is no doubt that information in terms of accumulation and repeat exposure to media by the same individuals can be more efficiently obtained by having diaries kept over a certain period by a sample of people. To find out by personal interview if a magazine advertisement or TV commercial which appears on two consecutive Thursdays is perceived both times by a person, only once, or not at all requires two personal interviews—one visit on each Friday to ask the respondent whether he or she noticed this advertisement "yesterday," that is, on Thursday.

It might appear that the task could be simplified by visiting respondents only on the second Friday to ask about "yesterday" (the second Thursday) and also about the Thursday of the previous week. The trouble is that this procedure taxes memory and therefore casts doubt on the reliability of the answer—perhaps more doubt than the problem under study can afford. A diary, on the other hand, self-administered by the individual respondent or representative of the household, can overcome the frailty of memory if respondents can be sufficiently enticed to make recordings in the diary on the day and at the time of day when the perception of advertising takes place.

Most research companies use personal interviews, diaries, and telephone interviews where appropriate in order to establish whether a given medium has made contact with a specific individual or with a member of a specific household. In some cases, all three approaches are combined in a single project.

The greatest amount of time and money goes into the execution of personal interviews. The interviewer visits certain households, usually in the latter part of the day when there is the greatest opportunity to find a representative sample of consumers at home. The consideration involved here is the importance of representing a most important segment of the population, those who are gainfully employed and are therefore rarely found at home in the earlier hours of the day.

The specific households which the interviewer has to contact are generally preselected by mathematical procedures applied at the home office. If the inquiry is related to individual reading or viewing behavior, a specific individual is selected within the household. A method has been developed by which this individual selection is accomplished without giving the interviewer any freedom of choice.

Next is the problem of obtaining accurate information. Taking magazine audience measures by personal interviews as an example, the interviewer tries to ascertain whether a specific copy of a specific magazine has been read by the respondent. It is obvious that the mere question, "Have you seen or read anything in the January 15th issue?" could hardly be answered with reliability. In order, therefore, to increase reliability, it is necessary to give the respondents some help. This aid consists of showing a copy of the specific issue under study and going through its full contents before the respondent is requested to state whether any part of the particular copy was seen or read before the interview.

In addition, data are gathered concerning demographic characteristics, such as the size of the household, income of the household, education of the respondent, and so forth. There is nothing original about this. However, the consumption of specific products enriches the information produced beyond the indirect conclusions to be drawn from demographic or socio-economic descriptions.

Further enrichment is achieved by examining certain psychological factors which have a bearing upon consumers' predilections for buying certain products and rejecting certain others. The same psychological traits which make consumers behave differently in their selection of products can also make them behave differently with reference to their selection of magazines.

While one segment of the field of psychology genuinely tries to approach the rigor of exact science, there are other segments which fall short of the degree of mental discipline required in a strict scientific approach. The latter segments are inclined to pursue information that is of little immediate relevance. In my opinion, the psychological part of the investigation should be confined to the exploration of such factors as the venturesomeness of respondents in response to new products, their propensity for spending or saving money, and their personal financial expectations.

When the interviewer has no freedom of choice, it becomes possible by mathematical procedures to direct the operation in such a way that the households or the individuals included in the sample constitute an unbiased sample of the American population. This means that one can project what is found in the sample to the total population. Since this includes, of course, behavior related to magazines, it should be possible to infer from the findings in the sample the total number and characteristics of the readers of a magazine in the total United States.

It is easy in the field of media research to substitute claims for actual quality of performance. In this regard, there is one figure connected with print media which, while not being completely accurate, at least comes close to the ideal of accuracy, as it deals only with objective quantities independent of human memory—that is, the Audit Bureau of Circulations figure. Wherever there is an opportunity, the introduction into a survey of measures of the act of *purchasing* a magazine permits a comparison with the ABC figure. In other words, although the purpose for which the media buyers use audience data is to acquire knowledge about readers and consumers, which ABC figures cannot provide, data can be added which are not related to the primary purpose but which perform the function of checking on the accuracy of the main information.

In situations where comparing the total number of magazine purchases (including circulation) is not feasible, the check data can be confined to copies subscribed to. The names of the claimed subscribers found in the survey are submitted to ABC, and ABC compares the names against subscription lists they confidentially obtain from the various magazines. If the comparison with ABC shows close agreement, it is safe to conclude that the information meets the media buyer's needs for accuracy.

Returning to the problem of criteria for evaluating media's contribution to sales, we logically start by searching for criteria and then selecting the techniques which could hopefully do justice to the criteria. A criterion which could obviously be expected to have a good correlation with a magazine's ability to contribute to sales is the number and kind of people who leaf through the magazine. However, this suggests the question of who is, after all, a reader of an issue. Thinking of the interest of the advertiser, we would say that the more the respondent has seen or read in the issue, the better.

This may suggest stipulating that a reader may be counted as such only if he has seen or read many items in the given issue. Then the question arises, how many? If the number of items is to be 10, it stipulates that 50 percent of an issue has to be read in a magazine which carries about 20 items and only 10 percent of an issue which carries about 100 items. This is a more severe criterion for the first magazine. Such an inequity is present with any arbitrary number, and there is only one solution: reduce the stipulation to one item only and define a "reader" as "a person who has seen or read at least one item."

At one time this definition encountered resistance in some quarters, based on the assumption that it was too lenient for the advertiser's good. Yet this definition of a reader on the basis of "at least one item" is the least of all evils.

To illustrate the problem of an arbitrary cutoff point in any continuum, it may be helpful to use an example from daily life. If an adult is defined as a person *at least* 18 years old, this does not mean that all adults are 18 years old. Needless to say, there are many more adults who are older than 18 years old than who are just 18 years old. Similarly, if a reader is defined as one who sees or reads at least one item, this does not imply that most readers so defined read just one item. This fact is borne out by experimentation that *Life* was willing to undertake in order to obtain actual numbers. It turned out that of those persons who saw or read at least one item in an issue, over 98 percent saw more than that. In fact, 80 percent saw nine or more items. The definition is today the standard definition in the industry.

In all measurements which do not isolate the actual sales contribution, there is a gap which can be filled only by assumptions and judgment. Research attempts to narrow the gap to a smaller margin than that achieved by what is nowadays traditional audience measurement. The fact is that establishing exposure to editorial content as a basis of readership measurement increases by implication the likelihood that ads are read; this in turn increases the seeming likelihood that a contribution to sales takes place.

The question, "Are ads read in a given magazine?" seems to be very plausible, but it is one loaded with fallacies. Whether a given person at the time the interview takes place remembers having seen or read a specific ad depends not only on the magazine which carries the ad but also on the content of the ad itself. That is, the event of remembering is the effect of two causes: medium and copy.

If the purpose is to study the performance of the medium, the influence of copy is a contamination of the measurement. (In this connection, it is worth noting that the recognition scores of two ads of the same size, appearing in juxtaposition in a magazine but with different copy, can vary in the ratio of one to five.) This, then, forces us to seek to eliminate the copy influence.

The solution is simple. What more can a magazine do than provide an opportunity for the reader to be sufficiently impressed with a given ad that he will remember it longer than a split second or a few days or weeks? The opportunity is offered if the page carrying the ad is at least opened. Thus the axiom follows: it is the obligation of a magazine to put open pages before open eyes.

The event of presenting an open page within the field of vision of a given person has to be given a name for the purpose of communication. The simplest name in the English language for this is "exposure." Exposure to a page which carries an ad, therefore, means that there is an opportunity for perception intense enough to be remembered for a split second or for weeks. This use of the word "exposure" happens to be remarkably close to the dictionary definition: "the act of laying open."

Thus research went to the next step and measured not only audience but exposure to ad pages as well. The exposure measurement is uncomfortably sensitive to the precision of interviewing and sampling, but the discomfort is worthwhile in the light of narrowing the room for assumption by one more degree.

Most important, the event of exposure denotes the only event which must be the common goal of all media, not only magazines but also TV, outdoor, newspapers, and radio. If there is a unit of measure equally applicable to all media, it can hardly be anything but exposure. It is the only step toward the ideal measure which does not suffer from the contamination due to differing copy effects. As an indication of the adaptability of exposure as a criterion, a sizable number of exposure studies have been made not only of magazines but also of the outdoor medium and of transportation advertising on the outsides of buses.

The following is an example of the way in which exposure to advertising on the outsides of buses was studied. Rather than count the pedestrians on the streets which are served by the buses, it was reasoned that everybody would be exposed to the poster who would see the poster. Since light rays travel the same straight line between two given points in both directions, it was concluded that everybody would be able to see the poster who could be seen by the poster.

So a camera was mounted on the poster. The camera provided pictures from which it was determined how many people—young and old, male and female—could be seen by the poster. If both eyes of the person could be seen by the poster, the head of the subject under question must have been turned in the direction in which ability to perceive the poster was highly probable.

In such a study, whether the copy on the poster is of such a nature that it is perceived and remembered is an irrelevant question.

In summary:

1. Advertising effectiveness cannot be measured solely on the basis of sales.
2. It is far simpler, and has been proved effective, to base the stipulation for a "reader" on a person who has read at least one item in a magazine.
3. It is the primary function of the magazine, from the point of view of the advertisers who buy space in it, to put the ad pages before open eyes. We have based much media work on this assumption, and we refer to it as "ad-page exposure."

Television Audience Research Basics •

GEORGE W. DICK

THE NEED FOR TELEVISION AUDIENCE MEASUREMENT has been an obvious reality since the first commercial broadcasts. The significance of research today has been greatly increased by the tremendous growth of the television industry itself.

Sampling must form the basis for widespread research, and it has come to be accepted as the foundation. However, there continues to be a great deal of confusion about application of the theory. The complex and highly specialized skills required to make sampling a practical and workable tool create uncertainties among many people.

The uncertainties are natural. It is for this reason that ARB has turned its attention to some specific questions regarding audience measurement: What is audience measurement? How is it obtained? How are its results reported? How can it be used?

WHY AUDIENCE MEASUREMENT?

Anyone communicating any idea must have some indication that the message transmitted is being received. In the context of product advertising, it becomes crucial for the advertiser to have some knowledge of who is receiving the message and how many people are.

The very idea gave rise to audience measurement originally; the growing complexities of media have spurred its growth. Television is a medium of tremendous power and influence and, without question, a highly complicated and expensive advertising tool. It is a field in which the most experienced are continuing to learn—and, though there have been some spectacular successes, most users are trying constantly to improve results further.

No other advertising medium can produce as many complex audience problems as television. In addition to those common to all media, television has an innumerable problem list all its own. Interestingly enough, no two people will have the same list—nor are the solutions always the same. But regardless of the problems that arise, no other medium offers the potential of television—combined sight and sound. To use television most productively, however, one must continue to place primary emphasis on the knowledge gained from meaningful research.

The first and foremost goal of anyone interested in the advertising aspect of television, or of any medium for that matter, is to obtain the greatest possible knowledge of and acquaintance with the medium. This goal ideally extends to each individual concerned to the slightest extent with television.

A second goal is a continuation of the first: constantly and regularly renewed acquaintance with the medium and the changes that occur within and around it. Never in the history of advertising has a medium moved so fast and changed so often and so dramatically. Patterns established yesterday are changing today—patterns in programming, commercial technique, selling, station operation, coverage, buying, planning, competition, and cost. The problems created by this constant change are as much a station's problems as an advertiser's problems; they affect everyone concerned with the medium.

Many of the problems of advertising in television arise at the buying stage. These are problems of selection—of making the best choice of broadcast vehicle, programs, announcements, stations, times, and markets. At this stage, particularly, research can mean the difference between good and poor choices. The number of choices and problems of selection in television is increasing every day as more stations and programs go on the air in more markets, as more films become available, and as different sales techniques develop. Obviously, as more possibilities present themselves, so does the necessity increase for means of measuring and identifying the relative values of each.

Research firms in the field provide a very close view of the estimated size and nature of viewing audiences, both locally and nationally. Close study of the basis quantitative estimates amassed by the measurement services enables both station and advertising planners to reduce considerably the chance for error in ad campaigns.

A different set of problems, usually occurring early in the planning stage, has to do with the nature and content of the commercial message that will be used. While it is not a primary function of audience research to provide data on "commercial effectiveness" or "impact," it is an area of growing concern and work. There are, as well, a number of firms that specialize in commercial and program testing, measuring the reaction of audiences to announcements and programs under laboratory test conditions. Once planning work such as this is accomplished and much thought and research have led to general profiles of the best audience for a certain product, past audience estimates are helpful for matching characteristics in planning buys.

Then, once advertising is placed on the air, other problems arise concerning following it up or checking results. Many times these are the most perplexing problems, and this is the area in which audience measurement is most often misused or misinterpreted. A few advertisers are fortunate in being able to check television results quickly and with accuracy where it counts most—at the cash register. By far the majority, however, cannot isolate the television results from the effects of other media advertising, or if they can, not until a great deal of time has passed.

This realistic problem of checking results comes in two parts: first, a *quantitative* question of estimated audience size, location, and character; second, a *qualitative* question of sales effectiveness. Television research services do a good job of providing answers to the first part of the problem. They can't however, tell too much as yet about what happened after —whether a sale was made.

The prime purpose of the research services is to provide specifically designed tools for the solution of television problems. Not only does research meet many needs from a purely economic point of view, but it also serves the viewing public. It is a natural and logical assumption that if advertisers truly wish to affect the public, their messages will accompany the type of television programming which people desire. However, they must know what this is. They must know what people do, not just what they say they will do.

WAYS OF MEASURING

There are a number of techniques for measuring audience, differing distinctly in procedure and purpose. But regardless of basic procedural differences, all audience measurements have a common characteristic: they are based on sampling.

Today almost everyone is at least vaguely aware of sampling and the effect that results of sampling have on our economy. But because many people are never asked to contribute information directly, except in a national census, it is totally inconceivable to many people that a sample can validly represent an entire universe—in the case of television, more than 50 million households.

To understand sampling fully, one would first ask the reason why sampling procedures were adopted in the first place—why they were necessary. Population growth, faster communications, mass production techniques, and more sophisticated management personnel are just a few of the factors that gave rise to sampling. It became apparent to the Federal Government years ago, for example, that conduct of its business and discharge of its responsibility required better and faster techniques for gathering essential statistics. How could it best meet the ever increasing demand for data on the cost of living, imports, exports, employment, income, taxes, and the hundreds of other factors with which it must deal?

Manufacturers, retailers, service organizations, and professionals needed measurements, too. Take the manufacturer producing thousands of items on an assembly line. How could he perform an accurate test of weight, size, and quality and do it quickly and economically? Suppose a large flour manufacturer had to know the average consumption of bread in New York? Or suppose a television advertiser had to ascertain how many people saw his programs each week?

All of these problems have one thing in common in that they cannot be solved practically—if at all—by a complete count or census. A tremendous amount of time, energy, and money would be needed to analyze the great mass of data these problems involve, even if, indeed, the data could be collected.

Sampling was developed and adopted to provide answers to these problems, and it works extremely well when properly applied. No statistician would ever doubt that the above problems can be solved by sampling. Proper sampling is an accepted, logical, and highly practical procedure used by people, governments, and businesses all over the world—not merely a technique conceived by the broadcast research companies.

But it is important to note, above all else, the modification, *when properly applied.* Poorly designed, inadequately controlled sampling and improper analysis have resulted in statistical chaos in situations where even an uneducated guess would have been the best solution. The key to the accuracy and value of any measurement based on sampling is threefold—the method, the sample itself, and what is done with it.

As mentioned above, there are a number of measurement techniques, and because they all differ, it has been a regular source of amazement to many people that one research company uses telephone interviews and another a diary. Yet the simple fact of the matter is that more than one research method is needed today to meet the varied demands of the communications industry.

There are primarily four classifications of audience measurement methods—each with advantages, each with disadvantages. To understand and appreciate the final audience estimates obtained from any one of the methods, it is an essential prerequisite to recognize the basis of the technique.

Diaries. Diaries are the primary source of audience information for practically every audience measurement firm. More station television time is bought and sold on the basis of estimates produced by the diary than by any other method. While the actual diaries used and the placement and sampling procedures differ from one company to another, the basic principle is the same: a selected sample of people are asked to keep a written record of a particular media activity, such as television viewing or radio listening.

The chief advantage of this method is that a diary can be designed to obtain a wide variety of information on the sample, in addition to specific media activity. It is also of importance that the diary can be adapted to an area of any size; it covers all broadcast hours; it is economical; and, in the case of television and radio, it can report individual activity—not merely set operations. The fact that it must be mailed to sample homes, used by the sample families, returned by mail, and then processed contributes to making it a somewhat slower method than some others.

Telephone interviews. With the high percentage of telephone homes today, telephone interviewing has become a much more reliable method of sampling than it was twenty or even fifteen years ago. Telephone surveys put the interviewer in direct contact with a person in the selected sample home so that questions can be asked directly. This advantage should, of course, be weighed against the possible interviewer bias that may be introduced. However, with trained and experienced interviewers and a professionally designed questionnaire, the limiting factors should not be great.

One of the main advantages of telephone surveys is that they can be conducted at the same time programs are broadcast. It follows that interviewees should be able to relate their media activity more accurately, since questions are asked when the activity is occurring. However, when surveys are conducted coincidentally with the broadcast, a time restriction is automatically set on the survey. Questions must usually be brief, and the resulting estimates are, therefore, not as comprehensive as those from a diary. Telephone interviewing is, nevertheless, quick and economical.

Mechanical devices. While a set's being on does not necessarily indicate actual viewers, mechanical devices have the advantage of being independent of people in the sample homes—in other words, the *device* indicates the tuning condition of the set. This frees the method from many interviewee biases that might occur because of inaccurate reporting, although it does limit the amount of basic quantitative data that can be obtained. Although machines are not immune to error, machine malfunctions can be spotted and identified more readily.

Mechanical systems are expensive to install and maintain. Therefore, research companies usually change sample homes less frequently than with other methods. But the speed with which estimates are reported by some mechanical techniques is so important and convenient in certain cases that objections to many of the limitations are diminished.

Personal interviews. Personal interviewing is expensive, time consuming, and subject to more interviewer and interviewee biases than the preceding techniques. However, excellent rapport can be created between interviewer and interviewee when a superior questionnaire is employed by a trained and experienced interviewer. There are many cases in which certain questions could only be asked personally, in which interviewers can *see* whether the questions are properly phrased and understood. Answers can be evaluated as they are given.

Unfortunately, the high cost and time consumption of personal interviewing has forced the application of recall techniques in those instances in which the method has been used. People must remember what they did—and in many instances one spokesman is asked to recall for the entire family. In addition, the recall technique creates an almost unsolvable problem of how to count families not available for interview who may or may not have been available for viewing during the period being measured.

Because of these advantages and limitations, most organizations use personal interviewing exclusively for special types of audience research rather than for broad and comprehensive coverage of audience measurement.

Within each of the four basic methods, biases can exist because of survey design, because of interviewers, and because of a hundred other factors that necessarily enter into such a complex operation as sampling. Together, these factors are a substantial reason why resulting estimates from two research companies may differ widely even though they both employ the same basic method. On the other hand, no practicing researcher employs any one of these techniques exclusively. And combinations are often used to gain the advantages or offsetting costs of each. Also, each research company has its own unique application of a technique, gained through its experience in adapting the method to audience measurement. That is why anyone who makes an evaluation of a research service should carefully examine the details of technique—the design of the survey, sample selection, placement procedures, interviewer competence, processing ability, accuracy control checks, and statistical capabilities.

Putting any of these basic survey plans into action requires detailed planning. Exactly what do we want to discover? What are we going to ask? Where and how are we going to select the people to be surveyed? How can the information be compiled, evaluated, validated? What form must it take to be most valuable to those who need the information? These are just a few of the questions any researcher must face.

The answers to these questions must inevitably differ from one research firm to another. But since the specific form the survey takes is such an essential part of research, it is impossible truly to evaluate the results of a survey without first considering how the information is obtained. Consider a finished statistical report on a survey. Unless one knows how the survey was conducted, what specific steps were taken to make it a reliable survey, and what criteria were used in analyzing the results, the figures actually have no meaning. For this reason the following section is devoted to a discussion of methods of obtaining audience estimates for each of the survey techniques used.

DIARY-BASED SERVICES

From the very beginning, we must recognize the importance of audience-size estimates in terms of individuals as well as homes reached. *People* watch television. *People* buy products. One selection of a technique which can most economically identify the people in the audience and, indeed, provide some indication of whether anyone actually viewed is the viewing diary. The diary provides the best opportunity for gathering the wealth of information which is increasingly required in automated media analyses.

The primary measurement tool for both local and national audience-research services is the interviewer-supervised viewing diary. The distinguishing factor of the diary technique is interviewer supervision. As the application of this supervision is outlined, the reliability added by the personal relationship between a skilled interviewer and the respondent will become apparent.

Diary design. The diaries are designed to collect extensive audience characteristics in addition to the basic viewing information. More specifically, diaries furnish complete and detailed instructions for recording separately, for each day of the week, the time when viewing occurred, the station, program, and audience composition.

In addition to viewing and audience-composition information, the diary is also designed to gather information on the age, sex, and number of school years completed by each person in the household; whether the housewife works outside the home more than 30 hours a week; occupation of the male head of the household and his type of employment; which commercial during the week was considered "best" by family vote; the number of television sets being used in the home; whether the home has a color television set; whether the home subscribes to a community antenna or cable system and, if so, the name of the company; the county and state of the diary-home residence; the time zone; the channel number, call letters, and city location of every television station that can be received; and comments and suggestions of the diary keeper. Also, one diary has a special section designed to gather information on the family's product usage—such as the number of wash loads per week and the consumption of instant coffee, headache remedies, hair spray, beer, and cake mixes.

Although this requires no small effort on the part of diary keepers, when properly approached and instructed as to the purpose of the survey families are usually quite willing to cooperate. In most cases no direct compensation is given for their efforts, although a token payment is made in areas where it has proved helpful in maintaining a satisfactory cooperation level.

Each sample used for diary surveys is composed of different families every week during a survey and from survey to survey. Experience has shown that families will keep one week's record of their viewing but that the viewing record becomes less satisfactory if the family is retained in the sample for a longer period.

To review briefly the advantages of the diary method: it provides a record of individuals viewing rather than merely set operation, it is adaptable to any size area, it can cover all broadcast hours, and it can provide a wide variety of information very economically. But these advantages lose their meaning if the original source—the diary itself—is lacking in accuracy or is invalid in any way. For example, some diary entries may be made on the basis of hearsay or the estimate of the diary keeper. As with any written questionnaire, the transcribing of information from the point of its inception to the final report is subject to human and mechanical error. And there is the question of possible differences in viewing habits between those who keep a diary and those who do not. For these reasons, a continuous program of testing, validation, and study is important.

Many of the errors do tend to be canceled out at least partially in the end results. Tests have been conducted which compare the results of a diary study with the results of other techniques of audience measurement, such as personal and telephone coincidentals, conducted in the same areas at the same time. By isolating the problems, information is gained as to the degree of statistical differences and their significance. For practical business decisions, the viewing diary has been found to be second to no other currently used technique in providing valuable audience estimates for industry use in television.

National diary surveys. While local market reports offer audience estimates on the basis of time periods by individual stations in local reception areas, the national TV reports provide a comprehensive analysis of network programs throughout the country—whenever they are telecast during the survey period. Even though the two types of reports cover different areas—and even report somewhat different information—the basic diary technique is the same.

The number of actual sampling points for a national report varies—from 300 during a period when no local market surveys are being conducted to 1,200 during nationwide sweep surveys. The national sample for each network report is composed of usable records received from approximately 2,500 different television families. Again, as in the local surveys, the sample is distributed throughout the 36 basic units in proportion to the television-homes estimates for each unit.

As in the case of local market surveys, a new sample of homes is selected for each survey and for each week of the survey. But unlike the local market surveys, national reports generally cover only a two-week survey period.

TELEPHONE SURVEYS

The telephone obviously plays a dynamic role in research plans as seen even in the discussion of the diary technique. But the telephone also serves as the basis for a separate survey technique—coincidental measurement. Coincidental measurement, of course, means that a survey is conducted at the same time that a specific program is being telecast.

Such a system, offering quick and economical measurement of audience for specific time periods, is an essential requisite for complete research. Because television is a dramatically changing medium, audience estimates are frequently needed on short notice as an aid in making decisions. Therefore, overnight surveys using a telephone coincidental technique are crucial.

Obviously, since the survey is coincidental the amount of information obtainable from respondents is, to an extent, limited. The prime functions of the service are, therefore, limited to determining ownership of at least one television set; assurance that there was viewing by one or more persons in the home at the time the telephone rang; and the channel number, station call letters, and title of the program being viewed. Other information can be obtained but is not a standard part of the service.

How telephone surveys are conducted. Telephone coincidental surveys are conducted largely on a local market basis and are designed to measure the population as represented by the nontoll sections of a particular market's telephone directory. The telephone directory being used is divided among all the interviewers in the market, so that each listing in the books theoretically has an equal chance for selection. In most cases, these interviewers are special telephone coincidental interviewers, as distinguished from the interviewing staff which places diaries. However, these interviewers are equally well trained in selecting homes to be called and in conducting interviews.

A minimum of 300 usable calls for any telephone coincidental survey is guaranteed—a usable call being defined as one which was dialed as many as five consecutive times during a measured time period.

Samples are selected, according to instructions, prior to the time period being measured. Interviewers are instructed to begin dialing the first sample homes 30 seconds after the start of the time period. Using the appropriate questionnaire, the interviewers are to record appropriate data for each telephone call.

MECHANICAL DEVICES

An instantaneous electronic measurement technique is used in the New York metro area. Essentially, the system operates through the use of small electronic units placed in several hundred television sets, representing a carefully selected sample of the New York area covered. These units connect by direct wire to an office that has a central computer.

At frequent, evenly spaced intervals during each quarter-hour period, an interrogation signal is transmitted to each of the units. Each unit replies instantly by indicating the tuning condition of the set to which it is attached. The computer receives this information, analyzes it, and tabulates it. Each time an interrogation is made, the computer records the number of sets tuned to each station and the number of sets reporting. This initial material is recorded on computer tape so that it may later be used by a larger computer which verifies data and provides quarter-hour rating estimates.

The sample: how it operates. Selection of the New York sample began with actual enumeration of more than 90,000 dwelling units in preselected blocks and tracts in the New York area. Specific homes were then systematically selected, beginning from a random starting point.

As in the case of any survey, some of the families chosen in the original sample refused to participate, not allowing the meter to be installed. However, substitute homes were chosen in the same way as the original homes, and taken from the same sampling tract.

The actual sample size fluctuates from time to time, although the objective is approximately 425 units in 340 homes. Fluctuations are caused at times by technical difficulties. But these are temporary variations, and, as they tend to be random, no specific bias should result.

Obviously, meters measure only set tuning and cannot determine whether anyone in the sample home is actually viewing at the times the set is reported on. However, the audience estimates are reported in these terms, and the need for swift rating estimates makes meters an essential method in the New York area.

Meters are used for national surveys of network programs for the New York metro area, while telephone coincidental interviews are conducted at sampling points throughout the country. The combination provides networks with audience estimates the morning after a program is telecast.

PERSONAL INTERVIEWS

The use of personal interviews is limited almost exclusively to radio reports and self-initiated research and development work. Personal interviewing is also valuable as a verification check against other survey methods, and it has been used in this capacity.

Expense is certainly a factor in limiting the use of personal interviewing, as is the time element, and TV media audience-research needs can be met with other reliable techniques. It is only in cases in which the universe to be measured is so specialized and precise that it requires something different in terms of sampling plans and questionnaires that personal interviewing is considered for use.

Consideration of the various measurement techniques points up the fact that choice of the one best approach depends upon the requirements of the user research—on exactly what the user wants to discover. Each technique has its own value and limitations. In evaluating the various research services which are available, the user must consider the versatility of each service and the firm's ability to handle each of his problem-area needs.

REPORTING THE RESULTS

The ARB Local Report service is designed to provide results of pertinent audience research on a regular basis to furnish television station, advertiser, and agency clients with a reliable aid in evaluating audience size and type for buying and selling decisions. The service provides reports of various kinds.

The *Television Market Reports* offer viewing estimates on the local level and are issued from surveys conducted in each of the 240 television markets at least twice a year. Depending on its size, a market may be surveyed as many as ten times each year. A report of basically similar design is published for each of the markets, based upon the information collected in viewer diaries returned from each survey area.

Local TV surveys are scheduled throughout the year for each market in such a way as to measure representative programming periods and also furnish reports during the seasons when they are most needed for buying and selling television time. Each survey is conducted over a period of several weeks, usually four. The sample is distributed equally over each of the survey weeks, and the results are combined for average-per-telecast audience estimates. This averaging is done to gain a broader time base for the surveys and add stability to the data. The broader time base more adequately represents all the conditions to which an audience during any specific time period may be subjected.

The audience information in the report is preceded by a map of the survey area; general information on the television stations in the market; the number of households and estimated television homes, color-TV homes, and multiple-set homes in the survey area; total sample characteristics; sample placement and return information; and counties included in the survey area.

In brief, each Television Market Report includes estimates of total homes reached, metro rating, metro share, and certain demographic data. These estimates are given for each time period (quarter-hours during the daytime and half-hours at night) in a broadcast week, and each supplies a mode of evaluating the television audience.

Specifically, the total-homes figure represents an estimate of the number of families who viewed a station at the designated time from wherever the station could be viewed. It is by far the most widely used yardstick for buying and selling local television time, because it gives an indication of the total audience delivered by a station during a given time period.

The metro rating is simply the percentage of all TV homes in the metro area which were reached by the station at the particular time. One hundred percent represents all homes within the metro area which have a television set.

Ratings traditionally have been based on the county or counties comprised by the metro area rather than the total survey area of a market, since the competing stations' broadcasting capabilities may differ. The differences are caused by differences in physical facilities, such as the amount of power and the height and location of the station's tower. The resulting differences in audience potential would cause the ratings base for each station to differ. The metro, on the other hand, provides a somewhat equal opportunity area and a common 100 percent base for all home-market stations. Thus the rating serves as an excellent estimate for evaluating program acceptance to compare with the same program's acceptance in other markets or with other programs in the same market.

While a rating expresses the percent of the television homes reached in the metro area, the share percentage relates to those homes in which television was actually viewed. The 100 percent in this case refers to all television homes in the metro area which had television sets turned on. Suppose, for example, that during a given time period half of the television homes in the metro area of a one-station market had their sets on. The station's rating would be 50, its share 100 percent. Now suppose another station is added which divides the same available audience equally between the stations. The rating for each station then becomes 25, and each station's share of audience, 50 percent.

Each Television Market Report also gives the broadcaster and advertiser certain demographic data which are of vital importance in delineating types of audience reached. From the total survey area the number of persons viewing is shown by several categories. The adult male and female classifications are both totaled and divided into age groups: 18 to 34, 35 to 49, and over 50. Two other age classifications are teens (12 to 17) and children (2 to 11). In addition, viewing housewives are shown by three important categories: (1) those with children under six years of age, (2) those with families of three or more persons, and (3) those employed at least 30 hours a week. Other demographics are offered by competing companies and are varied from time to time in accordance with requests from top clients or the AAA research committee.

The last section of the report is designed primarily to be of service in the process of spot time buying and selling. The "Spot Buying Guide" estimates audience size during station breaks—that period of time between the end of one time period and the beginning of the next. These estimates are arithmetical averages of the quarter-hour audience preceding and following each of the times listed. Therefore, a station's 10:00 P.M. spot audience is determined by averaging the station's reported 9:45-10:00 P.M. and 10:00-10:15 P.M. audiences.

The estimates provided in each market report are gathered from surveys scheduled simultaneously in every market during a particular month. Thus the same time span of programming is reported, and a greater degree of data comparability exists in market-by-market analyses.

Television Audience Profile reports are another important part of the local market service. Published twice each year, for November and March, the TAP report includes the audience estimates from the regular market report plus additional audience profile data—total viewing households; average number of homes viewing by three categories (1 to 2 members, 3 to 4 members, and more than 5 members); and number of homes viewing by education of the male head of the household (by 12 years of education or less and by 13 or more years of education). In addition, the TAP contains product-usage information by the following categories:

1. Number of housewives (adult women over 18) viewing from homes in which six or more wash loads are done a week.
2. Number of housewives viewing from homes in which at least one cup of instant coffee is consumed per day.
3. Number of housewives viewing from homes in which at least one package of cake mix is used a month.
4. Number of viewing housewives from homes in which hair spray is used at least seven times a week.

5. Number of viewing adults (men and women) from homes in which headache remedies are used three or more times a month.
6. Number of viewing adults from homes in which six or more cans or bottles of beer are consumed a week.

In addition to the above, there are a number of reports which serve to fill needs not met in the regularly issued national and local reports. These are largely annual and semiannual references which present key aspects of the standard reports—generally in a different way and for a specific group of clients. Another series of reports, designed for multi-market television planners and buyers, provides a wide scope of pertinent television-audience research material.

The *Television Market Analysis* (TMA) is published annually and is a unique research aid for evaluating and comparing individual stations and markets on the measures of audience, rates, revenue, marketing information, and other valuable data. This data is divided into eight sections:

1. Market rankings—television markets ranked by eleven different categories of audience data. Ranking by average quarter-hour night-time audience is augmented with average total audience and market's dominant station's average nighttime audience rankings. In addition, eight circulation rankings are provided—four based on net weekly circulation and four on average daily circulation.
2. Station rankings—station rankings by ten audience criteria (the same as the above minus the market's dominant station ranking).
3. Individual market data—television market definitions provided by four geographic areas: the metro; an exclusive marketing area; an effective area; and the "98 percent viewing area," which represents the total survey area for Television Market Reports. Basic marketing information on food, drugs, automotive, and total retail sales as well as consumer spendable income has been compiled for each area. Five categories of net weekly circulation estimates are included for each home-market station, and a special analysis of market report share pages shows metro shares, average metro ratings, average metro homes, average total homes, and the ratio in percent of metro homes to total homes.
4. Television market rate comparisons—analysis of the relative efficiency of markets, based on the relationship of network one-hour and 20-second spot rates and average homes delivered per rate period.
5. Television station rate comparisons—stations grouped by network

affiliation with information on the average-homes-reached ranking, average homes reached during prime time, network one-hour rate, and cost efficiency per quarter-hour per 1,000 homes. Similar information is provided for all stations using national spot rates.

6. Broadcast revenue analysis—a market-by-market comparison which details actual FCC revenue data by network, national spot, local, and total revenue and lists corresponding information on revenue per 1,000 homes reached during prime time. A four-year revenue analysis provides growth trends in all four categories of revenue.
7. Share of metro audience comparison—a three-year trend analysis from prime-time share-of-audience information, which provides pertinent audience data for individual stations. This information is grouped by network affiliation, time zones, and number of stations in the market.
8. Total households and TV homes—giving the most current county and state estimates of total households and television homes.

The *Network Television Program Analysis* offers information for evaluation of network programs on both a local and a national level. For each regularly scheduled network program telecast during the survey period, the report provides for all markets the total homes, total persons, total men and women plus three age breakdowns of each, teens, children, and housewives by three categories. The individual market data, except for the program's metro rating, are reported as percentages of the program's total national audience for all of the demographic categories above, facilitating a quick market-by-market comparison of how well a network program fared in each of the television markets surveyed. In addition to the individual market listing, network-program audience data are provided by market types according to nine geographic regions; market ranking groupings; market size (one station, two stations, and so forth); and spot TV efficiency (high, medium, and low CPM homes).

The *National Television Audience Composition Report* is actually a further breakdown of information collected on network program audience. It provides viewers per 100 homes and viewer demographic characteristics by day, quarter-hour, and half-hour time periods for the total United States and for the Eastern, Central, Mountain, and Pacific time zones. Demographic characteristics include the number of male and female viewers, family size, age of youngest child, age and educational level of the head of the household, and the percentage of working housewives for each audience segment. The section of the report giving audience characteristics by program type provides audience data by 18 types—for example, westerns, evening comedy, daytime drama, public affairs, and sports.

The *Syndicated Program Analysis* was instituted because of the increasing importance of syndicated programs to local television stations. This report provides a means for evaluating how well a certain program is doing in other markets during different time periods.

Audience Flow Analysis provides the estimated source and destination of the audience to a station or program during any given time period.

Viewing Group Analysis aids in evaluating a schedule of spots or programs by providing the estimated exclusive audience to each unit of the schedule and to every possible combination of units.

Special News Analysis combines several tabulations—the Cume, frequency-of-viewing, audience-flow, viewing-group, and station-loyalty analyses—to provide a special research package that will aid in pinpointing strengths and weaknesses in news programs. The station-loyalty analysis examines the portion of a station's late news audience which also viewed the early news, and vice versa, thus evaluating the degree of dependence on a particular station for news information.

The *Station Duplication Study* provides a selling tool for stations located in a market which lies within or partially within the area of another market. The Station Duplication Report provides the net weekly and average daily unduplicated circulation of each of the stations within the overlapping markets.

The *Special Market Report breakout* (1) provides tabulations of less than the standard quarter-hour measuring period to determine audience levels by five- or ten-minute segments for such programs as news, weather, and sports; and (2) provides an estimate of viewing to stations from adjacent markets whose audience may reach into the market under consideration but is grouped into "other" viewing in that market report because its level of audience does not qualify for individual listings.

Multimarket audience comparisons provide comparisons of audience estimates in several television markets. Also available are multimarket comparisons for syndicated programs, sets-in-use levels, commercial preference, and share of audience.

Color-TV penetration reports provide an estimated percent of TV homes in any market which are equipped to receive broadcasts in color.

Top 30 Programs reports rank the top 30 television programs in any market on the basis of total audience, most men, most women, and most children.

Special tabulations by computer are often undertaken. Most of the previously listed special tabulations are done for specific stations and markets. When larger and more complex tabulations are needed, a specially prepared computer program is often practical.

One such special computer tabulation is the spot activity report. Briefly, this involves a method for evaluating an agency's spot purchases. Traditionally, the evaluation—using the estimated audience and cost to calculate the cost per thousand—has been a monumental clerical task for agencies with substantial television billings. When the appropriate cost information is provided, a special computer program can perform the task, thereby lessening the clerical burden of the agency.

A number of special computer tabulations are currently being developed which stand a very strong chance of becoming future research products. One such program is the rate card analysis. This report offers the potential for a detailed cost evaluation of a station's rates based on the latest audience estimates for the station. For any spot times or participations it can provide a cost-per-thousand evaluation by total homes, men, women, teens, children, total persons, men 18 to 39 years of age, and women 18 to 39. These figures are based on each different rate classification.

Another such report is the sales territory analysis, which presents an advertiser's estimated audience in terms of his own marketing and sales areas. In other words, since many advertisers who have established sales areas would prefer to have audience estimates which are quickly comparable by these areas, the sales territory analysis is designed to meet this need.

A report on demographic characteristics by market is made up of an extensive tabulation and cross tabulation of many demographic characteristics of viewers in specific markets. It is similar in purpose to the standard Television Audience Profile reports but delves more thoroughly into the many possible viewing-audience breakdowns by various demographic criteria.

Special recall surveys are used to estimate viewing when it is impractical to obtain this information by the coincidental method—for example, for those time periods immediately after 11:00 P.M. and immediately preceding 8:00 A.M. Sample families are contacted by telephone on the day following the late-night time period to be measured and during the day of the early-morning time period. Interviewers attempt to contact these sample families a maximum of seven times between 8:00 A.M. and 10:00 P.M. Responses are then tabulated, providing ratings and share of audience, and results are delivered to the ordering client within one week of the date of the survey.

With the heavy concentration of various ethnic groups in many areas of the country, advertisers and broadcasters are becoming increasingly aware of the importance of reaching such groups on a selective basis. Ethnic group studies have been completed using bilingual diaries and bilingual interviewers to obtain television viewing estimates of Spanish populations in a number of markets. Surveys have also been designed using certain ethnic surnames as a target audience.

Reinterviewing families who have participated in diary surveys offers the potential for further study of particular viewer groups—people who watch a farm program, women who watch an afternoon movie, the audience to a special public affairs program, and so forth. Since it is possible to identify the audience to a particular program, reinterviewing can be designed to probe into facets of viewing activity not readily available by other survey methods. Such questions as "Do you make a point of watching the show?" or "Which member of the family selected the program?" provide a means of audience evaluation in terms of specific advertising objectives.

Other popular special studies are picture quality studies, color-TV studies, special radio research, and brand-share and product-usage studies. Special studies, of course, have very few restrictions, since they involve an individualized approach in each case.

PROBLEM AREAS IN AUDIENCE MEASUREMENT

Many problems have existed in audience measurement since the beginning, and there is every reason to believe that some of these will always be with us. This fact does not, however, negate the need for audience measurement or the value of audience measurement. But it does make it apparent that anyone who is concerned with the proper use of the estimates which are obtained through audience research should have a natural concern about these problems and their possible solutions. Great strides have been made. More will be made. How swiftly and how effectively steps are taken depends upon the understanding and attention the problem areas receive.

In addition to the *bona fide* problem areas, there are other areas where problems are needlessly created, simply by lack of understanding.

In both of these cases, something positive is being done—by the research firms involved, by trade interests, and by individuals. Most of the major trade organizations are working both together and independently to bring more facts to light. More and more, responsible and experienced people are writing, talking, and thinking about audience research, and many of the "mysteries" are becoming clear through objective and understandable analysis and discussion. More people are also studying audience estimates and using them more intelligently. And in doing so, they are discovering new uses and new meaning.

Two Congressional hearings have brought out many of the subjects of major concern for discussion and action. Following the 1963 hearings, the National Association of Broadcasters formed the Broadcast Rating Council to establish standards and provide auditing systems for audience research firms. This is a voluntary project for the research companies, but there has been a great deal of support for the effort, which has led to the Rating Council's becoming a separate corporation.

Let us consider a few of the problem areas in some detail.

Differences in data. Differences in data between one research service and another do not occur because of sampling theory but because of sampling practice. There is substantial evidence all around us that sampling is, indeed, the only solution to the marketing research needs of today. However, it is in implementing the sampling theory that differences in data will occur.

There are at least seven factors which can cause these differences in the audience figures published by the various research firms. These factors are measurement techniques; area measured; number of broadcasts involved; survey dates; manner of tabulation; sampling variations; and seasonal, geographical, and competitive program changes.

As for measurement techniques, there are four general ways of obtaining viewing information, and all four, plus some combinations, are in use today. The four, which have been discussed in detail above, are the mechanical recorder, the telephone interview, the personal interview, and the viewer diary. While all four provide a measurement of the audience, each one approaches it from a different angle.

The mechanical recorder is an excellent technique for measuring set tuning. It gives a good estimate of the volume of set operation and the nature of channel switching in a home. The recorder by itself, however, has no way of ascertaining how many or what kinds of people are watching the set—or even if anyone is in the room at all.

The telephone coincidental interview reveals what people who answer the phone *say* they are viewing at the time of the call. It has been found to be a satisfactory method for obtaining specific viewing information and answers to short, simple questions pertaining to television or, perhaps, product usage.

The personal interview, unless conducted coincidentally to the time period being measured, relates what people who are interviewed say they watched a number of hours earlier (or the previous evening) when aided in recall by a roster of programs broadcast.

The viewer diary reports what the respondent noted in written form at the time viewing—either by him or by others—took place.

Each one of these techniques is really measuring a different thing—set operation in one case, what people said under two conditions, and what people wrote in another. It must be expected that each of the methods will produce a different rating or audience estimate for the same program.

With regard to area measured, audience viewing information produced by measurement of, say, six counties constituting a metropolitan area must be expected to differ from information taken (even by the same system at the same time) in 40 counties around the same metropolitan area. This difference is caused by variances in signal reception, by the effect of outside stations which put a viewable signal into fringe counties, and by the different working, living, and viewing habits of rural and small-town viewers.

Since the sample size is so important in determining the precision of audience-research estimates, it should be understood that every user of television research data has a right to be informed of the effective size of the sample upon which each item of information is based.

With regard to the number of broadcasts measured, it stands to reason that viewing data for one particular broadcast on a certain date will differ from an average of the viewing estimates obtained by measuring two or more broadcasts of the same program.

As to survey dates, one service may publish, say, a July report using average figures based on a two-week survey conducted between July 4 and July 17. These data can easily differ from the July report of another service which happened to choose to measure the weeks of July 18 to July 31.

With respect to tabulation, there are a number of ways in which different results can be obtained from the same base data. The concepts of "average per minute audience" and "total audience" for a quarter-hour rating fall under this heading. In the former, one estimates the average viewing audience at any given minute of a program, and in the latter the audience that recorded seeing five or six minutes or more of the program during that quarter-hour is counted. Both are completely legitimate and useful audience estimates, as long as one recognizes what the estimates are based upon.

Even assuming that two research companies used the same interviewing methods for a survey, they would still come up with different figures. The differences in audience estimates are caused by variations in sampling. They become understandable when we realize that even two similar surveys by the same service, in the same area and at the same time, will normally produce estimates that are different. However, in this case both estimates may be expected to fall within the standard deviation or confidence range that applies. Yet they will appear as two different figures. That fact, in itself, in no way detracts from the value of either figure.

Seasonal, geographical, and competitive program changes, although linked to the factors of survey dates and area measured discussed previously, are sometimes overlooked as reasons for changes or differences in estimates often within the same service.

Misuses of data. We now shift our attention from the producers to the users of audience-research data. There are obviously cases when estimates are misused within the broadcasting and advertising industries—and these further compound the problems of audience research.

For instance, difficulties arise when audience estimates are used outside the environment in which they were obtained, as when a local rating is applied nationally or to another local area. Local ratings apply only to the area in which they were obtained, and by the same token, national ratings cannot be directly applied to various local areas. Before any survey begins, research companies have a clear understanding of the universe to be measured and, when that universe is so defined for the user, it is the only universe for which the estimates are applicable.

The use of ratings in a vacuum is another instance of misuse. Ratings alone cannot and should not carry the entire burden when an advertiser is appraising a show for sponsorship or continued broadcasting. Fortunately, the growing research sophistication on the part of advertisers and broadcasters has minimized this problem in recent years. In addition, the variety of audience information now provided by researchers has lessened the dependency on any one yardstick for determining television's success as an advertising medium.

Some of the best television campaigns, in terms of sale of merchandise, have been the lowest rated in a market. Probably the best examples of such shows are the daytime women's shows. The secret here seems to be that the program, the personalities, the commercial message, and the product are all extremely well matched to reach and sell a big part of a comparatively small, loyal audience of housewives.

Today's successful television advertiser recognizes the importance of audience types as well as audience size. He realizes that the lowest cost per prospect is not necessarily found among the higher-rated programs. He is increasingly aware of the climate for his commercials, in that programs which bring a favorable response because of their content bring a correspondingly favorable response to his product.

Similarly, the broadcaster has developed a keen awareness in serving all facets of the television audience. Station image is an important matter of concern, not only as a measure of responsibility to his viewing public but also as a salable value to his prospective clients. Through industry associations broadcasters are doing much to gain an understanding of all the yardsticks of a successful operation and to place each in its proper perspective. This increased attention to television's total potential has produced greater rewards for sponsors and broadcasters alike.

Closely connected to the overdependence upon ratings is the use of audience estimates as exact figures. Again, the tendency to switch schedules at the drop of a rating point is more a rarity than a common practice, but it deserves mention here. In every report and throughout every item of information there are carefully detailed descriptions of why the data should be accepted only as sampling estimates. This misuse has diminished and will continue to do so as more information is circulated on the proper interpretation of audience-research findings.

Standard deviation. A rating is an approximation. When a program is rated at ten (10 percent of the potential viewing homes) that means *about* ten, not exactly ten. The plus-or-minus range, or "confidence interval," around the rating which makes up this "about" depends upon the standard deviation. The important thing is that this range in a true probability sample can be measured mathematically.

All audience estimates, no matter who produces them, have a standard deviation, as does any measurement based upon sampling. The exact standard deviation formula, however, applies only to deviation expected in a theoretically perfect probability sample and does not take into account recording or processing errors that might occur or any limitations preventing a sample from being a perfect probability one. Inasmuch as it is impossible in a practical audience-measurement operation to obtain a perfect probability sample, because of the nonrespondent factor and the omission of nontelephone homes, actual deviations in audience estimates may, of course, be somewhat greater.

The plus-or-minus confidence range generally used is that having a reliability of 95 percent. This means that if one made the same survey 100 times, the rating results would fall within the calculated confidence range 95 times. (There are other reliability levels too, but 95 out of 100 is most frequently used in broadcast research because it seems to fill most requirements.)

Table 1 shows how this principle works in connection with ratings, using a local-area sample size of 300 homes as an example. These figures do not imply that a probability sample has been achieved or that the estimates are precise to the stated mathematical values. The point here is merely to demonstrate statistical variation to which all sampling is subject. Other errors which may occur are not considered.

Subject to these limitations, the tabulation shows that if a program has an actual audience of 20 percent, there will be a plus-or-minus range of 4.6 rating points around the 20 and that the rating estimate will fall between 15.4 and 24.6. Another way to look at it is this: with two identical surveys at the same time, one might show a 20 and the other an 18; still a third survey would produce another figure, perhaps a 21. But note that 95 out of 100 of these rating estimates would fall within the 15.4 to 24.6 range associated with the sample size of 300, with the majority of results tending to cluster around the actual audience of 20.

The size of the survey sample is important. (Size means the actual number of different base units measured, whether it is homes, wheat farms, or air-brake parts.) The plus-or-minus deviation range narrows as the sample is increased. Note in Table 2 how an increase in the sample of four times—from 100 to 400—cuts the range of deviation in half—from 6.0 down to 3.0. Notice also that to cut the deviation in half, it was necessary to increase the sample four times.

Naturally, a larger sample is more desirable since it produces a rating with a narrower margin of possible deviation. One can reach a point at which audience data are completely meaningless when the total number of

APPLICATION OF STANDARD DEVIATION PRINCIPLE

Program Audience (in rating points)	*Plus-or-Minus Deviation (in rating points)*	*Low Rating Limit*	*High Rating Limit*
10	3.5	6.5	13.5
15	4.1	10.9	19.1
20	4.6	15.4	24.6
25	5.0	20.0	30.0
30	5.3	24.7	35.3
40	5.7	34.3	45.7
50	5.8	44.2	55.8

TABLE 1

SAMPLE SIZE AND STANDARD DEVIATION

Sample Size	*Plus-or-Minus Deviation (for a rating of 10)*
100	6.0
200	4.2
300	3.5
400	3.0
500	2.7

TABLE 2

different homes used in the survey is too small. Conversely, while a sample cannot be too large from the standpoint of accuracy, it certainly can be too large in terms of the work required of it or the broadcasters' and advertisers' budgets that support it. Increasing the sample size four times means approximately four times as much in field costs for each survey. The practical solution is to use a sample that enables advertisers and broadcasters to make logical business decisions and still remain within a reasonable budget.

Since the confidence range for ratings exists, no advertiser should be upset when a program's rating drops a point or two (perhaps even five points) compared with the figures from the previous month, nor should a small gain cause excitement. A three- or four-time trend analysis should be developed in order to determine a significant direction of audience activity. If a program's rating rises from survey to survey, or continuously drops, then the research data can govern a broadcaster's or advertiser's action.

The nonresponse factor. Ideally, each home selected should participate in the survey in order to create, or maintain, a true probability sample. But, practically speaking, there are obviously some people who will never participate in surveys. Once a single person refuses, the sample is no longer really pure. The important consideration, however, is what effect a noncooperator has on the overall validity of the resulting estimates—and that is what we will discuss here.

It is often assumed that since the diary-keeping process—or any survey process, for that matter—requires *something* on the part of a selected family or individual, persons for whom television is a more significant recreational outlet are more likely than others to exert the effort of participating. In short, this suggests that returners of diaries will tend, because of their alleged greater interest in television, to do more viewing on the average than nonreturners, thus yielding higher values among returners than among nonreturners for estimates of "homes using television" and other estimates.

Interest in the validity of estimates has resulted in a number of studies which compare, among other things, the viewing of those families who cooperated in a diary survey and the viewing of families who did not cooperate in the survey. (Noncooperation indicates either refusal to accept a diary, acceptance and nonreturn of the diary, or return of an unusable diary.)

In the latest major study, an analysis of the diary technique using telephone coincidental surveys in 25 separate markets as comparisons, only one market was found in which there was a significant difference in the amount of television viewing by returners and nonreturners. The composite of the 24 market tested reported that 24.7 percent of the returners were viewing television at a given instant as compared to 23.8 percent of the nonreturners—not a statistically significant difference. A comprehensive report on the entire project was prepared, published, and distributed within the industry in order further to enlighten users of audience measurement regarding this important area of research. The report is by no means a final chapter on the nonresponse factor; rather, it is a pioneer project which opens the way to additional research.

Audience-measurement firms are constantly testing methods which will improve the cooperation rate. Although there will inevitably be those who will not cooperate in surveys, a firm and thorough knowledge of these people will certainly help to increase the validity of audience research.

Analyzing the service. There is some departure from theory on the part of all practitioners. Much that could be done comes at a higher cost than is now economically feasible. Fortunately, however, recent industry attitudes indicate an acceptance in many areas for improved and expanded audience measurement that has broadened this economic feasibility.

In studying TV research, the various services and their capabilities, one of the many considerations should be the degree of willingness on the part of the practitioner to put his own service to the test and to reach out for new research opportunities whenever they can help to clarify a media problem.

* * *

Every manufacturer of goods or purveyor of services using television to any degree, every advertising agency concerned with planning and placing television campaigns, and every television station concerned with profitable programming for its audience stands to benefit from familiarization with and intelligent use of television-audience research. It is not only the big-volume, big-name company that has a vital stake in efficient use of television. The new or the small sponsor buying his first announcement schedule in one market needs the same efficiency. And, as a matter of fact, for competitive purposes the small station or advertiser may well require more efficiency.

*The Marketing Value of Media Audiences: How to Pinpoint Your Prime Prospects** •

NORTON GARFINKLE

MARKETING HAS ENTERED the era of selective selling. Sophisticated marketing men are no longer asking the question, "How many people do I reach with my advertising?" They are now asking the more difficult question, "How many of my best prospects do I reach with my advertising?"

The Brand Rating Index Service provides advertisers, advertising agencies, and media with some of the data necessary to answer this question. These studies, conducted among a national probability sample of more than 10,000 adult men and women 18 and over, are designed to perform three tasks:

1. To identify the prime marketing targets for specific brands and products.
2. To describe the demographic characteristics of these prime target groups.
3. To identify the media that are most efficient in reaching each target group.

Marketing men have traditionally identified their targets as heavy users of the product category. Current studies confirm the findings of previous research—that the one-third of the households that can be identified as heavy users of a specific product category frequently account for two-thirds of the total product consumption. To go one step beyond this, in most product areas 50 percent of all households account for close to 90 percent of the total consumption of the product.

* The material in this chapter was originally presented at the Association of National Advertisers' January 19, 1965 Workshop on Advertising Planning and Evaluation.

The actual usage rates for a number of products are shown in Table 1. The figures indicate that in many product categories, such as car rental, air travel, hair-coloring products, and dog food, less than 20 percent of the population accounts for more than 80 percent of the usage. Even in the case of widely used products like soft drinks, facial tissues, coffee, and headache remedies, no more than 50 percent of the households account for close to 90 percent of the usage. No matter what the product is, therefore, advertisers almost always aim marketing efforts at no more than 50 percent of the population. In the light of these figures, it is not surprising that the stated objective of many marketing campaigns is to reach the heavy-user household.

The Brand Rating Index studies obtain information on the frequency of use of more than 150 major types of consumer products. This information provides a basis for:

1. Identifying the heavy users of each of the products studied.
2. Describing their demographic characteristics.
3. Identifying the media that are most selective in reaching these heavy users.

Here are some of the results of detailed analyses. The most important general finding is that the heavy users of the different products vary widely in their characteristics. Further, these differences in the characteristics of users of different products are carried over in the way different media vehicles select out heavy-user groups.

User characteristics vary by product categories. Automatic-dishwasher detergents, for example, are sharply oriented to upper-income families. Table 2 shows the sharp variations in usage of automatic-dishwasher detergents among different demographic groups. At the top end of the scale, the product is used by 35.9 percent of the homemakers in upper and upper-middle social class households and by 34.2 percent of the homemakers in households with $10,000 or more income. At the bottom end of the scale, the product is used by fewer than 1 percent of the Negro homemakers, the homemakers with low incomes, and the homemakers with grammar school education.

The same kind of variation exists among different media audiences. Table 3 presents the results of an analysis of 151 specific media vehicles: 91 nighttime network programs, 43 daytime network programs, and 17 major magazines. The table shows the ten most selective vehicles and the ten least selective vehicles. At the top end of the scale, 20 percent of the homemakers in the *Time* average-issue audience, 17.3 percent of the *Newsweek* audience, and 16 percent of the *Life* audience use auto-

PERCENT OF TOTAL PRODUCT USAGE ACCOUNTED FOR BY THE HEAVY USERS OF SPECIFIC PRODUCTS

(BRI December 1963)

	Heavy Users % of Population Group	*Heavy Users % of Total Usage*
Car rentals in past year (men)	3.6	89.6
Liquid dietary products	4.1	98.0
Air trips in past year (men)	7.8	87.3
Automatic-dishwasher detergents	9.0	100.0
Hair-coloring rinse or tint (women)	11.3	88.1
Scotch whiskey	12.6	98.6
Cigar smoking (men)	17.1	98.6
Rye or blended whiskey	18.4	98.5
Bourbon	18.8	98.7
Canned dog food	19.3	99.2
Dry dog food	20.7	99.2
Canned ham	22.8	83.0
Instant coffee	26.1	80.6
Cold or allergy tablets	27.0	84.3
Cigarettes (all adults)	27.2	84.1
Hair tonic (men)	27.8	76.8
Laxatives	28.2	92.8
Rice	28.8	82.7
Peanut butter	29.6	82.4
Cake mix	34.1	84.4
R.T.E. cereal	37.2	80.2
Upset stomach remedies	37.3	89.2
Shaving cream/pressurized cans (men)	38.7	98.0
Frozen orange juice	41.0	92.1
Soft drinks	41.8	84.9
Paper napkins	42.9	83.2
Bleach	43.7	81.6
Tomato sauce	44.9	90.7
Cleansing or facial tissues	45.2	82.9
Frozen vegetables	49.9	92.1
Regular ground coffee	50.5	92.7
H.H. laundry detergents	50.8	81.4
Headache remedies	52.6	93.1

[Note: The total population group is based on total households except for those products specifically designed otherwise.]

TABLE 1

HOW DEMOGRAPHIC GROUPS VARIED IN SELECTIVITY OF MARKETING TARGETS FOR AUTOMATIC-DISHWASHER DETERGENTS
(BRI December 1963)

	% of Group That Are Users of Automatic-Dishwasher Detergent	*Index of Target Selectivity*
Total female household heads	9.0	100
Upper & upper-middle class	35.9	399
$10,000 or more income	34.2	381
College-educated	23.1	258
Live in suburbs of SMSA	18.9	211
5 or more people in household	13.9	155
Homemaker 35-49 years of age	13.9	154
Youngest child 6-17	13.8	154
$8,000-$9,999 income	13.8	153
Western geographic region	12.9	144
Middle social class	12.6	141
Northeastern geographic region	10.7	120
3-4 person households	10.4	116
Youngest child under 6	10.1	112
North Central geographic region	9.5	106
High school education	8.1	90
Homemaker under 35 years of age	7.2	81
Homemaker 50 years & over	6.0	67
No children under 18	5.5	61
$5,000-$7,999 income	4.8	54
Southern geographic region	4.7	53
Live outside SMSA	4.5	51
Live inside Central cities	4.5	50
1-2 person households	4.3	48
Lower-middle social class	3.0	33
Lower social class	1.5	17
Under $5,000 income	0.9	10
Grammar school education	0.4	4
Negroes	0.4	3

TABLE 2

matic-dishwasher detergents. At the bottom end of the scale, fewer than 2 percent of the *True Story* average-issue audience or the "Queen for a Day" average-program audience use this product.

The reasons for this pattern are clear. The first table demonstrated that income was one of the factors most closely related to usage of automatic-dishwasher detergents. The same kind of variation is shown in Table 4 in the income profiles of the homemaker audiences of the different programs and magazines: 53.9 percent of the *Time* readers, 46.5 percent of the *Newsweek* readers, and 44.9 percent of the *Life* readers have incomes of $8,000 or more as compared to only 12.2 percent of the *True Story* audience and 10.4 percent of the "Queen for a Day" audience. Given these relationships, it is not surprising that usage of automatic-dishwasher detergents is more than four times greater among the women exposed to the more selective vehicles than among women exposed to the less selective vehicles.

This kind of information can be used by the advertiser to improve his media schedule by picking programs or magazines with above-average usage level. The table demonstrates vividly that the "marketing value" of the audience is an important factor that must be taken into considera-

HOW SPECIFIC MAGAZINES AND TELEVISION PROGRAMS VARIED IN SELECTIVITY OF MARKETING TARGETS FOR AUTOMATIC-DISHWASHER DETERGENTS

(BRI December 1963)

	% of Audience Who Are Users of Automatic-Dishwasher Detergent	*Index of Target Selectivity*
Total female household heads	9.0	100
1. *Time*	20.0	222
2. *Newsweek*	17.3	192
3. *Life*	16.0	178
4. *Saturday Evening Post*	15.9	177
5. *Better Homes & Gardens*	15.5	172
6. *American Home*	14.6	162
7. *Ladies' Home Journal*	14.3	159
8. Danny Kaye	13.6	152
9. *McCall's Magazine*	13.5	150
10. "Hollywood & The Stars"	13.0	145
. . .	. . .	. . .
142. "Love of Life"	4.2	46
143. "Temple Houston"	4.0	45
144. "The Doctors"	3.8	42
145. "The McCoys"	3.6	40
146. "Seven Keys"	3.4	37
147. "Secret Storm"	3.2	36
148. Lisa Howard—News	2.5	29
149. "Day in Court"	2.4	27
150. *True Story*	1.7	19
151. "Queen for a Day"	1.4	17

TABLE 3

HOW SPECIFIC MAGAZINES AND TELEVISION PROGRAMS VARIED IN SELECTIVITY OF FEMALE HOUSEHOLD HEADS WITH HOUSEHOLD INCOMES OF $8,000 OR MORE

(BRI December 1963)

	% of Audience with H.H. Incomes of $8,000 or More	*Index of High-Income-Group Selectivity*	*Rank on Selectivity of Users of Automatic-Dishwasher Detergents*
Total female H.H. heads	27.9	100	
Time	53.9	193	1
Newsweek	46.5	167	2
Life	44.9	161	3
Saturday Evening Post	42.6	163	4
Better Homes & Gardens	45.9	165	5
American Home	44.7	160	6
Ladies' Home Journal	44.1	158	7
Danny Kaye	37.0	132	8
McCall's Magazine	42.1	151	9
"Hollywood & the Stars"	35.2	126	10
"Love of Life"	16.7	60	142
"Temple Houston"	22.2	80	143
"The Doctors"	15.7	56	144
"The McCoys"	15.1	54	145
"Seven Keys"	15.7	57	146
"Secret Storm"	12.4	44	147
Lisa Howard—News	10.6	38	148
"Day in Court"	9.5	34	149
True Story	12.2	44	150
"Queen for a Day"	10.4	37	151

TABLE 4

tion along with the traditional factors of cost and impact. Since there are sharp differences in the degree to which different programs and magazines select out users of the product, the cost savings in using some of the more selective vehicles can be substantial.

The detailed information developed on this product illustrates another important point. The process of selecting media that offer high prospect potential must ultimately focus not on general media classes—like magazines or television—but rather on specific media vehicles. Even in the case of a sharply focused product like automatic-dishwasher detergents, there are a substantial number of television programs, as well as magazines, which afford the advertiser an unusually good prospect potential. For example, the detailed tables on this product indicate that not only are the *Time* and *Newsweek* audiences above average, but the Danny Kaye television program audience is 52 percent above average in selecting out users of automatic-dishwasher detergents.

The important point here is that an analysis of prospect potential does not restrict the advertiser to the use of only one general medium. The advertiser can find specific vehicles within each of the general media—television, magazines, newspapers, and radio—that will afford high potential for his specific product. The advertiser who feels he can get greatest impact by using both magazines and television programs or any other combination of media can achieve his objective by using the highly selective vehicles from each medium. Whatever the advertiser's general approach, the greatest dividends can be gained not from a simple analysis of cost per thousand homes but by building a schedule around vehicles that provide a substantial number of prospects at a minimum cost.

There is a marketing myth that selectivity exists only for high-income products, but some products find heavy users among low-income groups. Now let's examine a product that has the opposite pattern from that of automatic-dishwasher detergents—laxatives.

As Table 5 indicates, laxatives are used regularly by 49.7 percent of the Negro households and 36.9 percent of the households with incomes under $5,000 as compared with only 15.0 percent of the upper- and upper-middle-class households and 14.5 percent of the households with incomes of $10,000 or more.

The specific media pattern shown for users of laxatives in Table 6 is an almost complete reversal of the pattern shown for users of automatic-dishwasher detergents. "Queen for a Day," which was the lowest-ranking program in selectivity of users of automatic-dishwasher detergents, is the top-ranking program in selectivity of regular users of laxatives. At the other extreme, *Time,* which was the top-ranking vehicle in selectivity for automatic-dishwasher detergents, is the lowest-ranking vehicle in selectivity of regular users of laxatives.

The two examples cited so far have been fairly clear-cut. In both cases, the single most important dimension producing the variations in media selectivity was the dimension of income, education, and social class. Now let's examine another product—men's hair tonic—where the operative demographic factor is age.

Table 7 shows the same pattern for this product as for those presented earlier. There are very sharp variations in usage among different popula-

HOW DEMOGRAPHIC GROUPS VARIED IN SELECTIVITY OF MARKETING TARGETS FOR LAXATIVES
(BRI December 1963)

Regular-User Households— Those Using Laxatives at Least Once a Month	*% of Group That Are Regular Users of Laxatives*	*Index of Target Selectivity*
Total female household heads	28.2	100
Negroes	49.7	177
Grammar school education	39.3	139
Lower social class	38.8	138
Under $5,000 income	36.9	131
Homemaker 50 years & over	36.4	129
Southern geographic region	34.9	124
1-2 person households	34.1	121
No children under 18	33.8	120
Lower-middle social class	33.1	118
Live in Central cities	30.9	110
Live outside SMSA	30.1	107
High school education	26.7	95
Northeastern geographic region	26.4	94
$8,000-$9,999 income	25.9	91
5 or more people in household	25.6	91
North Central geographic region	25.3	90
Respondent 35-49 years	25.0	89
Youngest child 6-17	24.6	88
Western geographic region	24.0	85
$5,000-$7,999 income	24.0	85
3-4 person households	23.9	85
Live in suburbs of SMSA	23.2	82
Youngest child under 6	22.6	80
Homemaker under 35 years of age	20.9	74
Middle class	18.9	67
College education	16.2	57
Upper & upper-middle social class	15.0	53
$10,000 or more income	14.5	51

TABLE 5

tion groups. At the top end of the scale, 35.8 percent of the men in the 18-to-35 age group use hair tonic daily. By way of contrast, only 15.2 percent of the men in the over-50 age group use this product daily. Table 8 shows that there are equally sharp variations in usage patterns among different media audiences. At the top end of the scale, 36.8 percent of the audience for "The Fugitive" and 36.8 percent of the *TV Guide* audience use hair tonic daily. At the other extreme, only 19.5 percent of the "To Tell the Truth" audience and 20.5 percent of the "Today Show" audience use hair tonic daily.

Table 9 shows that these sharp variations result primarily from the influence of the age factor both on product usage and on media exposure. The table shows vividly that the programs and magazines that are highly selective of regular hair tonic users also tend to be the programs with large concentrations of young men under 35. The table also adds weight to the conclusion that the analysis of selectivity should focus not on broad media classes like television or magazines but on specific programs and specific magazines.

All television programs are not alike and all magazines are not alike. One group of television programs, like "The Fugitive," is among the

HOW SPECIFIC MAGAZINES AND TELEVISION PROGRAMS VARIED IN SELECTIVITY OF MARKETING TARGETS FOR LAXATIVES

(BRI December 1963)

	% of Audience Who Are Regular Users of Laxatives	*Index of Target Selectivity*
Total female household heads	28.2	100
1. "Queen for a Day"	43.9	157
2. Lisa Howard—News	41.0	146
3. "Day in Court"	40.0	142
4. *True Story*	39.9	141
5. "The Great Adventure"	39.0	139
6. "The Virginian"	38.4	136
7. "Rawhide"	38.1	135
8. "The Doctors"	37.6	133
9. "Who Do You Trust"	37.3	132
10. "General Hospital"	37.1	132
142. "Captain Kangaroo"	24.3	85
143. *Redbook*	23.9	85
144. *Better Homes & Gardens*	23.6	84
145. *Saturday Evening Post*	23.3	83
146. "Tonight Show—Carson"	23.2	82
147. *Life*	23.0	82
148. "Hollywood & the Stars"	22.7	80
149. *Woman's Day*	22.6	80
150. *Family Circle*	22.4	79
151. *Time*	18.9	67

TABLE 6

HOW DIFFERENT DEMOGRAPHIC GROUPS VARIED IN SELECTIVITY OF DAILY USERS OF HAIR TONIC

(BRI December 1963)

	% of Adult Men in That Group Who Use Hair Tonic Daily	*Index of Target Selectivity*
Base: total adult men (18 & over)	27.8	100
Under 35 years of age	35.8	129
Age of youngest child under 6	34.8	127
Single men	34.5	124
35-49 years of age	33.5	121
High school graduate	33.3	120
Age of youngest child 6-17	32.8	118
H.H. income $5,000-$7,999	32.6	117
5 or more in household	32.2	116
H.H. income $8,000-$9,999	31.7	114
Blue-collar workers	31.5	113
Some college	31.5	113
3-4 in household	30.5	110
Some high school	29.9	108
Executive & professional	28.5	103
Income $10,000 or more	27.5	99
College graduate	26.8	96
Married, widowed, divorced	26.6	96
Negro	23.3	84
Income under $5,000	22.5	81
Grammar school or less	20.5	74
1-2 in household	18.7	67
No children under 18	18.0	66
50 years & over	15.2	55

TABLE 7

most selective vehicles; and a different group of television programs, like "To Tell the Truth," among the least selective. Similarly, one magazine, *TV Guide,* is among the most selective vehicles; and another, *National Geographic Magazine,* is among the least selective.

The table illustrates one further point. In the past, there has been little information available on television program audiences other than ratings data describing the number of households tuned in. Consequently, programs have been dropped from the air on the basis of simple household ratings with little reference to the marketing value of the actual people exposed to the program. There is a sharp difference between a "household" rating and a "people" rating, and there is an even sharper difference between a "household" rating and a "marketing target" rating. If the effort is made to match specific products to appropriate programs, the "ratings game" may produce different results as to which programs are kept on the air as well as more efficient media buying for individual advertisers.

The above illustrations provide some insight into the direct ways in which demographic factors such as age or income can produce sharp variations in the selectivity of media for different products. The next examples illustrate a somewhat different point. There are equally sharp variations in usage among different population groups. But in each of

HOW SPECIFIC MAGAZINES AND TELEVISION PROGRAMS VARIED IN SELECTIVITY OF DAILY USERS OF HAIR TONIC

(BRI December 1963)

	Ranking of Media Vehicles by % of Adult Men in Audience Who Use Hair Tonic Daily	*Index of Target Selectivity*
Base: total adult men (18 & over)	27.8	100
1. "The Fugitive"	36.8	132
2. *TV Guide*	36.8	132
3. "Breaking Point"	36.7	132
4. "The Lieutenant"	36.2	130
5. Jerry Lewis	36.2	130
6. "Outer Limits"	35.8	129
7. "Eleventh Hour"	35.5	128
8. *Playboy*	35.5	128
9. "McHale's Navy"	35.4	127
10. *Sports Afield*	35.1	126
109. *National Geographic Magazine*	25.0	90
110. "The Price Is Right"	23.6	85
111. "Sing Along with Mitch"	23.3	84
112. "Password" (night)	23.2	83
113. "International Showtime"	23.1	83
114. "Bell Telephone Hour"	23.0	83
115. "Meet the Press"	22.8	82
116. "I've Got a Secret"	21.8	78
117. "Today Show"	20.5	74
118. "To Tell the Truth"	19.5	70

TABLE 8

HOW SPECIFIC MAGAZINES AND TELEVISION PROGRAMS VARIED IN SELECTIVITY OF ADULT MEN WHO ARE BETWEEN 18 & 35 YEARS OF AGE

(BRI December 1963)

	% of Adult Men in Audience Who Are Between 18 & 35	*Index of Selectivity of Young Men 18-35*	*Rank on Selectivity of Daily Users of Hair Tonic*
Base: total adult men (18 & over)	34.2	100	
"The Fugitive"	48.1	141	1
TV Guide	45.0	132	2
"Breaking Point"	50.7	148	3
"The Lieutenant"	42.3	124	4
Jerry Lewis	40.1	117	5
"Outer Limits"	56.3	165	6
"Eleventh Hour"	41.7	122	7
Playboy	73.0	213	8
"McHale's Navy"	43.8	128	9
Sports Afield	52.0	152	10
National Geographic Magazine	31.8	93	109
"The Price is Right"	22.3	65	110
"Sing Along with Mitch"	19.6	57	111
"Password" (night)	22.1	65	112
"International Showtime"	25.7	75	113
"Bell Telephone Hour"	25.5	75	114
"Meet the Press"	17.4	51	115
"I've Got a Secret"	18.1	53	116
"Today Show"	24.1	70	117
"To Tell the Truth"	14.8	43	118

TABLE 9

these cases there is no single demographic dimension which accounts for all or even the major part of the variation in media selectivity. Rather, a number of different factors combine to produce the variations.

Table 10 shows the sharp variation in usage of cold tablets among different demographic groups. Among the factors related to cold-tablet usage are age of youngest child, size of family, and race and age of homemaker. The demographic groups with the highest usage levels are the households in which the youngest child is in the 6-to-17 age group, households with five or more people, and Negro households. In addition to these identifiable variables, there may well be other psychological and nutritional factors which do not show up in a normal analysis of population groups.

The variety of factors involved suggests that a demographic analysis can provide only a partial clue to media selectivity. The only effective way to account for all of the factors that influence cold-tablet usage is to

HOW DEMOGRAPHIC GROUPS VARIED IN SELECTIVITY OF MARKETING TARGETS FOR COLD OR ALLERGY TABLETS

(BRI December 1963)

Regular-User Households— Those Using at Least 3 Tablets a Month	*% of Group That Are Regular Users of Cold or Allergy Tablets*	*Index of Target Selectivity*
Total female household heads	27.0	100
Youngest child 6-17	34.8	129
5 or more people in household	34.2	127
Negroes	32.8	122
Homemaker 35-49 years of age	31.7	117
3-4 person households	30.4	113
Homemaker under 35 years of age	30.2	112
Youngest child under 6	29.9	111
$5,000-$7,999 income	30.0	111
Lower-middle social class	29.9	111
High-school education	29.1	108
North Central geographic region	29.1	108
Southern geographic region	29.0	108
$8,000-$9,999 income	27.8	103
Live outside SMSA	27.4	102
Live in suburbs of SMSA	27.3	101
Lower-social class	27.1	101
Grammar-school education	26.4	98
Live inside Central cities	26.1	97
Western geographic region	26.1	96
$10,000 or more income	25.9	96
Under $5,000 income	25.1	93
Middle-social class	24.2	90
Northeastern geographic region	22.7	84
College education	22.6	84
Upper & upper-middle social class	21.4	79
No children under 18	20.7	77
Homemaker 50 years & over	20.4	76
1-2 person households	18.8	70

TABLE 10

HOW SPECIFIC MAGAZINES AND TELEVISION PROGRAMS VARIED IN SELECTIVITY OF MARKETING TARGETS FOR COLD OR ALLERGY TABLETS

(BRI December 1963)

	% of Group That Are Regular Users of Cold or Allergy Tablets	*Index of Target Selectivity*
Total female household heads	27.0	100
1. "Father Knows Best"	40.8	149
2. "Loretta Young Show"	36.5	136
3. NBC News—Newman	36.4	135
4. "General Hospitals"	35.9	133
5. "Outer Limits"	35.6	131
6. "Seven Keys"	35.4	129
7. "Make Room For Daddy"	35.4	129
8. NBC News—Scherer	35.2	129
9. "Queen for a Day"	34.6	128
10. "The Flintstones"	34.5	128
142. Danny Kaye	26.1	97
143. Garry Moore	25.8	95
144. *Redbook*	25.7	95
145. Judy Garland	25.7	95
146. "I've Got a Secret"	25.6	95
147. "To Tell the Truth"	24.6	91
148. Jack Benny	24.2	90
149. "To Tell the Truth" (night)	24.2	90
150. "Bell Telephone Hour"	23.2	86
151. "Meet the Press"	23.0	86

TABLE 11

measure this usage directly among the audiences of each of the major media vehicles.

This direct measurement shown in Table 11 indicates that there is very sharp variation in usage among viewers of different nighttime television programs. Programs like "Father Knows Best," "The Loretta Young Show," "Outer Limits," and "The Flintstones" are among the most selective vehicles, while others like "The Jack Benny Show," "To Tell the Truth," and "The Bell Telephone Hour" are among the least selective of cold-tablet users. This complex pattern holds true for the great majority of products.

Information on the characteristics of regular users of facial tissues is given in Table 12. The regular users of facial tissues differ substantially in characteristics from the regular users of cold tablets. Despite the fact that these two products appeal to different population segments, the information on both products illustrates the same general point about media selectivity. The detailed data in Table 12 denote sharp variations in usage of facial tissues among different demographic groups and indicate that there are a number of different factors related to usage of this

HOW DEMOGRAPHIC GROUPS VARIED IN SELECTIVITY OF MARKETING TARGETS FOR FACIAL TISSUES

(BRI December 1963)

Regular-User Households—Those Using at Least 401 Single Tissues a Month	*% of Group That Are Regular Users of Facial Tissues*	*Index of Target Selectivity*
Total female household heads	45.2	100
$10,000 or more income	63.5	140
5 or more people in household	61.3	136
Upper & upper-middle social class	60.4	133
Homemaker 35-49 years of age	57.6	127
Northeastern geographic region	56.9	126
Youngest child 6-17	56.2	124
Youngest child under 6	54.2	120
$8,000-$9,999 income	54.2	120
Middle social class	53.8	119
College education	53.7	119
Suburbs of SMSA	52.6	117
$5,000-$7,999 income	52.4	116
North Central geographic region	50.7	113
High school education	49.7	110
3-4 person households	49.4	109
Homemaker under 35 years of age	48.2	107
Live inside Central cities	46.9	104
Western geographic region	41.4	92
Lower-middle social class	39.6	88
Live outside SMSA	38.0	85
Negroes	37.3	83
Lower social class	36.0	80
No children under 18	33.2	74
Homemaker 50 years & over	32.1	71
Southern geographic region	31.9	71
Grammar school education	31.1	69
Under $5,000 income	30.8	68
1-2 person households	30.3	67

TABLE 12

HOW SPECIFIC MAGAZINES AND TELEVISION PROGRAMS VARIED IN SELECTIVITY OF MARKETING TARGETS FOR FACIAL TISSUES

(BRI December 1963)

	% of Audience Who Are Regular Users of Facial Tissues	*Index of Target Selectivity*
Total female household heads	45.2	100
1. "Tonight Show"—Johnny Carson	59.4	133
2. *Good Housekeeping*	58.1	129
3. *Redbook*	57.6	127
4. *American Home*	57.5	127
5. *Woman's Day*	57.1	126
6. *Life*	56.9	126
7. *Parents' Magazine*	56.8	126
8. *Time*	56.8	126
9. "DuPont Show of the Week"	56.2	124
10. "Breaking Point"	55.9	123
142. "General Hospital"	42.7	94
143. "Father Knows Best"	42.6	94
144. Lawrence Welk	42.4	94
145. Lisa Howard—News	42.1	93
146. "Secret Storm"	42.1	93
147. "To Tell the Truth" (night)	42.0	93
148. "The Doctors"	41.5	92
149. "Seven Keys"	41.2	91
150. Tennessee Ernie Ford	40.3	89
151. "Queen for a Day"	40.2	89

TABLE 13

product. In this case, both income and family size contribute directly to heaviness of use of facial tissues, along with a number of other factors including age, education, and geographic region. As for the data in Table 13, the same factors that produce sharp differences in consumer product usage also influence the consumer's media habits—the programs that she watches and the magazines she reads.

The most important points that emerge from these tables are: (1) there are a number of different factors that combine to influence usage of each product and exposure to each program and magazine; (2) consequently, the demographic data alone are not sufficient to predict the selectivity of each vehicle for each product.

Mathematicians have looked into the question of how well the demographic data can be used to predict the product-usage levels of specific media audiences. In general, multiple-correlation analysis indicates that, in most product categories, demographic data alone can predict no more than 50 percent of the variation in usage levels among different media audiences and in most cases can predict only 20 to 30 percent of the variation.

Even in the first three product areas examined—automatic-dishwasher detergents, laxatives, and hair tonic—where simple factors such as age and income are the major influences, there are enough other factors operating that there is no one-to-one correspondence between the media-planning result that would be secured through profile matching and the result secured through direct examination of the product-usage pattern of each audience. (See Table 3 versus Table 4 and Table 8 versus Table 9.)

The sharp differences in product usage among different media audiences require taking account of product-usage levels in formulating media schedules. But the complexity of the factors that influence usage of most products makes it both difficult and hazardous to make important media commitments solely on the basis of limited demographic data.

There are several general conclusions that emerge from these data:

1. There are sharp variations in the degree to which different media vehicles select out marketing targets for specific brands and products.
2. The selectivity of different programs and magazines will vary sharply from product to product.
3. For any product, there is substantial variation in the selectivity of different vehicles within the television medium and within the magazine medium, as well as between media classes.
4. The most effective way to measure the selectivity of media vehicles for specific products is to do so directly—by analyzing the product- and brand-usage levels of the people within each specific audience.

The last point is particularly important. Until recently, the standard method of selecting media has been to match the demographic profile of the product derived from market studies with the demographic profile of media audiences derived from independent media studies. This procedure was a major advance over the simple application of cost-per-thousand criteria to total audience figures. However, the data presented in this paper indicate that the technique of profile matching has two major limitations.

For one thing, profile matching of necessity is limited to the few demographic characteristics which were covered in both previous market studies and previous media studies. As a consequence, the specific demographic factors selected for matching may not be the critical ones—and in all cases they will not cover all the demographic and psychological variations related to purchase behavior.

Second, and equally important, the procedure of looking only at demographic variables overlooks the fact that the consumer's previous exposure to advertising for the brand is one of the critical factors influencing her purchasing behavior. If a consumer is a regular reader of a magazine in which brand *X* has been advertised, she will have a greater likelihood of buying brand *X* than a customer with the same demographic characteristics who has not been exposed to the magazine. Since exposure to advertising is an independent variable which has no necessary relation to demographic characteristics, there is no way to account for the advertising-exposure factor through profile matching. The only way to account for previous exposure to advertising as well as all the other demographic and psychological factors is to measure the product- and brand-usage levels directly within each specific media audience.

The essential point is that profile matching is a substitute for direct examination of the media habits of the product's prime marketing targets. In the past, the indirect method of profile matching was the best technique available because direct data matching media to markets were not available. Now that there are marketing and media data on the same consumers, one can utilize media-selection procedures which go directly from a definition of marketing targets to an analysis of the media habits of these target groups.

The first step is the definition of the marketing target group. As shown above, in a number of product categories (such as automatic-dishwasher detergents) all brands are competing directly for the loyalty of a limited group of total users or heavy users. In these categories, it is appropriate to utilize "total users" or "heavy users" as the marketing target group. In many other categories, however, the various brands have directed their appeals to different segments of the total-user market. To take only one example, in the laundry soap and detergent category, low-suds detergents like Ad, All, and Dash appeal to a very different segment of the market from high-suds detergents like Tide, Cheer, Oxydol, and Fab. Among upper-income households (incomes of $8,000 or more), 26 percent use Ad, Dash, or All, as compared with only 9 percent of the households with incomes under $5,000 and only 5 percent of Negro households. Sharp differences like these—which are the rule rather than the exception in many product areas—indicate that in many cases the advertiser's prime marketing targets must be identified not simply in terms of heaviness of product-category usage but rather in terms of responsiveness to the specific brand being marketed.

The prime targets for many established brands generally consist of two groups. Current users of the brand are one of these. They are valued customers, and advertising to them serves to confirm their commitment to the brand. A careful analysis of brand-switching behavior in a number of product categories indicates that in our dynamic economy between 20 and 40 percent of the regular purchasers of a brand (those who say it is the brand they buy most often) will switch away from that brand within a six-month period. Marketing efforts that are effective in reaching current customers can minimize this switch-away rate to less than 20 percent.

Consumers who consider the brand their second choice make up another prime target group. These people are almost, but not quite, convinced. Reaching them with advertising can convert them into users. Our studies have indicated that the largest group of new customers comes from this second-choice group. The "conversion rate" among consumers who consider the brand their second choice is more than four times greater than the conversion rate among consumers who rate the brand lower than second choice. Equally important, the rate of switching from second-choice to regular user can range between 10 and 30 percent for different brands in the same product category in a six-month period. Marketing and advertising efforts that are effective in reaching the second-choice group may be able to maximize the conversion rate at the 30 percent level or even higher.

To meet the need for information on marketing targets, the Brand Rating Index gathers data not only on heaviness of product-category usage but also on consumer usage and acceptance of all the major brands in the major product categories studied. These data enable the advertiser to identify the prime marketing targets for his own brand: current customers, in order to retain their loyalty and keep the switch-away rate to a minimum; and consumers who consider the brand their second choice, so as to maximize the conversion rate and thereby gain the largest possible group of new customers.

The most important finding of analyses of the characteristics of the prime marketing targets for different brands is that these groups vary widely both in demographic characteristics and in media habits. The critical point is that an analysis of media patterns which starts with a definition of marketing targets in terms of the brand itself shows the same sharp variation as an analysis which starts with the definition of the heavy user of the product category.

The kind of information presented here has a wide variety of applications to specific media decisions. The implications of the data are clear. If the differential marketing value of media audiences is taken into account, then it is possible for the advertiser to increase the efficiency of his media-selection process not by 5 or 10 or 15 percent but by substantially more than 20 percent.

One of the more interesting applications of these data is in the scheduling process. Many multibrand advertisers have available to them a number of media vehicles which have been bought on an annual corporate basis. In many cases, the process of matching brands to vehicles has been done largely on a random basis. For example, there was one case where the top-ranking vehicle in selectivity for one of the advertiser's brands was not being used for that brand, but, rather, was being used for another one of his brands for which it was below average in selectivity. By simply rescheduling his own brands on the vehicles he had already bought, the advertiser was able to increase the efficiency of his schedule by 28 percent.

Another important area of application of data of this kind is in the analysis of the net reach of alternative media schedules. Since there are cumulative audience data for all major media vehicles from the same individuals, computers can determine the net reach and frequency of alternative media schedules in reaching marketing targets for specific products. An advertiser who builds a schedule around highly selective vehicles for his product can frequently reach his target groups at a rate that is at least 50 percent higher than the reach against groups that are not targets for his product.

Different media vehicles vary sharply in their marketing value for different brands and products. Given this fact, it is extremely important to utilize the concept of marketing value in building a media schedule. It is equally important, however, to recognize that marketing value is only one of four elements in building a media schedule. A complete media selection system must take account of:

1. The size of the audience.
2. The marketing value of the audience—the number of marketing prospects per hundred viewers, readers, or listeners.
3. The advertising impact value of the vehicle—the number of advertising impact units (number of viewers, readers, or listeners exposed to an average advertisement in the vehicle times the impact value of each exposure) delivered per hundred viewers, readers, or listeners.
4. The cost.

A formula which could be used to evaluate alternative media vehicles and schedules would have to include all four elements. It might be stated in the following way:

$$\frac{\text{Size of audience} \times \text{Marketing value of audience} \times \text{Advertising-impact value of vehicle}}{\text{Cost}} = \text{Marketing target impact units per dollar spent}$$

For a number of years, reasonably good estimates of audience size and specific information on advertising costs have been available. During the next few years, the industry will sharpen its techniques for using information on marketing value, and researchers will be able to allocate more and more of their creative effort to the next problem area: measuring the advertising-impact value of alternative media vehicles.

SECTION IV

MEASURING THE EFFECTIVENESS OF ADVERTISING •

AT THE PRESENT TIME it is safe to say that the field of media measurement is quite stable. Sampling procedures and various methodologies in the composite offer quantitative measurement which is adequate for an advertiser's needs. By scientific study the costs of various media can be appraised and the potential reach and frequency estimated to a point where the advertiser can obtain maximum efficiency for his advertising dollar in terms of his target audience. But when this has been done, there is no assurance that the advertiser has made a single sale.

Despite the theme of the avant-garde school headed by Marshall McLuhan, no marketer believes that media ever sold a nickel's worth of merchandise. Media only represent an opportunity to sell. The message determines the impulse to buy the product itself. Pricing, quality, distribution, and packaging modify that impulse to buy and to repurchase the product. Since all other factors can be evaluated, the most pressing need in advertising today is a certain way to measure effectiveness of the advertising message.

The advertising message falls into two broad categories: electronic—radio and TV commercials; and print—newspaper, magazine, and outdoor advertising. The problem is how to examine these messages and their impact on the eye and the ear, the attention-getting factors of the message, the penetration of the product claims, and the resulting intent to buy.

The reason why this information is elusive is that it is impossible for researchers exactly to simulate the psychological conditions of the prospect as he reads a newspaper or a magazine, or listens to the radio or watches television. Consequently, all known measurements today are necessarily artificial and only roughly relevant to the ultimate advertising impact.

In the following chapters leaders in each of the media-research fields discuss their technology and certain results they have achieved. Unspoken will be the disbelief of most advertisers in these methods, as well as their hope for a "brave new world" that may never come true.

Two distinguished motivational research practitioners, Emanuel Demby and Louis Cohen, discuss the use of depth interviews as a necessary adjunct to quantitative marketing research. They use case histories to illustrate the effect on purchasing behavior of nonrational factors that can only be identified through depth research.

The oldest form of media research is in the print field. For one reason, the print field has been with us longest and more time has been available to develop technologies of measurement. Daniel Starch has established a generic name for readership studies in the newspaper and magazine fields. The basic method that Starch uses is to interview respondents in an attempt to determine whether they remember seeing or reading an advertisement and what impressions were retained. The second stage is to try to learn from the respondents their degree of reading of the body copy. Obviously, this information is subjective, generally elicited via aided recall or prompting by an interviewer, and relatively reliable in the respect that reactions to all advertisements are equated by this technique.

A further advantage of this technique is the more than 40 years of experience the Starch company has had in gathering responses to the same type of questions. In the aggregate, this type of information can be used by a sophisticated advertiser to determine the success of a message in the broadest of terms. It is possible to determine that something is very good or very bad. It is almost impossible to measure shades of gray or to determine the true sales effectiveness of the message.

Since newspaper advertising is predominantly local in nature except for a corporate-image campaign or the introduction of a new product, the magazine studies are of paramount importance to national advertisers. It is somewhat easier to measure magazine advertising because there is less volume than with newspaper advertising and less variation in the size of the advertisements. Because of the vast amount of advertising dollars going into many magazines, magazine publishers as well as advertisers have encouraged the development of studies in their field.

Foremost among these are the services offered by Gallup & Robinson, Incorporated, Alfred Politz Research, Incorporated, and W. R. Simmons & Associates Research, Incorporated. In essence, they have refined and developed the Starch techniques, adding multiple questions, word associations, and depth interviews and making other modifications. Gallup, Politz, and other services have been able to give more precise answers to advertisers, including "reasons why" theories of brand switching related to advertising effectiveness and trends.

Advertisers, however, have had and still do have mixed feelings about the validity of these findings. Advertisers of all persuasions, from the late George Washington Hill to the scientifically oriented Procter & Gamble management, concluded that quantitative measurements were adequate but qualitative measurements were unreliable. George Washington Hill decided that he would simply repeat a major slogan such as "Lucky Strike means fine tobacco" as many times as he could during a half-hour program. His idea was to "brainwash" the listener by repetitiveness and, whether current philosophical schools of advertising agree with him or not, he was enormously successful with this technique. Procter & Gamble followed a similar course in clearly stating the name of the product a number of times and impressing the public with the broadest, simplest, and most powerful brand claims that could be supported for any of their brands. Obviously, the Procter & Gamble approach was equally effective.

While a similar case can be made for the new school of advertising, which has a greater appeal to the increasingly better-educated public by using humor, surprise techniques, subtleties, negative approaches to brand claims, and shock values, there is no evidence that either of these schools is completely correct. A sound advertiser will examine the information supplied by the research companies and use his judgment in conjunction with fact to reach a proper conclusion.

Perhaps the most perplexing search for truth in advertising effectiveness is in the TV commercial field and, secondarily, in measuring the impact of radio commercials. Since radio is a secondary national medium at this stage, there is less radio research being done. Because radio is a personal medium that accompanies other activities, it is possible to conclude that subtle advertising cannot be effective on radio stations because the listener's attention is not completely directed to the message. Driving an automobile, reading, talking, walking, and other activities which are performed in conjunction with radio listening are distracting to the extent that only a loud sound or strong claim can penetrate the subconscious. It should be noted, however, that there is a popular new school of humor in radio commercials, appealing to sophisticated listeners. This technique is much admired but little measured.

The portions of this section that are devoted to the broadcast media will be confined to the television commercial. Horace Schwerin, chairman of the Schwerin Research Corporation, describes pretesting of TV commercials and discusses its value to the advertiser. Once again, the researcher finds it impossible to duplicate the home viewing conditions. The major technique used in measuring TV commercials is the assembly in a theater or large hall of several hundred people—who have been lured to come to this meeting place by the promise of premiums, a free show, a door prize, or other inducements—and having these people express, either vocally, by notation on a sheet of paper, or by means of an electronic device, their like or dislike of a commercial shown to them in the body of a TV program and between several programs. A composite graph is made of their opinions and compared to previous experiences. From this norm a rating is given to the commercial, which attempts to denote its range of acceptance. Refinements of this technique include asking the audience to select merchandise on the way out of the theater as well as on the way into the theater, which purports to determine brand switching because of the commercial shown to them during the course of the program.

There are many variations of this technique. Some companies assemble five to ten housewives at a supermarket center in a large van for an hour or more of viewing and questioning. Other companies invite selected members of the public to view television in a series of small living rooms and interview them in some depth after showing them programs and commercials. Other techniques involve a portable TV projector carried from house to house; after screening a program and commercial, the interviewer uses a word-association technique to determine attitudes.

All of the techniques share the same failings. In the first place, in order to test a commercial, it is necessary to produce a commercial. This involves a large outlay of money on the part of an advertiser—from $10,000 to $50,000. It is highly unlikely that a commercial representing such an expenditure will be junked because of the findings of the survey. In some cases, advertisers test rough commercials made from a series of photographs linked together on film or slides, or a series of rough-drawn cartoons which are similarly reproduced. Here again, a true condition is not simulated.

One cause for advertisers' reservations about this challenging area of research is its assumption that people, influenced by the behavior of other people in a testing situation, can be properly subjective in giving a reaction. It is also difficult to gather a representative sample in a single theater or assembly place. Sometimes people who attend this kind of performance tend to be exhibitionists and may not be a cross section of the viewing public. For these and other reasons, there is considerable controversy about the testing of TV commercials before they go on the air.

An advantage of this testing is that it provides an indication of whether a performer used to sell a product is acceptable. Since this performer may be used for many weeks, or even years, the results can be quite productive.

In conjunction with controlled testing of commercials, most advertisers themselves use some form or other of audience testing of commercials. This research may consist of a telephone survey of viewers of a program to determine, after a commercial has been shown, the sales points remembered and intent to buy the product. Again, this information is a rough indication at best, but in conjunction with other facts it can be used as a guidepost.

What then is the current state of qualitative-effectiveness research for an advertising message? At the present time, it is only possible to predict that there will be continual refinements of the methods reported in these chapters by the practitioners of these methods. A dean of this field of opinion research, George Gallup, has hopes for using a method of electrically probing the cortex of the brain to extract specific information pertaining to products. He points out that the human brain, like the computer, retains all information fed into it, and that methods may be devised to tap the brain for this information. At this time, however, it seems unlikely that an eager cross section of consumers will make itself available for brain tapping.

Measuring Advertising's Sales Effectiveness: The Problem and the Prognosis •

GEORGE GALLUP

THE CREATION OF ADVERTISING has often in the past been surrounded with an aura of mystery. Good advertising was good because it was described as good by its producers, and not because it met any objective tests of goodness.

Virtually all professions and sciences have gone through this art stage. Until the turn of the century medicine was more of an art than a science. Advertising is now passing through—and to some extent out of—the art stage. While it is not accurate to say that it has entered the science stage—advertising will always, of course, depend to a very great extent upon creativeness—it has reached a stage when management is requiring more and more objective evidence that amounts spent are justified in terms of proved results.

Advertising space and time costs have moved steadily upward in recent years, and as a consequence advertising budgets have grown larger and larger. Along with them has grown the necessity on the part of responsible management of seeing that these large sums are spent wisely. Top management men today are increasingly requiring that as much guesswork as possible be taken out of advertising decisions and that evidence of effectiveness be produced to show that an advertising program is actually achieving the specific goals for which it was designed.

Of course, many factors in addition to advertising influence sales curves. Consequently, one of the most important functions which research can perform is to help single out and weigh these various influences. If sales are good, it is important to know why they are good; if they are bad, it is even more important to have the analytical tools to diagnose the reasons.

In today's highly competitive market, advertising is often the dominant variable in many product fields—especially those where product features and prices are comparable and leading brands are widely distributed.

The problems involved in producing advertising are many. Reduced to simplest terms, however, they fall into five categories:

1. What to say—what sales ideas to present to win new customers and hold old ones.
2. Where to say it—what media to use.
3. How to say it—how to present sales arguments in the most interesting and convincing manner.
4. How to relate the advertising to sales results—what proof of sales can be found?
5. How much to spend—at what point do added advertising dollars not pay their way?

These are the specific problems to which the staff of Gallup & Robinson has addressed itself during the last 18 years.

A significant step toward providing advertising management with answers to these problems was the development by Gallup & Robinson of the Impact research method. In the course of this research we have studied the impact of advertising on a continuing basis for many of the major advertisers in the United States. We have worked closely with advertisers and their agencies on all of the problems outlined above, and have followed many campaigns from their conception to their ultimate effect upon sales. Our files currently contain more than 60,000 case histories of print advertising and 16,000 case histories of television advertising—all with quantitative scores and qualitative verbatim playback gathered under actual reading and viewing conditions—representing the tested experience of more than a billion dollars worth of print and television advertising. The primary function of our research staff has been to analyze these data for the guidance of advertisers in producing more effective advertising.

The amount of money spent by different advertisers for a page of space in a given magazine—or a minute of time on a given television program—is a constant. What they receive in return for their expenditure is a variable. And this variable can be shockingly large. It is not unusual to find one advertiser registering his sales message on ten times as many prospects as his competitor in the same issue of a magazine and in the same amount of space.

In brief, the heart of the Impact idea is this: if a reader or viewer is exposed to an advertisement or commercial under normal conditions where his processes of selectivity have free play—where he can accept or reject the advertising message—then the effectiveness, or impact, of that ad can be gauged by the ability of the respondent to play back the advertiser's message at a later date without re-exposure. This method involves a long interview in depth, the only aid to recall being the advertiser's name and product. The data obtained in this manner permit evaluation of the effectiveness of an ad in terms of both its ability to register the name of the advertiser and the degree to which it was able to communicate selling ideas and create conviction. By studying the content and execution of ads which have been successful and unsuccessful in terms of these criteria, analysts are able to distill out from these data those principles of communication which make for the most effective advertising.

That this type of research has had a great influence on advertising practices can readily be demonstrated. In magazine advertising, for example, the use of the news approach, which our researchers indicated in 1952 could produce performance premiums of some 20 percent, has virtually doubled in the period since 1952. Conversely, advertisements which rely heavily on mechanical devices such as printing on tint block, sketch art, copy patches, and trick headline typography have shown a marked decline since the penalties for this approach were revealed as early as 1950. At that time this type of gimmickry was found in virtually a third of all advertising. In the period from 1950 to 1966 it declined from that level to something less than 5 percent of all advertising.

As a result of this type of research, management today is in a much better position to decide what to say in its advertising and how best to say it. But until recently there has been no basic-research technique capable of determining how well a campaign is actually working to produce sales—of indicating whether, in the final analysis, the huge sums committed to advertising are being wisely spent.

Oddly enough, this was long a neglected area, but in recent years the demand for such a system has become particularly insistent. One of the outstanding leaders in the advertising agency world has stated, in fact, that "the number one obligation of our business" today is to find a way to measure the relationship between advertising and sales.

In this search sales records can often be misleading. Total sales reflect many influences—some under the direct control of the advertiser, such as advertising, price, product, packaging; some under indirect or long-range control, such as distribution, dealer and consumer loyalty; and some under no control, such as the activities of competitors. To state the problem simply, it is entirely conceivable that an advertising campaign can be effective while total sales are declining, or it can be grossly ineffective even though the sales curve is moving upward.

Management has frequently to answer these questions about advertising expenditures:

- How can we justify to our stockholders the large sums spent for advertising? What proof do we have that our advertising is doing the job it is supposed to do?
- We have just started a new advertising campaign. Can we find out whether it is working or not?
- Our sales curve on product *X* has been flat for many months. Should we kill the present campaign and try a new one?
- Our chief competitor is gaining a larger share of the market for his product; our sales have been declining. Is his advertising responsible? Is our advertising responsible?
- We must decide soon whether to renew our contract for our TV show. What evidence is there that our present effort is paying off?

These are but a few of many such questions, and there are, unfortunately, no easy or perfect solutions to such complex problems.

Gallup & Robinson has developed a new research procedure to determine the sales effectiveness of advertising and, in particular, how well it is performing in creating new customers for a product and in winning back old ones. The procedure is concerned primarily with the relationship between advertising stimulus and buying behavior and is called Activation. The Activation method relates the two variables of sales effort and sales result.

The initial conception began with the classic research approach to the problem, wherein persons exposed to a given brand's advertising are compared with a control group of persons not exposed to the advertising for the brand under consideration. Data on usage of the product by both groups are obtained and analyzed and if, as expected, usage is higher among the exposed group, the presumption is that the brand advertising is the causal factor explaining the difference.

However, this approach, which is theoretically sound, is fraught with difficulty, since it requires an arbitrary decision to include or not include a given individual in the exposed group. What constitutes exposure? Is it seeing any one issue of a magazine or one TV program? The entire research design can founder on the difficulty of subjectively defining exposure.

In the course of searching for ways to make the results more meaningful, some very simple and basic facts were discovered, one of the most important of which was the realization that a typical person, put in a structured interviewing situation, can report the sequence of events leading up to a purchase.

One of the great medical discoveries of recent decades was made by Dr. Wilder Penfield of McGill University who, by electrically probing the cortex of the brain, discovered that a patient can and does retain every conscious experience of his life. The mind, like a tape recorder, retains an imprint of the experiences. A patient whose brain has been exposed in the course of surgery can perform unheard-of feats of memory when brain areas are stimulated by an electric needle. He can recall, for example, the names of the other children in his first grade class at school or the batting order at a baseball game attended many years ago. Practical use of this principle is to be found in psychiatry, where by careful questioning the psychiatrist probes back into a patient's early childhood in an attempt to discover a cause of his present behavior.

Significantly, the present era of copy research was an outgrowth of my discovery as early as 1928 that under certain conditions newspaper readers could report accurately and in detail what they had seen and read in a given issue. They could do this because the newspaper itself provided many memory cues. In much the same manner it was later discovered that with the right questioning procedure respondents could perform impressive feats of memory in playing back the selling messages from magazine ads and TV commercials. This discovery brought to advertising the Impact method used in copy research.

The foundation of the Activation method is this same basic technique—a carefully structured interview with many memory cues. And it is based on the common sense assumption that while total sales of a given product are the result of all the available influences—advertising, price, product, package, distribution, competition, and so forth—a single, individual purchase of a given brand will rarely be affected by all of them.

All too frequently, we find, there is a tendency to think in opposite terms—to rationalize that since total sales are normally affected by all influences, single purchases must be similarly affected. Yet differences in individual buying motives must surely prevent this situation from occurring.

From a research standpoint this is very important. It means that the comparative simplicity of a single buying act makes investigation of that act easier than many might expect.

There is, of course, a way to go about this and a way not to go about it. And the way not to do it is to follow the usual questionnaire design and ask the respondent why he made a given purchase. By asking a person why he bought a given item, one will never discover the true role advertising played. Obviously, advertising does influence sales. Yet when the interviewing situation is structured in this manner, it is rare to find more than a negligible percentage of all respondents acknowledging that advertising had any influence whatsoever on their choice of brand or product.

The last thing in the world that anyone cares to admit is that he has been influenced by advertising. People react in a strange way even to the suggestion of advertising influence. They become annoyed or evasive. Before the words are out of the interviewer's mouth they reply, "No, advertising doesn't influence me." Even for such products as toothpaste, where advertising is a demonstrably important factor, the respondent will say that he buys a certain brand because his children prefer the taste, or because his dentist recommended it, or because of other product qualities.

I am sure that it is primarily because of this basic error in research approach that many advertising people, perhaps largely in self-defense, have developed the mistaken theory that "people do not know what makes them buy."

The truth is, as can be demonstrated, that people can retrace the mental steps that led to a purchase, and in doing this they can give the researcher useful evidence as to the part which advertising did or did not play. Obviously a large proportion of respondents will still report that they purchased brand *X* because of the recommendation of a neighbor, or they might reveal that when they went to the store the sales clerk told them it was a better product for less money. Importantly, however, in response to the Activation interview consumers give advertising due credit for the sale. In the case of the purchase of all brands not heretofore used, nearly half of all respondents report that they got the idea for buying from advertising.

Particularly in the case of small-ticket, women-directed items, the question arises: is such a purchase activity normally of sufficient importance to be memorable?

The answer is "Yes," under certain circumstances. There are two buying situations which permit relatively easy recall of purchase influences: (1) when a brand has been purchased for the first time, and (2) when the current brand purchase constitutes a change in brand from the previous purchase.

In these cases the purchasers can be identified as "new/switch" buyers. They have reason to be conscious of what influenced their recent purchase behavior by virtue of the factor of change.

It is difficult to obtain similar testimony from repeat purchasers, chiefly because a decision of the same order is not required on the part of the buyer. But even in this situation indirect evidence can be revealing. If the purchaser has not been exposed, and if he has no awareness of current advertising for the brand he continues to buy, it can reasonably be assumed that the advertising has played an unimportant part in the repeat purchase. Rather, the product itself has brought the customer back. If the repeat buyer is aware of current advertising, then it can be presumed that advertising deserves at least some credit for the buyer's continued loyalty.

Fortunately from the researcher's standpoint, there are a sizable number of new/switch buyers among a given brand's total buyers at any one time. Our pilot work suggests that, as a result of the continuous brand warfare for new customers, 25 percent of all current buyers of the average brand are in the new/switch category.

So if the line of questioning described above is used in a sufficient number of cases, one can obtain from the new/switch purchasers a relative cross section of all the influences at work at that time. Then systematic analyses of many case histories taken over a period of time will produce meaningful indications of the changes in the ability of any of the various influences to produce sales.

With such intelligence an advertiser can, for example:

- Continuously observe the selling power of a given advertising campaign, so that a worn-out campaign can be replaced. The new campaign can be audited to determine if it is an efficient replacement.
- Compare one against another the selling power of individual TV shows, so that the weaker properties can be culled out of the program lineup.
- Continuously observe the effectiveness of competitive marketing tactics, so that only those tactics actually doing some damage need be countered.

Activation is not a cure-all. But enough progress has already been achieved to indicate that we are on the edge of a solution. The method is a workable one, and the data have, in recent years, pointed unerringly to the advertising campaigns which have had outstanding records for moving goods.

So I am confident that we shall, within the next few years, uncover the means by which to measure, with a high degree of accuracy, just how much advertising contributes to sales. When this is accomplished, the final gap in advertising research technology will have been bridged, and management will have in its kit of tools the information necessary to eliminate completely the guesswork which, even today, remains a factor in so many major advertising decisions.

Advertisement Readership Studies •

DANIEL STARCH

FOR MOST COMPANIES advertising is intended to do three things: to inform people concerning a product, to create a favorable buying attitude toward it, and to induce people to buy it. Advertising is a form of communication, and its effective performance rests on the postulates that only those who perceive the advertising message can be influenced by it and only those who buy the product are the final measure of advertising performance.

Obviously, the first step in measuring advertising performance is to measure the perception of the advertising message. In the case of printed advertisements, this means readership. Readership studies aim to answer the question, Who and how many persons read specific advertisements of a given product?

Today it may seem superfluous to ask whether people read specific advertisements of a company's products. However, managements are not always sure that enough people read their advertisements for the expenditure to be profitable. Because of sharp competition, managements look closely at every item of cost. They want evidence of how well their advertising communicates. They want measurements of their advertising's performance in readership and sales.

At the depth of the depression, in the early 1930's, managements wanted to know whether anybody read their advertisements and, consequently, whether advertising was profitable for them. It was generally assumed that people read the advertisements, but there was no proof they did, or that enough did so for it to be worthwhile. In the early depression years Daniel Starch and Staff had just started its continuing readership studies and was reporting to clients how many persons read specific advertisements in specific media. In 1922 Daniel Starch devised the method for measuring readership of advertisements which since then has come into wide use. The continuing program was begun in 1932 with 13 consumer publications and has grown since that time to cover advertisements in practically all magazines of general distribution as well as in about 60 business, industrial, and professional publications and selected newspapers.

The first obvious value of readership studies to managements is to reassure them that people do read their advertisements. A manufacturer of automobiles wants to know and measure the performance of his automobile under actual conditions of usage. The food processor wants to know and evaluate the acceptability, taste, and convenience of his coffee or cereal. The maker of a refrigerator or toaster needs to know how well his appliance performs under home usage. Likewise, managements need to know and measure how well their advertising messages communicate and help sell their products.

The second and highly important value of readership studies is to ascertain what kind of advertisements people stop to look at and what kind they read through. The value of such analyses is to help advertisers create more effective advertising.

The third value is to find out to what extent perceivers of advertising messages own, use, and buy specific brands or makes; to help measure actual present markets; and to estimate prospective market potentials. Readership research can ascertain who and how many among the advertisements' readers own, use, and buy a company's brands.

The fourth value of readership studies is to determine what kind of advertising messages induce purchase and use of the advertiser's products. Information on these points is of never ending interest and value to management.

What have readership studies discovered over these many years? To begin with they have shown that there are two sets of factors that determine who and how many persons read an advertisement. The first set of factors consists of the inherent interests of men and women. By inherent interests we mean the interests which are a natural part of human nature or develop out of one's environment and experience. Men, for example, have high interest in sports and automobiles and low interest in food preparation and child care. On the other hand, women have high interest in child care and food preparation and low interest in sports and automobiles.

A list of 18 items of potential interest was submitted to men and women in 11,000 households. They were asked to indicate the three items of top interest. Eight times as many men mentioned automobiles as food preparation, whereas eight times as many women mentioned food preparation as business and finance.

The effect of these wide ranges of interest is that nearly twice as many men as women look at automobile advertisements and nearly four times as many men read half or more of the text. In a 1964 study, tabulation of the readership scores of 549 one-page four-color automobile advertisements in four magazines read equally by men and women showed that 53 percent of men and 28 percent of women stopped to look at these advertisements and 11 percent of the men and 3 percent of the women read most of the text. Just the reverse was true for food advertisements. Data for 831 one-page four-color food advertisements showed that they were seen by 28 percent of the men and 53 percent of the women. Half or more of the text was read by 4 percent of the men and 10 percent of the women.

Little can be done about the inherent interests of people except to realize that they exist, to understand them, and to appeal to them constructively. These interests are fundamental elements in human nature; they are more or less fixed and change slowly.

The second set of factors that determine what persons, and how many, look at and read specific advertisements consists of the characteristics of the advertisements themselves: what they say and how they say it. Readership studies made possible the significant discovery right at the beginning of these studies that, at the various levels of inherent interests, advertisements differ enormously in readership. Some advertisements for the same kind of products attract two or more times as many readers as others and induce five or more times as many to read them through. For example, two one-page four-color syrup advertisements appeared a few pages apart in the same issue of a woman's magazine. One was looked at by more than twice as many women readers of the issue and read half or more of the way through by seven times as many.

Readership scores measure three levels of reading:

1. Noted, the percentage of readers of the current issue of a publication who remember, when interviewed later, that they saw the advertisement in the issue studied.
2. Seen-associated, the percentage of issue readers who saw the advertisement and associated it with the name of the product or company. This is usually indicated by the respondents' having seen or read

some part of the advertisement which clearly indicates the product or company.

3. Read most, the percentage of readers who read half or more of the text of the advertisement.

In these terms the scores of the two syrup advertisements were as follows:

	Size and Color	*Page Location*	*Noted*	*Seen-Associated*	*Read Most*
Karo	1-page, 4-color	52	51%	49%	21%
Sweetose	1-page, 4-color	58	25	21	3

What makes for such wide differences? Both were attractive advertisements. Both pictured mouth-watering dishes of pancakes, waffles, toast, and biscuits, amply flooded with syrup. The Karo advertisement pictured the "Karo Kid" as a chef baking and flipping pancakes. The headline was, "Now to give the folks a 'break' for breakfast." There was an average amount of text, including a recipe at the bottom. The Sweetose advertisement pictured four appetizing dishes, with the headline, "Here's a new way to serve them." Apparently the important difference in this instance was the picture of a person engaged in action centered around the product.

This is not an isolated instance. Readership scores for high- and low-scoring advertisements of competing pairs of brands were compiled for ten pairs of products. These pairs of advertisements appeared in each instance in the same issue of a given publication. They included pairs of advertisements for competing brands of cheese, cosmetics, soap, soup, margarine, furniture, refrigerators, china, and television receivers. The average scores for the high- and low-scoring advertisements were as follows:

	Noted	*Seen-Associated*	*Read Most*
High 10	55%	48%	9%
Low 10	34	25	4

What are the characteristics of advertisements that explain such wide differences in their ability to stop readers and induce them to read the copy? First, as to stopping readers, generally speaking, advertisements that have high Noted scores usually have a dominant focal area. This area may consist of an outstanding picture or headline, or a combination of the two. An analysis of 30 top advertisements as compared with 30 low-rated ones among 474 one-page advertisements showed that 93 percent of the top advertisements had a dominant attention center as against only 33 percent of the low-scoring ones.

A second potent element in causing readers to stop and look is picturing people in action centered around the product. The same analysis of high- and low-scoring advertisements showed that 70 percent of the top advertisements pictured people in action centered around the product as against only 23 percent of the low-scoring ones. The situation that not all advertisements in the top group had dominant focal centers or pictured people in action is due to the fact that every advertisement is a mixture of several determining elements with varying amounts present in any one advertisement.

Our next question is, What induces readers to read on? As stated previously, top-scoring advertisements may induce four or five times as many persons to read on through most of the text as low-scoring advertisements. Several characteristics appear to induce lookers to read on further. One is an action picture, the same characteristic that at the beginning causes many readers to look. Among the 30 advertisements with high Read-Most scores 70 percent had action pictures, whereas only 7 percent of those with low Read-Most scores had.

A second powerful factor that leads lookers to read on is a curiosity-arousing headline or picture. Of the 30 high-scoring advertisements 67 percent had curiosity-arousing headlines or pictures, but only 3 percent of the low-scoring ones had. Many provocative, curiosity-stirring headlines or pictures convey news, or tell about a new product or bring news about a known product, or picture known persons or celebrities in action centered around the product. For example, advertisements of Bufferin that pictured Arthur Godfrey speaking about the product attracted 50 percent more readers than the usual run of advertisements for the same product. Advertisements that pictured family groups using Maytag washing machines induced nearly twice as many lookers to read most of the advertisements as those which pictured only the appliance or one person standing beside the appliance. Those that pictured brides or celebrities attracted the most readers.

Another device that tends to induce stoppers to read on is a continuity layout which conveys a story of action in a series of panels or successive pictures. Action begun in the first and continued in successive segments tends to induce readers to follow on through. Such advertisements usually do not stop any more readers but as a rule lead many more stoppers to read on.

Various other findings uncovered by readership studies may be of interest. For example, as regards the use of color, four-color advertisements attract about 50 percent more readers than black-and-white ones. Two-color advertisements attract about the same number of readers as black-and-white. These findings are corroborated by inquiry returns reported in *An Analysis of 12 Million Inquiries.* Color in newspaper advertisements increases readership over black-and-white fully as much as in magazines.

Two-page advertisements do not attract twice as many readers as one-page advertisements. However, in proportion to opportunity the additional page attracts approximately its proportionate share of readers. By "in proportion to opportunity" is meant that if 30 out of 100 issue readers note a one-page advertisement, the second page of a double-page spread will attract approximately 30 percent of the remaining 70 out of 100 issue readers. A similar relationship exists with regard to half-page and one-page advertisements.

Number of pages or thickness of issues has a relatively moderate effect on readership scores. For issues within the range of 80 to 160 pages, Noted scores may range from 45 to 35. For very thin issues of 40 pages or less, scores tend to be substantially higher; and for issues of 200 pages or more, scores tend to decline relatively little.

Advertisements on second and third covers and on page 1 obtain about 30 percent more readers than advertisements in middle-section positions. Advertisements on the fourth cover attract around 65 percent more readers. Space rates, however, are usually the same for all positions with the exception of the outside fourth cover, for which the rate is about 30 percent higher than for other locations.

Full-column quarter-page advertisements tend to stop somewhat more readers than rectangular quarter-page advertisements on the lower half of a page. A reader's eyes are more likely to sweep across the upper half of a page and hence are more likely to be stopped by a full-column quarter with a part of its space on the upper half of the page. Sideways positioning on a page is a disadvantage rather than an advantage. To read an advertisement in a sideways position requires the partial turning of the magazine being read, which is more likely to be an obstacle than an advantage for reading the advertisement.

Repetition of the same advertisement at intervals of a month up to six or seven insertions apparently does not cause decline in readership. A high-scoring advertisement continues to score high and a low-scoring one is likely to continue to score low. If advertisements are repeated, more readers are consistently reached by the initially high-scoring advertisements.

High- or low-readership advertisements tend to attract a correspondingly high or low number of current users, buyers, or prospective buyers of the product advertised. For example, high-scoring Texaco advertisements had a correspondingly high number of current buyers of Texaco gasoline and oil among their readers. Advertisements that attracted 50 readers per 100 issue readers had 11 current buyers among them, whereas advertisements that scored 32 had 6 current buyers among them.

To create advertisements that are likely to attract high readership is therefore a worthy aim. The number of users, buyers, and prospective buyers increases correspondingly with increase in readership. Automobile advertisements in newspapers which were read by 75 out of 100 issue readers had among these readers six in-the-market prospects, persons who expected to buy a new automobile within six months. Advertisements which attracted only 25 readers had among them two in-the-market prospects. The high-scoring advertisements attracted three times as many readers and reached three times as many in-the-market prospects.

The problem of measuring product sales produced by advertising has become increasingly important. Managements demand to know what their advertising produces in sales and what it adds to profits. Substantial progress has been made in this direction. A study by McGraw-Hill Incorporated revealed that among 893 companies manufacturing industrial products, the ones whose share of advertising expenditure in the total sales expenditure was higher had a lower overall sales cost as compared with the companies whose advertising expenditure represented a lower share of the total sales costs.

Numerous studies conducted by Daniel Starch and Staff have shown that about 15 percent more issue readers of a publication buy a brand within the immediate period when issues contain advertisements of the brand than when issues do not. These studies also found that the proportion of issue readers who buy is influenced by the level of readership of the advertisements and by the persuasive, activating power of the advertisements. The Bufferin advertisements featuring Arthur Godfrey not only attracted 50 percent more readers than the average Bufferin advertisement but in addition they induced more than a proportionately larger number of purchases.

Next the crucial qestion is, What kinds of advertisements impress, persuade, and activate people to buy? Three things, I believe, stand out above all others: informativeness, helpfulness, and believability.

First, advertisements that are informative, that convey news about the product, are likely to create product and buying preference. The reader feels he has benefited by reading the advertisement.

Second, advertisements that contain helpful information, suggest helpful ways of using and enjoying a product, and, in the case of food advertisements, show helpful ways of preparing and serving foods are apt to induce buying preference. For instance, advertisements that stressed ways of serving apples induced twice as many to buy apples as advertisements that stressed health. Soup advertisements that stressed taste and enjoyment in eating soup caused three times as many additional persons to buy the brand of soup as advertisements that stressed ingredients.

Third, possibly the most effective characteristic of all is believability. Advertisements that state fairly and believably, that understate rather than overstate, that may even point out moderate negatives about a product instead of reiterating clichés and stock phrases, are likely to produce maximum persuasion and buying activation.

Such advertisements are hard to create. Reiterating and rearranging "arty," "addy" generalities are easy ways to fill advertising space or time. It takes head-scratching study and observing and questioning of people as they buy and use products to find out what triggers buying action. No doubt, widely used, low-priced brands—so-called impulse products—may need merely a reminder to the reader in order to be bought. But even for such products informative, helpful, believable advertisements may be a refreshing and rewarding change.

A motorist had never been fully persuaded of the effectiveness of snow tires until a friend told him that he regularly put on his snow tires on Armistice Day in November and took them off in April and had always found them effective. This motorist bought snow tires the next day. Believability is of the essence of persuasiveness and activation.

Pretesting Television Commercials •

HORACE S. SCHWERIN

REGARDLESS OF THE MEDIUM USED, top management is more concerned these days than ever before with finding out in advance of making massive budget commitments whether the company's specific advertising campaigns will pay off. This is particularly true of television advertising, for two reasons.

First of all, it costs more to produce a finished TV commercial than to turn out an equivalently polished piece of advertising in any other medium. Stanley Kubrick, producer of *Dr. Strangelove,* is an admirer of many of the creative devices of TV advertising. He is quoted in a recent interview in *The New York Times* to the effect that it would take $50,000,000 to complete a full-length movie matching the best commercial work in technical proficiency. But even a comparatively mundane commercial is apt to run into five figures, and sometimes the sky is the limit.

Second, and generally even more important, it takes a good deal of money to put a commercial on the air even once. The price of a single minute of network nighttime prime time has been estimated at anywhere from $30,000 to $50,000. The going rate for spots on the popular professional football games has now soared past $100,000.

Faced with these harsh realities, the prudent advertiser knows that he cannot simply emulate Mrs. Gamp when she threw up her hands and exclaimed, "Oh Sairey, Sairey, little do we know what lays afore us!"

The first absolute necessity under any conditions, of course, is to have the best possible agency. But with three or more brands seriously competing in nearly every conceivable field these days, obviously not all of them can have one of the agencies described in the trade press as the "hottest." In fact, what we mainly detect from testing thousands of joint client-agency efforts each year is that some common attitude of mind regarding how to evaluate the advertising is even more important than brilliance alone.

Beyond harmony in the client-agency relationship, therefore, some orderly course of procedure for evaluating the advertising in advance seems desirable. Broadly speaking, there are two possibilities which are considered by sophisticated managements. These are test marketing and pretesting. One or the other, and usually both, are utilized to varying degrees by nearly every leading company at the present time. The point is to know why, when, and how—to take three of Kipling's "six honest serving men" —rather than whether.

An instance where both procedures were applied to finding out which of two commercials would be the better opening gun in a national campaign may be illuminating here. The study was undertaken six years ago by the Alberto-Culver Company with the twin objectives of securing information on which to base its decision and of checking whether test marketing and pretesting would lead to the same conclusion.

The two approaches were tested in rough form by Schwerin Research. It was found that, while commercial *A* caused an additional 7 percent of women viewers to choose the brand, commercial *B* was even stronger: it produced an 11 percent preference change.

Simultaneously, Alberto-Culver began broadcasting the commercials in two carefully matched Midwestern cities, each exclusively in one of the cities. Store purchases were regularly audited during the next half-year. Midway through the proceedings, sales were running neck and neck. By the end of the test-market period, however, the commercial that was the victor in pretesting had registered an indexed sales gain of 212, against 133 for the alternative possibility. In other words, it was outselling the weaker commercial at a rate of three to two.

This study, which is archetypal of others made during that period, led to certain conclusions. It had long been known that setting up a test-market situation under proper conditions was costly and time consuming and that it took many months to be sure that the results were predictive. Meanwhile, in the case of an existing product, the test areas selected were open to counteraction by rival brands; and when it came to a new product, the manufacturer was committed to manufacture it in sufficient quantities to meet the demand.

If the lesson learned from the Alberto-Culver and other studies was correct—that pretesting could predict which campaign would succeed better in the test-market situation—management and its agencies could short-cut the process. They could use pretesting to identify the strongest campaign and then employ test marketing, which then became simply a method of exploiting the new brand or the novel claim for the old brand in the most efficient manner, by building up regionally toward a national success.

Another case history is relevant at this point. A few years after the study just described, we were pretesting an equal number of commercials apiece for two large companies in similar product fields but with different advertising philosophies. About one-third of the efforts of each proved to be substandard in effectiveness (an excellent batting average, by the way, in the pretesting league). Company *A* nevertheless chose to broadcast nearly all its output, while company *B* rejected all but a few of the inferior commercials without ever putting them on the air. By the most conservative calculation, the sum expended by the former to place its below-average advertising on television was just about equal to the company's profit for that particular year.

The logic arising from investigations such as the above is reflected in today's management philosophies. To quote J. Emmet Judge, vice president of marketing research, Westinghouse Electric Corporation:

> A few years back many advertising men would have been startled at the idea that creativity and accountability could be linked closely. Results indicate that we, along with a number of other companies, are making substantial progress.
>
> We have found that research, properly used, or properly oriented, can make creativity more effective and channel it in the direction we want.
>
> We think that in all areas of advertising we ought to put into research between 2 and 3 percent of our total communications investment. I would put money into research even if it meant reducing the amount of exposure.[1]

And this is how the National Industrial Conference Board summarizes part of what the Campbell Soup Company's official pretesting manual has to say on the subject.

> The program does not cover every print and TV ad; but whenever a proposal for a new campaign or for a revision of an existing campaign or for the introduction of a new product is in the offing, the ads in question are pretested.
>
> The company-agency pretesting program has led to more effective advertising, in the opinion of Campbell's management. A number of factors have contributed to this end. One is the interest management has steadily mani-

[1] Judge, J. Emmet, "Ad Mood Changes," *New York Herald-Tribune*, August 17, 1965.

fested in the pretesting program since it was first initiated. A second is the joint development of the program by the company and its agencies.

The use of agreed-upon third parties to carry out the research has also been a source of vitality to the program. This assures an unbiased (in terms of interest in the results) viewpoint towards the test ads.[2]

Before turning to some of the ways in which companies like Westinghouse and Campbell use pretesting, it is necessary at this point to go briefly into the manner in which the research is conducted.

To begin with, as was mentioned previously, rough commercials are the subject matter of the most of the pretesting we carry on today. Our research has shown that such roughs can be tested and that the test results are reliable—"reliability" simply meaning that tests of the rough and of a finished counterpart come out the same. Experimentation over the years has shown that, in experienced hands, either live-action roughs or still-photo roughs (the latter often done in rapid sequence, as in the "squeeze frame" technique, to simulate action) are satisfactory. The most elementary level, filming agency storyboard panels and adding a sound track, is chancier, except in cases where the final version is to be in cartoon or other animated form.

Roughs are produced at a fraction of the cost of commercials designed for actual broadcast. Some of the economies possible are described by The Toni Company, whose experience spans the whole period of development:

For example, nonessential music or optical effects are virtually eliminated; still photographs may be used in places where motion is not necessary to the message; also, whenever possible, test films make liberal use of existing film scenes available from Toni's extensive library of past film productions.[3]

Once prepared, the rough commercial is tested in exactly the same manner as is a finished commercial about to be broadcast or already on the air. (The latter is usually referred to as post-testing.) Audiences of from 300 to 450 people are attracted to a theater by a random mailing. The sessions are held regularly in New York, Chicago, Toronto, Montreal (for French-language advertising), London, and Hamburg, and frequently in other localities.

After filling out a questionnaire giving their personal characteristics and

[2] Wolfe, Harry D., James K. Brown, Stephen H. Greenberg, and G. Clark Thompson, *Pretesting Advertising,* National Industrial Conference Board, New York, 1963.
[3] The Toni Company, "How Toni Pre-tests TV Commercials for More Effective Advertising," *Toni Topics,* Chicago, 1963.

information on what products they use and other matters, the audience members turn to a list of all the major brands in the product field. On this they check the brand of merchandise they wish to receive if they are the winners in a drawing. A substantial supply is offered—for example, $10 worth of a frequently purchased food item—so that the choices will be carefully considered.

Next the audience sees a half-hour pilot film that has never been on the air. The commercial for the pretest brand appears in this show, along with two other commercials for noncompeting products. This program is kept constant from test to test, thus serving as a control vehicle when various commercials for the same brand are being tried out.

At the conclusion of the control show the viewers are given another opportunity to choose from the same list of brands, and another drawing is held. The percentage difference between those choosing the advertised brand before and after exposure to the commercial is the Schwerin Competitive Preference score. Incidentally, about a third of all the commercials we study fail to achieve any significant change in preference. Occasionally, indeed, a definite negative or boomerang effect will be encountered, as in the case some years back where the wife in the commercial nagged her husband for not shaving on Saturday morning and succeeded in driving male viewers away from the advertised brand.

The way in which pretesting such as this operates in practice can be seen from an actual case history of Puss'n Boots cat food, a product of the Quaker Oats Company, which was reported in detail by *Printers' Ink*. The current campaign was showing signs of having run its course, and the Lynn Baker agency experimented with various possible replacement ideas. The approaches tried included an emphasis on ingredients, a mood story centered on a little girl and her first kitten, and an attempt to blend a sentimental opening and straight sell. None of these achieved a satisfactory score. The format that did prove outstanding was built around the cat as the star—playing with a ball of yarn, chasing its reflection in a mirror, and then enjoying a dish of Puss'n Boots. Reports *Printers' Ink:*

> . . . the test results have been confirmed by sales results. In the first year of the cat action commercials the rate of sales growth for Puss'n Boots was twice that of the previous year. It was all a matter of finding the right theme —and the right cat.[4]

[4] "Selling the Hard Way—with a Trained Cat," *Printers' Ink,* August 4, 1961, p. 30.

Besides answering the fundamental question—Is the commercial worth putting on the air?—pretesting also provides guidance on various specific problems. One of these is choosing the strongest copy theme or motivator, as was done in a series of tests for a television-set manufacturer.

In this particular study, the same announcer and the same background—a display of the sets—appeared in all seven instances, but the copy and the accompanying legends were different on each occasion. The themes included the diversity of the line of models, the rugged construction, the fact that servicing was seldom required, and the clarity of the picture. The weakest of the motivating ideas secured no significant preference change. The strongest, which proved to be the beauty of the sets—their "fine furniture" styling—brought about a preference change of 10 percent. The lesson appeared to be that people, by that particular time, had developed confidence that most television sets would work properly and were more interested in whether the set they bought would fit into the decor of their homes.

Instead of changing the idea, one can keep it constant but vary the method of presentation, as in the case of a new household product that had a new packaging feature. The advertiser first tried an amusing all-animated approach, in which a bumbling little cartoon pitchman declaimed on the virtues of the product. The animated character ran away with the commercial but in doing so performed an indifferent selling job. The advertiser then produced an all-live action commercial, which demonstrated the package feature in terms of realistic consumer benefits. The latter approach scored five times as highly as the former and was the most effective commercial yet tested in this product field.

A third possibility is to choose a presenter, perhaps a company spokesman, for a brand or for the whole product line. A large number of studies of this type have been run, with all the candidates for the part following exactly the same script. Often there is a considerable difference, even when the actors are not well-known personalities, in how well they go over with viewers, as was true in four screen tests for a company spokesman assignment for a food advertiser: the two top candidates secured preference changes of 9 percent, against 4 and 2 percent for the other pair.

No discussion of this subject would be complete without mentioning the particular advantages of television pretesting where new products are concerned. Utilizing the rough-commercial technique, clients are constantly trying out new product ideas at every stage of development.

In today's business world, as a former chairman of a giant consumer-products manufacturing company has remarked, "the race is always between speed and quality"; and pretesting often contributes the swiftest accurate answers.

The possibilities extend back even to a point before actual manufacture of the product, assuming the company's R&D technicians know that it can be made if a proper market exists. For example, one manufacturer who was debating whether to introduce a unique appliance tested a rough commercial filmed around a mock-up design. He learned, first of all, that the new product would have good acceptance. More pertinently, it was found that it appealed particularly to the middle-income group, whereas it had been feared that its price would make it attractive only to the extremely well-to-do. Still more specifically, the built-in selling promise of the appliance emerged when it was discovered that those most interested in having it were parents of young children.

At the other end of the spectrum, pretesting via the rough commercial has often been worthwhile in deciding what to name a new brand. A well-known household-products advertiser had developed a new form of one of his existing products. Although it was in part a replacement for an established product, he decided to market it under the company name, hoping to draw upon reputation. He produced a strong commercial but noted one side effect: the new product was drawing support away from the established brand. He then shifted to emphasis on the brand name, with only incidental reference to the fact that it was made by the parent company. There was a happier result: the new brand did just as well as before, but the original product gained choosers rather than losing them.

There are, then, many ways in which pretesting can be used to advance the objectives of management; and, as I have tried to indicate, they are not limited entirely to finding out whether one commercial is better than another. That, however, with the ramifications that grow out of it, is truly the heart of the matter. And perhaps the best summary is that of the National Industrial Conference Board:

> The cost of preparing an advertisement is usually just a fraction of exposing it to the intended audience. And the cost of determining, in advance, whether or not an advertisement will do the job desired is generally even less. Yet many millions of dollars (which could have been invested in productive advertising) have failed to yield results. . . . Often, simple and inexpensive pretests can prevent such losses.[5]

[5] Wolfe *et al.*, *op. cit.*

Motivational Research •

LOUIS COHEN
and
EMANUEL DEMBY

MOTIVATIONAL RESEARCH HAS DEVELOPED during the past 20 years as a bridge between marketing facts and consumer actions. While the gathering of facts is an essential marketing research function, the direct application of the results often creates what appears to be a paradox.

For example, some years ago a large mail order house sought to discover why catalog customers failed to make repeat purchases. The firm undertook a marketing research study, only to discover that the customers claimed that they were repeat buying. Seventy percent of those who bought only once reported they were repeat buyers. Understandably confused, the firm engaged Motivational Programmers, Incorporated.

Our study revealed that while the customers were steady catalog purchasers, they failed to distinguish among mail order houses. In their frame of reference, they were "repeat" purchasers. Today the company enjoys a high repeat business by differentiating itself from the other companies through various promotions.

While the explanation may seem obvious in retrospect, the typical closed-ended marketing research questionnaire (with fixed questions and where choice of answer is limited) often fails to shed light on the underlying causes for consumer action. The reason for this failure is not poor research. It simply reflects the limitations of marketing research which is based on the assumption that the consumer understands and will state the cause of his actions. Questionnaires are framed to consolidate this information, while, in fact, the consumer is often unaware or unwilling to speak of his motivations for acting one way or another.

Motivation research has been slow to be recognized by marketing executives because its early "womb and tomb" psychological jargon was abstract and even suspicious. Today, however, psychologists are as marketing conscious as the executives who employ them. A typical study report will contain few, if any, psychological terms, but behind its "plain talk" may be volumes of psychological interpretations and analyses of data.

The high-speed computer has greatly expanded the ability of marketing researchers to gather data, analyze them, and project the results of various marketing alternatives. A few years ago a representative national study was limited to one or two basic problems, since the amount of hand labor required to tabulate results made more comprehensive studies impractical. High-speed computers now permit us to tabulate several thousand questionnaires with hundreds of separate answers in a matter of days. As a result, the research firm is no longer a passive participant in the marketing program. Its findings and mathematical projections are vital ingredients in the decision-making process.

A full-scale study involves two primary elements: motivation research and marketing research. Each element provides an independent result of worth to the company, yet each is related in an important way to the other.

A third technique, still in a developmental stage, is the use of mathematical marketing models. This is a means of establishing on paper a viable mathematical representation of the company and its markets. The model can be used to simulate marketing moves and test them through the computer model without actually going into the field. Though some of these techniques have been available for a number of years, they have become feasible only since the advent of the high-speed computers. A mathematical model which formerly took several people a number of years to complete, by the use of desk calculators, can now be completed in a matter of minutes. We have completed a number of these marketing models at MPI, and we can say that this new technique is an extraordinarily powerful new resource for marketing science.

THE ROLE OF MOTIVATION RESEARCH

Motivation research is probably the most practical, the most realistic tool of attitude and behavior research. People rationalize—they say things to save face, give "socially desirable" answers to questions. In short, they often are not aware of or else will not admit the reasons for their opinions and actions. In questioning a subject, the researcher must take into account what a person has to gain or lose by a specific statement of "fact" or "opinion." He must be aware of the anxieties and social pressures—all the inhibitions to knowing and stating accurately and objectively what one's reactions are to stimuli.

Motivation research unearths the frame or frames of reference through which to develop the proper marketing research questions and through which to view and analyze accurately the responses and their meanings and implications in ways that are operationally useful to marketers. And its use as an indispensable tool in the study of behavior is by no means limited to consumer purchasing behavior. In the following case histories, the role played by motivation research in both consumer and industrial purchasing studies is demonstrated.

A processed-meat case history. The need for motivation research—as well as the special effectiveness of coordinated marketing and motivation research—is shown in a project given us by a meat packer who, specifically, wanted to know how to market a processed meat. The meat product was also sold in nonprocessed form by the company.

In the first stage, we met with marketing management and marketing research to discuss the problem. We learned that this company sells the processed meat at two levels: the regular grade at a regular price and a premium grade product (fat trimmed, a better cut, and so forth) at a considerably higher price. This premium product was in direct competition with an imported product, which sells very successfully at the higher price.

Management told us it could make a decent profit only on its premium product, since the regular-priced product was treated by the supermarkets as a "commodity." As a result of price pressures, there was little net return on the regular-grade product, despite its huge sales volume. The company therefore wished to expand the sales of its premium product. It believed the natural market for this higher-priced product to be the consumers who purchased the imported product.

During the previous five years the company had conducted research projects on the product, including package, copy, and product-placement research. Among these was a comprehensive large-scale study of several thousand housewives. The study concluded that the processed product was seen as inferior to the fresh meat version. The latter was seen as far more wholesome, good tasting, and so forth, than the processed product. The advantage of the processed meat was its convenience in terms of time and effort to prepare.

After meeting with management, our next step was to reanalyze the studies already done. In examining the comprehensive study, we noticed a paradox. The processed product did, indeed, have an inferior image to the fresh product, despite the fact that the latter sold at a lower price. However, the processed product was used more for company and special occasions, while the fresh product was used more for everyday meals. Several other studies showed the same findings. We knew this was unusual, since women tend to put their best food forward when cooking for guests; they know they will be rated for a long time on their cooking ability, depending on the success of the meal. Why, despite the poor image of the processed product, was it used so often as a meal for company?

We began to interview homemakers in depth. One reason so many used the processed product for company was that it was quick and easy to prepare and allowed them to concentrate on other parts of the meal. Probing further, we discovered that despite the "wholesomeness" and "good taste" of the fresh product, there was always the possibility that the product would be too salty. When this happens, the best cook cannot avert a disaster. The processed product was seen as far less salty. The homemaker felt that she could depend on the processed product on this count. We checked back to the large-scale study and discovered that, indeed, the processed product was seen as far less salty.

The seeming paradox was now understandable. While an occasional salty product is all right in the everyday meal situation, the housewife cannot take this chance when cooking for company. This knowledge has been useful in advertising, promotion, and packaging of the product.

In our depth interviewing of housewives, we made a surprising finding: although the company considered its premium product to be in a premium-product category and, indeed, could point to several domestic competitors with products in this category, the vast majority of homemakers were not even aware of this premium domestic category. They knew only that there were domestic and imported products, and they thought that the word "premium" on the package was just puffery. Those in the trade knew about the premium domestic category; it was just the consumers who did not.

(This problem of "noncategory" categories exists in a number of product areas. For example, the Canadian whiskeys were not in the frame of reference of consumers until recently. Seagram's VO was seen simply as a higher-priced blended whiskey by most whiskey drinkers. The recent campaign for the brand, which stresses that Seagram's VO is a Canadian whiskey and that it is imported, may relate to a recent research finding indicating that many drinkers did not know that VO was a Canadian, imported whiskey.)

We were able to show the meat packer the large potential market for its premium product and were able to demonstrate how to market the product because we learned the consumer's frame of reference—through depth research.

To summarize the above case history, housewives could not overtly tell us the full reason why they bought the processed version of the product for special occasions. Marketing research could learn only part of this reason. The processed product's advantages in speed and convenience of preparation were plainly evident; this was certainly a contributing factor toward its purchase. However, to admit that the processed product was safer (never too salty) for guests than the fresh version was something not easy for the housewife to do, assuming she was even aware of this reason, for it detracted from her ability as a cook. Only skilled, in-depth motivation research could unearth this finding.

A surgical supplies case history. In this case, company managers wanted to know the effectiveness of a publication which they distributed mainly to surgeons. They wanted to know if they were spending their money effectively, since it represented a high percentage of the company's marketing dollars. Were surgeons influenced in the company's favor by the publications? An advertising agency had done marketing research on the subject, but only on attitudes; the company wanted to know the effect on sales.

Our first step was to study all the previous research conducted by the company. After completing this step, we still did not feel that we knew enough about the process of purchasing the company's products. We therefore suggested:

1. That we not take it for granted that the surgeon was responsible for the purchase of the company's products (the company was spending three out of four promotional dollars to influence the surgeons).
2. That we do depth interviews before we began closed-ended research.

The company having agreed, we proceeded to conduct depth interviews in hospitals with mainly three groups: surgeons, the purchasing department, and nurses who are operating room supervisors. The early results showed all three groups stating that the surgeons did have the responsibility for naming the brand in the company's main product line, and the surgeon said that he selected his brand on the basis of quality, service, and so forth. However, we noticed that the operating room supervisors appeared to have far more knowedge about the product than did the surgeons, who seemed to be mouthing clichés.

We tried an experiment: we interviewed the surgeons and nurses just after an operation. This broke the study wide open. We found that the doctors almost never knew the brands they had just used, while the nurses quoted chapter and verse about brands. Probing deeper, we found that the surgeons were often not even aware of the brands being used in the hospital, let alone those used during the last operation.

We found that while the surgeon did indeed have responsibility for selecting the brand, he tacitly delegated responsibility to the operating room supervisor, who in most cases picked the brand to be used. The surgeon thought any name brand to be fine, just as a carpenter may feel that any nail is fine. On the other hand, the nurse considered brand selection to be an important decision.

As a result of this study, management reoriented its promotional policy to concentrate on the operating room supervisor rather than the surgeon. The company now directs a publication specifically to these nurses, and its detail men now spend more time with them. The detail men have become enthusiastic about the new approach because they see that as they convince the nurses about their product, sales increase. The change in orientation is currently paying off in increased product sales, since the nurse is the key.

Now, in a later phase of the research, we are quantifying the data and developing a mathematical marketing model of the hospital field for the products of the client.

In summary, had it not been for motivation research, it is doubtful we would have learned that the central figure in choosing surgical-product suppliers is the operating room supervisor. Very capable marketing research had missed this finding.

An industrial purchasing case history. MPI recently completed a study, *Industrial Purchasing Influences: How Industry Buys*, in association with the College of Business Administration, Fairleigh Dickinson University. We analyzed in depth 49 purchases made by 11 large companies in northern New Jersey. This entailed 181 depth interviews, as everyone involved in each purchase studied was interviewed. Three stages of purchasing influence were considered: initiation of the purchase, naming of the supplier pool, and the final choice of supplier.

We found that the influence of top management and the purchasing department had been overstated in previous studies of purchasing influences, while the influence of middle management had been understated. Previous researchers had studied specific purchases in a closed-ended marketing research framework, rather than in the motivation research manner. It had been found that in most companies any relatively big-ticket purchase must have the O.K. of someone in top management. In 16 of the 49 purchases we studied, there was, indeed, an O.K. by top management. However, when we interviewed in depth, we discovered that 15 of the 16 O.K.'s had been "automatic."

One controller told us that if he studied the requisitions which came across his desk, he would have time for nothing else. He took it for granted, he said, that the people responsible for the purchase knew what they were doing. On the other hand, we found in our depth probing that middle management often selects the supplier in a very informal manner—by a telephone call or perhaps a face-to-face mention while handing the requisition to purchasing—and, as a result, this often does not show up in marketing research studies.

We made another finding in this area: almost invariably the person interviewed regarding a purchase placed himself in the center of the situation—as though the purchase revolved around him. This was especially true in interviews of purchasing executives, who are loathe to admit the influence of others. Only by studying all the interviews related to a purchase and returning to those interviewed for in-depth probing could we pinpoint what really led to the purchase.

Previous research in the area of selling to industry contributed in part to certain misinformation suppliers have about who in industry is actually influential in purchasing. In one phase of our investigation, we interviewed every supplier who was considered for the purchases studied, whether or not he was the supplier finally selected. We found that suppliers overstated the influence of top management and the purchasing department and were not aware of the degree of influence of middle management.

The central finding we made in this study indicates the need for motivation research in industrial marketing. We found that companies do not purchase products, *people* do—and that people do not check their emotions at home. We found that the executive who, as a human being, is influenced by many nonrational factors in purchasing his automobile or whiskey is equally influenced when he purchases something for his office or factory.

In summary, then, motivation research unearthed the key finding that much of top management's "influence" in industrial purchases was really nothing more than an automatic, disinterested O.K. Motivation research discovered the central influence of middle management in selecting suppliers. It also showed the possibilities of selling industrial products from a more creative, consumer-oriented frame of reference. Closed-ended marketing research questionnaires, without the use of motivation research, were simply not equipped to learn the whole story.

The toothpaste case history. In studying the marketplace, whenever we see a brand that has dominated for years have its position suddenly threatened by a new brand, we find it useful, as researchers, to investigate this phenomenon. The following case history is an example of just such a phenomenon.

Crest was the first toothpaste to be recognized by the American Dental Association as a caries preventative, and it was highly successful. Prior to this, the brand dominating the toothpaste market was Colgate. We wanted to know why certain people made the switch to Crest and why others remained with Colgate. The existing findings did not seem to provide the answer. Toothpaste research tended to show taste as the key factor. However, this did not explain the precipitous climb in Crest's share of the market after the ADA approval.

Probing, we discovered the motivational key: those who remained with Colgate were in large part people who were more afraid of mouth odor than of the dentist. Colgate had "invented" mouth odor many years ago ("cleans your breath as it cleans your teeth") and, as a result, had retained a dominant share of the toothpaste market for many years—until the ADA approval of Crest. But while many will purchase a product to prevent mouth odor, few will speak about it. This must be learned through expert probing—in a depth interview. Also through depth interviewing we found that many of those who made the switch to Crest were people who either had problems with their teeth or were afraid of the dentist. This constitutes a considerable segment of the population.

To summarize, it is doubtful that in a closed-ended marketing research questionnaire one can be expected to admit being insecure about one's breath. These people may even have been unaware that a chief attraction to Colgate was the product's promise to prevent offensive breath. And Crest users may not have been fully aware of why they used that brand. Without motivation research these findings, which are so central to the marketing of the product, might not have been unearthed.

The expensive wrist watch case history. A client who manufactures expensive watches asked us to find out why fewer expensive watches were being purchased than in former years, when people were considerably less affluent. We asked consumers this question directly, but they could not tell us. All they could say was that they did not especially want to have an expensive watch.

It was not until we asked how many people they knew who owned expensive watches that we began to get to the bottom of the problem. Respondents knew very few, if any, people who owned expensive—or cheap—watches. They did not notice watches. And consumers today tend to purchase expensive products which are noticed, like luxury automobiles, mink coats, or big diamonds.

Until recent years, prior to Timex, an inexpensive watch was believed to be functionally inferior and, therefore, an unwise purchase. For practical purposes then the more expensive watch was the only "worthwhile" watch to buy; but the situation has now changed. (The present success of the relatively high-priced Accutron watch is probably due to its being "different.")

To summarize, the client now had two courses of action, one or both of which he could take. To succeed with an expensive watch, a way would have to be found to make the watch's high cost recognizable to others (as Accutron with its unique identity has done). The other direction was to put a heavier concentration of effort into the low-priced wrist watch market.

Something to be learned from this case history is that people often do not know why they do or do not do something. They do not generally analyze their behavior. Only expert depth probing can get at the "why" of their behavior.

A bourbon case history. Marketing research indicated that bourbon drinkers wanted a "strong and smooth" drink, and a distiller had geared its labels, its advertising, and the strength of its whiskey taste to the study responses. Despite this, sales had declined. Obviously, something was wrong, and we were called in.

Examination of previous sales and earlier approaches to the market provided the first insights into the problem. The pilot-platform interviews substantiated the guess that while bourbon drinkers liked to think of themselves as masculine and therefore enjoying a he-man drink, what they really wanted was a "strong" drinker image with a "smooth" (which really meant "mild") taste image. They wanted to retain the masculine image but enjoy a mild drink. With this knowledge the company regained its sales level and increased its market penetration.

In this case, motivation research was able to learn the true meaning to drinkers of the words "strong" and "smooth." Previous marketing research questionnaires had taken drinkers' responses literally. They assumed that drinkers knew (or if they knew, would admit) what they really wanted in their brand of bourbon.

THE STRUCTURE OF MOTIVATION RESEARCH

The basic motivation study is the key to effective marketing research. However, no information is better than its interpretation.

A motivation study begins with the client's outlining his problem. Then in-depth discussions are held with members of the firm. Later, a detailed and often exhaustive analysis is made of the company's files.

Using previous research. Most companies, inexperienced in motivation research techniques, are completely unaware of the gold mine of information available in their files to a trained motivation researcher. Invoices, product guarantee cards, letters from customers, newspaper clippings, and sales records provide a substantial picture of the firm's marketing program and often will suggest promising leads to the researcher. Previous marketing research studies which have been filed and long since forgotten often can be reinterpreted in the light of additional information and can be an invaluable guide to the new study.

The pilot depth interviews. Having gleaned as much information as possible from within, the researchers then turn to depth interviews to help substantiate or assist in the formulation of a line of questioning. These initial external interviews are called the "pilot platform" phase of the study. This phase generally entails one- to two-hour taped interviews with no less than 20 subjects, who may be consumers, stockholders, salesmen, or purchasing agents, depending on the problem.

The purpose of these interviews is to allow the researcher to get behind the quick answer which often confuses the ordinary marketing research interview. A good depth interview series will provide many insights into the marketing problem. It will enable the researcher to formulate questions for later use that will produce significant answers.

The final depth interviews. Following the first interview stage is the "final platform." Here the insights obtained during the pilot stage are put to the test. Depth interviews of a shorter duration, running perhaps an hour, are established with from 100 to 200 persons. At this point the researcher refines and sharpens the questions that will produce significant answers. These may be as few as 10 or 15. These questions are being framed for the marketing research questionnaire, although the study may be completed at this point—having achieved its purpose.

Sampling. Marketing research is necessary to qualify findings in the marketplace. Thus probability sampling, enabling one to project findings of the sample to the entire market, is necessary in marketing research.

But sampling in motivation research is much different. With a sample of 100 to 200, one hasn't enough for a probability sample. In fact, one cannot "waste" interviews on nonpotential customers. For example, to study a whiskey brand, one would interview a number of users of the brand, some who had left the brand, and some who drink it once in a while. If the brand is losing young drinkers, then one would make sure to interview a number of these. If the problem is regional, then one would interview in both strong and weak areas. The total sample design should find and solve the problem at hand. Findings can then be quantified and validated in the general marketplace in a large-sample marketing research project.

The project team. A psychologist is central to the motivation research project. He must, however, be versed in marketing; then the chances are high he will find realistic solutions to real marketing problems. But the marketing orientation is needed not only by the motivation researcher. The marketing researcher without a marketing orientation is likely to come up with a research design which, however, elegant from an academic point of view, is unlikely to produce the necessary answers for the brand manager. And the mathematician without a marketing orientation will come up with a mathematical marketing model which will work well in a vacuum but not in the marketplace.

From the research company's side, there are other members of the team—statisticians, interviewers, and coders. One generalization we can make is that a simply technique-oriented researcher is not too likely to hit pay dirt, but a problem-oriented one will.

The team must also include members of the client company's management, for at least three reasons:

1. In any project, the first interviews should be held with management. Preliminary insights for the project can be developed from depth interviews of marketing men, store managers, and so forth. For example, in our salesman-selection system we have a research bank of hundreds of questions which have proved successful for certain other companies. We interview sales management to determine which questions are likely to distinguish between potentially good and potentially poor salesmen for their specific company.
2. As the project develops, preliminary insights will develop. Some may be useful, some perhaps impractical. Research must rely on management to keep it on the right track. Management lives the

business every day, and its experience must be used. While we would not expect the management of a client company to be able to conduct a series of skilled depth interviews, neither should they expect research to be as knowledgeable as they are about their own business.

3. Management's involvement with the team is necessary to insure that the results and recommendations are accurately communicated to the company and then used.

There is really only one kind of good research: that which learns, in practical terms, the truth of a situation. Although usually thought of as separate, independent techniques, motivation and marketing research are often inefficient one without the other. The complete approach to attitudinal and behavioral research is a proper blending of the two into a single approach. These two techniques, correctly used, complement rather than conflict with each other.

At MPI we utilize the gamut of research techniques, from the most sophisticated computerized mathematical models to the more conventional marketing research techniques, to the delicate, beneath-the-surface probing of human motivation. We can present equally strong cases for any of these research tools. If we have an "ax to grind" for motivation research, it is because we know it is absolutely necessary to the efficient solution of marketing problems.

SECTION V

INTERNATIONAL MARKETING RESEARCH •

IT BECOMES INCREASINGLY apparent that a considerable portion of American industry's future profit is going to come from international marketing. There is scarcely a major U.S. company today that is not importantly engaged in a search for worldwide markets. Although the vast continents of Asia and Africa still remain relatively untapped, Europe, Canada, Australia, and Japan have become "annexes" of U.S. business.

Despite this historical fact, the entry into a foreign market by a sophisticated U.S. company can often be incredibly naïve. The junkyards of Europe are full of products that never should have been introduced to these markets.

Because of the large investments necessary for expansion into foreign markets, American management has become more cautious about plunging into these markets without knowledge of methods of reaching the consumers. As a result, international research companies specializing in the knowledge of foreign fields are beginning to arise.

The Nielsen Company is, of course, expanding into the European field to give the same kind of information on movement of food and drug products that it provides in the United States. But there is still relatively little information before the fact that can make the difference between introducing an item properly and failing miserably.

Foremost among the companies specializing in the foreign field is International Research Associates. Another leader in this field is the Motivational Research Institution. Almost all U.S. research firms are available to do special studies overseas, and some European marketing research firms are beginning to arise. Advertising agencies abroad, usually subsidized by or affiliated with U.S. agencies, are becoming increasingly adept at research, following practices developed in the United States and Great Britain.

There are also individuals with prior U.S. experience who have become established in various overseas companies and are currently developing consumer information in some quantity. It is essential that an experienced researcher examine and validate these data before they are used as the basis for any substantial decision, however.

An experienced practitioner in the foreign field, Elmo C. Wilson, has provided the chapter for this section. His experiences should be profitable to any American company planning to enter a foreign market.

The problem in the past has been the reluctance of American industry to pay enough money to obtain good research in the foreign field before entering the market. It is strongly recommended that marketing budgets include a substantial amount of money for research before a company enters any country with its U.S. product line.

The sources for research-founded guidance to marketing management do now exist. And it is to be expected that as American business becomes more active in the foreign field, good research will follow that business in proportion to the investment made in each country.

Marketing Research in the International Field •

ELMO C. WILSON

IN THE EARLY 1950's one of the largest manufacturers of processed foods in the United States embarked on a major program of investment overseas. An international division was established and staffed, and the leading seller from the company's broad product line—a "surefire" item—was launched in a European market, using marketing systems which had proved successful in the United States.

Despite tremendous investment, it failed. For four years the new branch hovered on the brink of bankruptcy. A second effort was made with the same product in another country, and the results were virtually identical.

At the top corporate level, serious consideration was given not only to eliminating these two failing companies overseas but also to the elimination of the international division per se. However, it was decided to make one further attempt. A third market was selected for investment; but this time, nearly two years were spent in prior research within that country, probing in detail into every aspect of the marketing problem. Thorough studies of the retail distribution system were made; consumer habits were analyzed; motivational research was employed; the product itself was modified, through a series of careful tests, to achieve maximum appeal to local tastes.

The product was a resounding success. Not only was it successful in this third market; when similar techniques were applied in the first and second areas, the trend was changed there as well. Now, many years later, the product is successful in virtually every market around the globe in which it is manufactured.

It is axiomatic in marketing that the seller must know his buyer. The effectiveness of any marketing program is often in direct relation to the empathy which exists between the marketer and the consumer. This empathy is difficult enough to achieve domestically; with the growth of mass marketing, the personal intimacy that used to exist between an entrepreneur and his customers—the intuitive "feel" that distinguished the successful marketer of only a generation or two ago—has largely disappeared. At the very least, it has had to be buttressed and supplemented by other means—largely by marketing research.

In domestic marketing, however, the gap in understanding that has to be bridged is not nearly so great as it is in the international field. Within the United States, regardless of the region of the country or the type of person, there is a certain community of experience in education, language, cultural heritage, and a multitude of national institutions, which provides a bedrock of shared environment. A marketer in Denver is not that radically different from the consumer of his product in Milwaukee; an advertiser in New York can intuitively feel what at least some of the reactions to his campaign will be in San Francisco and Dallas. And where instinct fails because differences in outlook or habits are too great, there is at least some common ground for understanding them and changing the marketing program to fit.

In international marketing the situation is radically different. There are many superficial problems in conducting overseas business: statistical data may be inaccurate or nonexistent; politics and governmental restrictions may seem to hinder the operations of American companies; laws and the different concepts of law may be strange and unfathomable; language must always be a major obstacle. But more important than any of these, the fundamental problem is the lack of that common background of experience which any domestic marketer shares with his consumer. Without it, the accuracy of any empirical intuitive decision must be questioned.

Bridging these immense gaps in understanding and providing accurate statistics where none have existed before are the vital roles that survey research plays in international marketing. And today, a generation after World War II, the demand for research has grown to such a point that there is virtually no part of the free world in which surveys—indistinguishable from those carried out in the United States—are not conducted.

Twenty years ago it would have been unthinkable to find professional research facilities in almost any area of the globe. Demand and need have brought these facilities into being.

Literally thousands of studies are conducted throughout the free world every year, in markets that range from the most sophisticated to the most backward. Their objectives and their scope vary enormously, but their fundamental purpose is the same: to provide for management the understanding that it must have of the markets in which it operates.

As in the above example of the food manufacturer, research is used more and more to determine the advisability of an investment before it is ever made. And at times research of this type serves a double purpose: it is used not only to permit management to make an accurate decision, but also to elicit permission or concessions from the local government, without which the investment might not be possible.

Such a case recently occurred in Pakistan. A major American petrochemical manufacturer sponsored a study throughout the Indus Valley to determine the advisability of investing in a fertilizer plant—and to demonstrate to the Pakistani Government that the national fertilizer monopoly would need help if the country's agricultural program were to achieve its goals. Thirty-five hundred personal interviews were conducted among Pakistani farmers, covering their planting methods and crop expectations, their attitudes toward change, and the whole complex of behavioral and attitudinal data which a decision of such magnitude required. Today a major fertilizer plant is in successful operation there, with the blessing and support of the Pakistani Government.

Studies to determine the size of a market and its growth trends, the nature and strength of the competition, and the opportunities for entry by a new manufacturer have been conducted by the hundreds. Both consumer and industrial markets have been evaluated, at times under circumstances that skeptics might have believed impossible. (Both usage and attitude studies on sanitary napkins have been conducted in Latin America, for example, although it had been believed that no Latin American woman would discuss problems of feminine hygiene with an interviewer.)

But the evaluation of an initial investment is of course only a first step in the use of research in a foreign market. All of the information which is required domestically is also needed abroad—and frequently more, because of the lack of data from other sources and the gaps in personal knowledge on the part of American management. Product and package testing, advertising pretests and post tests, general marketing studies, store audits and continuing sales measurements, media research, and the great variety of related studies are continually under way around the world.

Often in the less developed countries American marketers find it necessary to begin a research program with a study of fundamentals that would be completely unnecessary in the United States. Surveys to determine the number and types of retail outlets are sometimes needed, as are studies to evaluate the penetration of the major advertising media among different segments of the population. In many countries of Asia, Africa, and Latin America such fundamental data must be developed by the marketer himself. And even where these data are known, the first efforts of the marketer in his own direct behalf are of course focused primarily on the fundamental aspects of the market—the number of consumers, shares of market, usage habits, and the like.

Yet while the newer or less imaginative marketers are concentrating today on fundamentals of this type, others who have been involved in international business for years have moved ahead to more sophisticated requirements. Thus it may be that at the same time one manufacturer is just beginning to determine his market position, another is completing his tenth annual trend study on that subject, having accumulated a research library on virtually every aspect of his marketing program during the ten years.

A major American manufacturer of soft drinks has developed a program of core research which is administered uniformly in more than 30 countries around the world, providing data which are comparable for all countries and which permit the development of standards of comparison that are truly meaningful in an international context. This same program of repetitive fundamental research pinpoints problem areas within a market and permits the application of special research as needed on a country-to-country basis. This company was one of the pioneers in applying research to foreign markets, and its competitors are only now beginning to appreciate the extent of the knowledge gap that they must overcome in order to be able to compete on an equal footing.

The demand for research data has also stimulated the growth of research by those who service the marketer. Primary examples, abroad as at home, are the advertising media. Continuing radio and television rating studies are in operation in most of the sophisticated markets and in many of the less developed ones. Audience surveys for print media have been conducted by both magazines and newspapers in a great many countries. And where the media themselves have failed to provide such data, combinations of marketers have often been formed to sponsor the work that is necessary. The need for the individual marketer to supply such data for himself is becoming less and less each year.

A list of specific services that are available or specific projects that have been conducted would be of little use. More meaningful to management is the fact that some services and facilities exist almost everywhere; and where they do not exist locally—as, for example, in such underdeveloped countries as Paraguay or Sierra Leone—they are available through a growing body of international specialists who may operate from a neigboring country or from a regional headquarters somewhere nearby.

Technique is of course a major factor. Survey research is only as good as the level of technical competence of the personnel involved and the ability of these personnel to apply accurately the tools of research which are required. Great advances have been made in this area as well, as facilities have grown to meet the demand.

Fundamental to good research is the ability to design an accurate sample of the population to be studied—a sample which is accurate within appropriate and known levels of statistical reliability. In a number of key countries outside the United States it is possible to draw samples which are actually both far more reliable and far more efficient in terms of cost than it is possible to obtain within the United States. In Italy, Sweden, Great Britain, and Germany, for example, the governments maintain population rosters which are highly dependable and up to date, so that random samples of individuals may be drawn which are more precise than those based on the probability methods used in this country.

Yet at the other extreme, in the underdeveloped countries, census materials are often either out of date, unreliable, or nonexistent. Research organizations, over the years, have circumvented these problems, either through traditional methods, at great initial cost, or by developing novel but statistically reliable sampling schemes that are peculiarly adapted to the particular circumstances under which the research is to be conducted. In some Latin American countries, for example, survey organizations have spent thousands of dollars compiling data from materials which had been in existence in census bureaus but not tabulated. In others, actual block censuses have been taken in the major cities; in others, aerial photography has been used to pinpoint dwelling units, or to make up maps where none had previously existed. And special systems have been developed to compensate for sampling problems which rarely if ever have to be faced in the more organized societies.

At times the problems involved in achieving an accurate sample are so great that to a casual observer the effort would hardly appear worthwhile. In Bangkok, for example, field teams work for weeks every year mapping by hand the individual dwellings which cluster indiscriminately in random patterns in the poorer sections of town. Yet, as a result of these efforts, it is possible to design a sample in Bangkok with as great precision as in Cincinnati. And, with difference only of detail, the same results are being achieved in Nairobi, Rio de Janeiro, Singapore, Bombay, and dozens of other cities.

The ability to ask questions that are meaningful and to analyze responses accurately is of course just as fundamental to good research as is the sample of people of whom the questions are asked. This involves not only a thorough knowledge of the language, but also an understanding of the people who use it and their culture. Again, the demand for accurate research has caused the creation of facilities to accomplish it. A new generation of competent research technicians has begun to emerge in almost every major country to complement those who pioneered the field in the more sophisticated markets before and just after World War II. It would be deceptive to say that there is a great depth of talent in this field in every country; but the nucleus has been formed and is expanding rapidly, and professional research is available where none was available before.

Questioning techniques which are adapted to local idiosyncrasies have been developed for different areas of the world. In Southeast Asia, for instance, comparative research has found that the use of projective techniques is essential in certain types of research to bypass the tendency of many people to avoid or soften negative or critical remarks. (In India, a respondent will often tell an interviewer to ask the village mayor for information about his personal background—on the grounds that the mayor knows more about it than he does.) In the more backward countries, American-style scaling devices in questionnaires are often useless because the respondents have no concept of the sort of numerical evaluation with which every American school child is familiar. These examples only hint at the full extent of special knowledge which is requisite to the optimum conduct of research in societies which are basically different from the United States.

The rate of expansion of international marketing research will inevitably be attuned, as it has been in the past, to the rate of growth of the world economy. This growth will be fostered and stimulated not only by the foreign aid of the developed countries and the United Nations, but also by the expected rise in trade and investment. According to a study by Booz, Allen & Hamilton, for instance, it is estimated that the sales generated by direct investments of American firms overseas will rise from the recent level of $42 billion per year to approximately $100 billion by 1970. This extremely rapid rate of growth will require an ever increasing amount of highly varied forms of marketing and opinion research—for which the necessary facilities are either in being or in process of creation.

In all of this world trade, American business firms have taken a leading part. Their need for marketing research has been the primary factor in the growth of research facilities. To an extent, their needs have been responsible for the creation of research agencies which operate within the national boundaries of overseas territories and have no ties of any type with American research firms. To an extent, too, their needs have stimulated American research firms to send teams of researchers abroad to conduct specific projects, although the domestic firms may have no overseas branches or affiliates.

More importantly, however, a third type of facility has come into being which has been specifically designed to fulfill the needs of the international marketer whose corporate headquarters are in the United States. This is the international research network based in the United States, which operates overseas through the coordination and supervision of the work of interconnected research agencies that provide the required knowledge of the local market and the local culture. Through this unique type of organization, the direct communication of client and researcher at the directive level is available, and the imposition of high technical standards is insured—without risking the errors that might be incurred from lack of detailed familiarity with local culture and conditions.

The approach that networks of this type have taken in recent years has been to offer considerable flexibility in operational methods, which have been adapted to the varying needs and structures of American firms operating abroad. In some cases, research planning has been basically decentralized, and the local office of the client firm works directly with the local branch of the research network. In other cases, the research is designed and controlled by the U.S. home offices of the client and the research network, working together. Between these two extremes a wide variety of procedures have been developed which are geared to the structure of the client company and its research requirements.

The impact of research on the foreign consumer has not as yet reached the level that has been achieved in the United States, of course—simply because the volume concentration in any single market has not reached the intensity that has been reached in the United States. Yet in specific instances, related to specific marketing areas, the effects of research have been just as profound. Audience measurement techniques, for example, have had as great an effect on radio and television programming in some foreign markets as they have had in the United States. Product design specifications have been adapted to local needs and desires in numerous instances, providing not only greater profits to the marketer, but also greater satisfaction to the consumer. Retailing methods, consumer credit structures, the content of entertainment media, and many other factors have been geared to consumer demands, with much greater accuracy—and much more rapidly—than would ever have been possible without the introduction of American research methods to the foreign scene.

Foreign marketers have not been far behind their American counterparts in adopting these techniques, with the result that competition is more effective and intensive abroad than ever before. In some markets, and in some product areas, local marketers have actually been the first to employ modern research techniques to improve their market positions or to increase the efficiency of their advertising—to the embarrassment, at times, of their American competitors.

The combined research efforts of American firms and foreign businesses make it a virtual certainty that the foreign consumer will find his life affected more and more by the survey method as the years go by.

In highlighting the effects of research on the populations of foreign countries, however, it would be wrong to mention only those commercial surveys which have caused changes in products or marketing procedures. Perhaps the firmest indication of the levels of professionalism which have been achieved abroad, as well as of the acceptance of research in other countries, is the increasing rate at which the survey method is being used by foreign governments. Such research is sometimes for a purely political purpose; but often it is geared to improving the lot of the underprivileged, to correcting social and political evils that have existed for years in many nations.

Perhaps the most dramatic case of government use of survey research abroad occurred some years ago when a political poll averted a revolution. The study took place in a small, politically unstable country, in a highly charged atmosphere of intrigue and potential violence. A special election was to be held to determine the successor to a president who had recently been assassinated. Three candidates were in the field; one, the candidate of the assassinated president's party, which still controlled the Congress; the second, a general in the country's armed forces, who controlled the loyalty of the military; and the third, a candidate whose only claim to importance was the fact that his candidacy would almost surely prevent either of the others from attaining a clear majority of the vote. Under the constitution of that country, if no candidate achieved a majority of the vote, the president would be selected by congress—an assured victory for the government party's candidate. But the military candidate threatened a revolution if he were to obtain a plurality and not be selected by congress. The entire electoral machinery was called into question, and charges and countercharges of rigging the forthcoming election were made.

The two leading candidates, foreseeing the results of their irreconcilable differences, met through intermediaries to arrange a unique solution. Though they mistrusted each other completely, they agreed to call in a survey research firm which was known to and trusted by both. The research firm was called upon to conduct a pre-election poll, the results to be delivered to each candidate on the eve of the election. If the results of the election were generally similar to the results of the poll, each candidate agreed to accept the election as honest. And further, each agreed to resign if the other secured a plurality in the election, certified by the poll.

The study was done on these terms. The full facilities of the government and the military were made available to the research firm, and a whirlwind poll was conducted. The results of the election were within one-half of 1 percent of the results of the poll: no candidate received a majority, but the general secured a clear plurality. The government candidate, who could still have been elected by the congress if he had so chosen, resigned from contention, and the general was elected. It was surely the first time in history that a revolution had been avoided by the application of modern marketing techniques.

While opportunities for revolutionary surveys still arise, it is not likely that this particular need will be fulfilled by foreign research firms with any regularity. But it is symptomatic nonetheless of the strides that have been made abroad in a field which, a generation ago, many believed could never be extended beyond the orderly markets of a few rich nations of the world.

SECTION VI

MANAGEMENT GUIDEPOSTS •

TOO OFTEN MANAGEMENT uses research in an opportunistic manner bordering on the haphazard. The pressure of time—the urgency of introducing a new product—causes hasty improvisation; and hasty research is too often poor research with misleading results. The following section presents some guideposts for advertisers and their agencies in the profitable employment of professional research services. The questions for which management must have answers are:

- How much research should I use?
- Which research company should I use?
- How much time should I allow for research?
- How much should the research cost?

A summation of the practical use of research has been written by an officer of a major advertising agency, whose responsibility it is to make recommendations to a diverse group of clients concerning the above questions. An advertising agency generally counsels its clients on the practical use of marketing research, from establishing the corporate brand image to test marketing new products, packaging them, preparing a test campaign, projecting test-market advertising to national advertising, and, finally, testing copy and maintaining an audit of the success of the product in the marketplace. The suggested guideposts in a systematic approach to research as recommended by Stephens Dietz, executive vice president of Kenyon & Eckhardt, should serve as a working model for marketing research for any product or company.

Modern techniques, including the use of the electronic computer, offer means of integrating and coordinating marketing research data so as to assist management in making decisions such as the choice of the most effective media mix. Herbert W. Robinson, president and chairman of the Council for Economic and Industry Research, points out the importance of management awareness and understanding of how these data can be used and their value determined.

Management has an additional recourse in evaluating the variety of research methodologies and the sources of marketing research data that may be employed in seeking answers to crucial marketing questions. This "final arbiter" for many areas of marketing research, particularly advertising research, is the Advertising Research Foundation, a nonprofit research organization that pools the talents of leading advertiser and agency research executives as well as employing a research staff of its own to counsel and aid management in making sound appraisals. It is fitting and suitable that a "primer" on marketing research for top management should contain a history of the ARF and an outline of the diversity of services which this organization offers within the advertising industry.

The Untapped Power of the Scientific Approach to Marketing Problems •

HERBERT W. ROBINSON

OTHER CHAPTERS OF THIS BOOK make it clear that an ever increasing wealth of data is now being collected on a systematic and regular basis in the field of marketing research. The sheer volume of statistics being produced on all aspects of consumers' behavior and activities is so immense that its intelligent integration and application to concrete marketing problems has become a formidable task. How can we put to work this mass of information, collected at tremendous cost, so as best to achieve the objectives of our particular business?

It may be well at the outset to try to establish what a business is really trying, basically, to accomplish. As chief executive officer of a company I am inclined, myself, to crystallize the main problem into the simple goal of making the greatest possible profit in a certain restricted period of time. In order to accomplish this objective, I have at my disposal the whole array of corporate resources—productive capacity, financial resources, skilled professional and technical labor forces, and, especially important, the ability to launch marketing programs of various types.

When the situation is viewed in this way, it is obvious that my corporate plan must comprise a consistent set of planned activities for each and every department of the company, including the marketing department, dovetailed in such a manner as to produce the greatest profit. The day has passed when I can afford to set a separate independent goal for my marketing department, such as maximum sales or maximum sales per unit of expenditure; quite obviously the marketing activity is only one of the many activities involved in my business, and what I am really seeking is an optimum set of activities, all of which have intricate interconnections. For example, if I have a plant in one location which is underutilized, my marginal profit will be high in that plant and marketing efforts in that particular area will at that point of time be much more valuable than marketing efforts in an area where a plant is already being used to capacity.

Thus it is not enough to leave the marketing executive in a watertight compartment, charged with the vague mission of "marketing the company's products." There have to be intercommunication and interaction among the vice presidents of production, finance, research and development, marketing, and so on; unless we have the cooperation of the departments of the company as a team playing out a particular comprehensive strategy, rather than as separate star players, we cannot possibly get the most out of our corporate resources.

An obvious implication of this way of thinking—a comprehensive total optimization of the profit from all our resources considered simultaneously—is that we need a more scientific approach to the problems of managing the business, and especially to managing the marketing activity. Fortunately, the past 30 years have seen a revolutionary development of analytical techniques with which to tackle this problem and at the same time, by a fortunate coincidence, the development of the electronic computer as a tool with which to put new concepts into practice at reasonable cost. The analytical techniques I am referring to come from a variety of disciplines: mathematics, mathematical statistics, logic, and computer technology. In the field of mathematics, the mathematician has emerged from his ivory tower and has begun to help in the application of mathematical technology to those business problems in which a large number of variables interact in complex ways. Almost a new science of mathematical model building has been evolved, whereby we can take a complex operating problem, identify the variables and interrelationships involved, and then set up a set of mathematical equations which faithfully represent all the quantitative aspects of the problem. It should be noted that I say *quantitative* here, the qualitative aspects being, of course, still entirely the domain of the executive and an area where he alone, thanks to his long experience in the business, can provide the overriding considerations or constraints within which the business must operate. In the case of mathematical statistics, the past 30 years have seen fantastic progress in the development of this technology, to the point where virtually every last ounce of information regarding interrelationships and underlying developments can be squeezed out of the available data by the application of sophisticated mathematical techniques based upon the application of the laws of probability. Moreover, this discipline also enables the mathematical models mentioned earlier to be so structured as to take account of the random fluctuation which arises in practice in most of the variables with which the businessman has to deal.

Finally, only in the past ten years have we seen the development of the computer, with its ability to store, retrieve, and manipulate vast quantities of information and its ability to perform logical and arithmetical operations on the data at speeds of hundreds of thousands per second. It is now a realistic possibility to manipulate and operate upon a vast mass of information at amazingly low cost. The computer, in effect, has given a completely new dimension to the possibilities of managerial analytical work, and unless the executive is able to leap forward in his thinking and fully comprehend the new cost-performance ratio that prevails in the manipulation of masses of data, he cannot fully exploit the fruits of this modern technology to its optimum extent. Unfortunately, few executives have in fact been able to master the essentials of these new techniques and computer hardware to the point where they can say with truth that they know they are applying the latest scientific methods to their problems in an optimum fashion. In other words, there are vast untapped resources of technique and machines now available to tackle the management problem, but the fact of the matter is that few top executives today are properly using the new resources available to them.

Part of the scientific approach, and one of its great assets as a discipline when dealing with complex problems, is to define concepts and measurements with logical precision. And in the field of marketing research the importance of definition is much greater than in many other fields. Frequently, however, the definitions have become blurred by the purposes for which the measurements have been used—or even by the availability of the data themselves—rather than serving as objective, scientific building blocks.

To clarify the problem, let us consider the concept of "potential exposure," the maximum possible number of persons who might conceivably be reached by a particular medium. The "actual exposure" is simply the smaller population of persons actually exposed to the ad in the particular medium. However, if I pick up a newspaper or magazine I am exposed to all its advertising matter, but there is no guarantee that I will even look at the page on which the *XYZ* company has placed its ad. The certainty that the exposure will succeed in attracting some conscious attention on the part of the exposed person will vary from class of media to class of media and from one member of a class of media to another member of the same class. Yet, obviously, we have no chance of achieving actual sales unless we do in fact turn "exposed" persons into "attentive" persons, ready to buy our product or service; and our success here will depend upon:

1. The general "climate" created by the media themselves.
2. The actual content of the ad.
3. The product or service itself.
4. The demographic, social, and economic profile of the person involved.

Obviously, we must be meticulous in our logical reasoning when we put to work the masses of data now available. We must also bear in mind that the data must be clearly labeled as to their definition and scope. And we must be prepared to acknowledge that some of the data we really need may not exist or may have to be developed by various means, either by deduction from data presently being collected or by additional data collection. Unfortunately, past lack of clarity in analysis has resulted in huge gaps in the required data, which are bound to be costly to fill in.

It becomes clear, when we recognize all these facts, that the problem of selecting a media mix which does the best job for our company's profits is, in reality, an extremely complex problem. It requires for its solution not only all the facts about all our company's resources and their interrelationships, but all the relevant facts about media and the people they reach, the people they make attentive, and the people they make ready to buy.

Fortunately, it is possible today, to a quite advanced degree, to formalize the inherent logical problems involved into manageable "mathematical models" and with the aid of large high-speed computers either to simulate the effects of various alternative media strategies or even to evolve an "optimum" strategy. To be practical, however, such models must be fully engineered to fit the company's particular needs, and there must be plenty of room within them to allow for the qualitative judgments experienced executives alone can provide. Likewise, the computers and the elaborate computer programs needed to implement such models as practical tools for the executive are also readily available, though few marketing and advertising specialists are fully aware of their capabilities.

On the other hand, the lack of experience in using such techniques in the past has prevented the development of a complete, consistent, and accurate body of data to support fully the application of these modern analytical techniques. Most of the data being collected are the result of past oversimplified approaches to marketing problems and do not fit well into this new scheme of things. It is clear, however, that as all the parties involved—the advertiser, the advertising agency, the media, and the data researcher—became more indoctrinated and experienced in the scientific approach and demand adequate supporting data, the accuracy and completeness of the data being collected will improve. No doubt expenditures on data research will have to grow markedly, but this should be more than compensated for by the lower cost of achieving the optimum program or by the greater efficacy of a particular level of expenditure on media.

The Art of Using Marketing Research •

STEPHENS DIETZ

MARKETING RESEARCH is a relatively new tool to most companies, since it has achieved acceptance as a major marketing technique only in the post-World War II period. It should therefore be no surprise, nor any discredit to anyone concerned, that today's managers have serious problems in using marketing research services productively in the conduct of their business.

They are not sure that they are using the right amount of research; on the one hand they fear they are buying too much research, and on the other hand they are afraid that they may be overlooking a particularly valuable service a competitor is using. This is their *quantity* problem.

Nor can they find any general agreement on the validity of research techniques; they receive conflicting recommendations and advice from supplier, staff, and agency researchers. This is their *quality* problem.

Nor can they be really sure that they understand the research jargon in which too many research recommendations are phrased. While they, as managers, are decision-oriented, the researchers are technique-oriented; and the combination of different frames of reference and different technical meanings of words is a major barrier to understanding and agreement. This is the *semantics* problem.

The quantity problem. To illustrate the quantity problem, we have listed below some of the research techniques and services available for use in the marketing of a packaged-goods product:

Basic market study.
Concept test.
Motivation studies.
Name test.
Package-design test.

Blind-product test.
Identified-product test.
Advertising-concept test.
Advertising-execution test.
Merchandising-placement test.
Advertising-weight test.
Alternative-media test.
Sales audit.

The problem with this list is how to decide where to start and where to stop. How much research makes sense in a given situation?

The quality problem. In the qualitative area today the manager is confused and befuddled by the conflicting claims made for the value of competitive services. Is eyeball movement a true measure of advertising effectiveness? or Starch readership? or television ratings? or magazine circulation? How valuable is pretesting of advertising copy? Are monadic product tests better than paired comparison tests? Realistically, how valuable is research in the process of selection of a product name or corporate identification symbol? How does the manager with a nonresearch background evaluate the qualitative contribution of competing research services, even with the advice of his own professional technical people?

The semantics problem. And how is the manager going to equip himself to cope with the researchers' technical jargon? Like the members of other professional fields, marketing researchers have a language all their own, and they are—and in most cases justifiably—proud of their special techniques for finding information, for validating their results, and for confirming that they have a technically superior product. But top management does not understand their language, and the researchers make very little effort to translate their services and techniques into terms that management can understand. There is some suspicion that they prefer not to make the effort because they wish to preserve a professional mystique. While this may be partially true, the real fault undoubtedly lies in the difficulty that scientific people have in projecting themselves into the business manager's frame of reference, for professional research people consider themselves to be scientists and not businessmen. The gulf between the two and the lack of understanding can be compared to the gulf between the scientists and the humanists which C. P. Snow commented on so effectively several years ago.

The man who uses marketing research productively in the making of business decisions has somehow learned to cope with these three problem areas. He has learned to select from the many services and techniques available to him those which apply to his problems. While he is alert to new techniques, he has by a process of trial and error found the suppliers and the methods in which he has been able to place confidence. And he has learned how to communicate with research scientists, either by getting his professional advisers to couch their recommendations in business terms or by being able to make the translation for himself.

ESTABLISHING A SYSTEMATIC MARKETING RESEARCH PROGRAM

How has he done this? By establishing a systematic, programmed use of marketing research as a part of his marketing decision-making process. The use of this systematic approach is the basic distinction between the manager who is using research productively and the manager who isn't. The manager who has the most trouble with research usually approaches it on an *ad hoc* basis as an aid to instant decision making and the resolution of arguments in committees.

In some large companies, as a matter of fact, both approaches—the systematic and the *ad hoc*—are in use, with most of the problems being encountered with the *ad hoc* projects.

The first step in establishing a systematic marketing research program is to lay out the frame of reference—draw up a model—of the decision-making process in the area of business activity for which the research program is being set up. Typical areas of activity are: selection and evaluation of advertising campaigns, new product development and introduction, and selection and evaluation of merchandising and promotional devices.

As an illustration, we have traced the process of new product development and introduction in the accompanying chart. Each activity is identified by a line and a number, and the process flows from left to right—starting with activity 1, the decision to embark on the program, and proceeding to activity 35, where the decision is reached on whether or not to expand out of test markets.

The key to the chart is given in the lower left corner. Circled numbers represent activities. The numbers under the line indicate time in weeks. Lines marked by a diamond denote critical path—that is, the longest time required by a single activity in an area. For example, in the first area of the chart, "Category Evaluation to Establish Priorities," the critical path is the line leading to activity 4, described as "Agency isolates consumer characteristics for product categories." This is given a time value of five weeks. Activities 3, 5, and 6 are given time allowances of three, three, and two weeks respectively. But since activity 7 depends on evaluation of 3, 4,

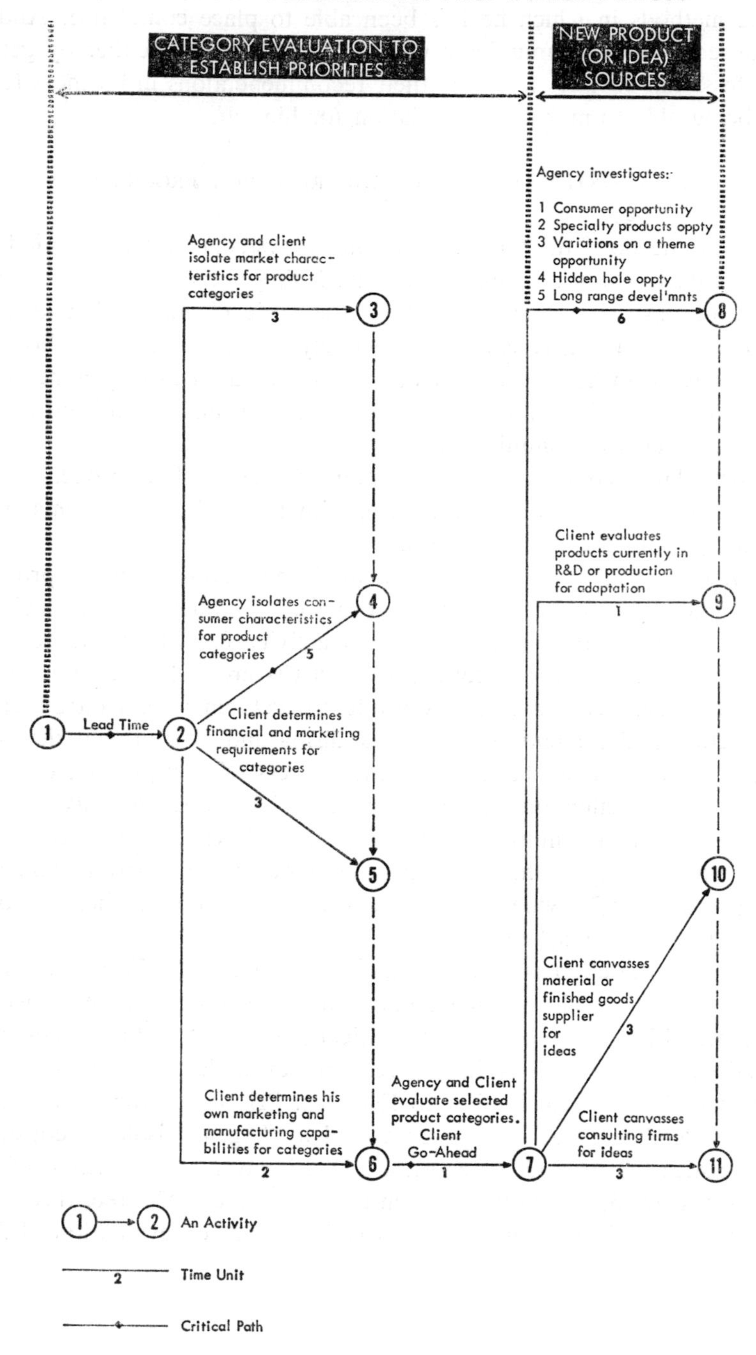
CRITICAL PATH ANALYSIS
NEW PRODUCT DEVELOPMENT AND INTRODUCTION
CATEGORY EVALUATION TO ESTABLISH PRIORITIES
NEW PRODUCT (OR IDEA) SOURCES
Agency investigates:
1 Consumer opportunity
2 Specialty products oppty
3 Variations on a theme opportunity
4 Hidden hole oppty
5 Long range devel'mnts
Agency and client isolate market characteristics for product categories
Agency isolates consumer characteristics for product categories
Client determines financial and marketing requirements for categories
Lead Time
Client evaluates products currently in R&D or production for adaptation
Client canvasses material or finished goods supplier for ideas
Client determines his own marketing and manufacturing capabilities for categories
Agency and Client evaluate selected product categories. Client Go-Ahead
Client canvasses consulting firms for ideas
An Activity
Time Unit
Critical Path

CRITICAL PATH ANALYSIS (CONTINUED)

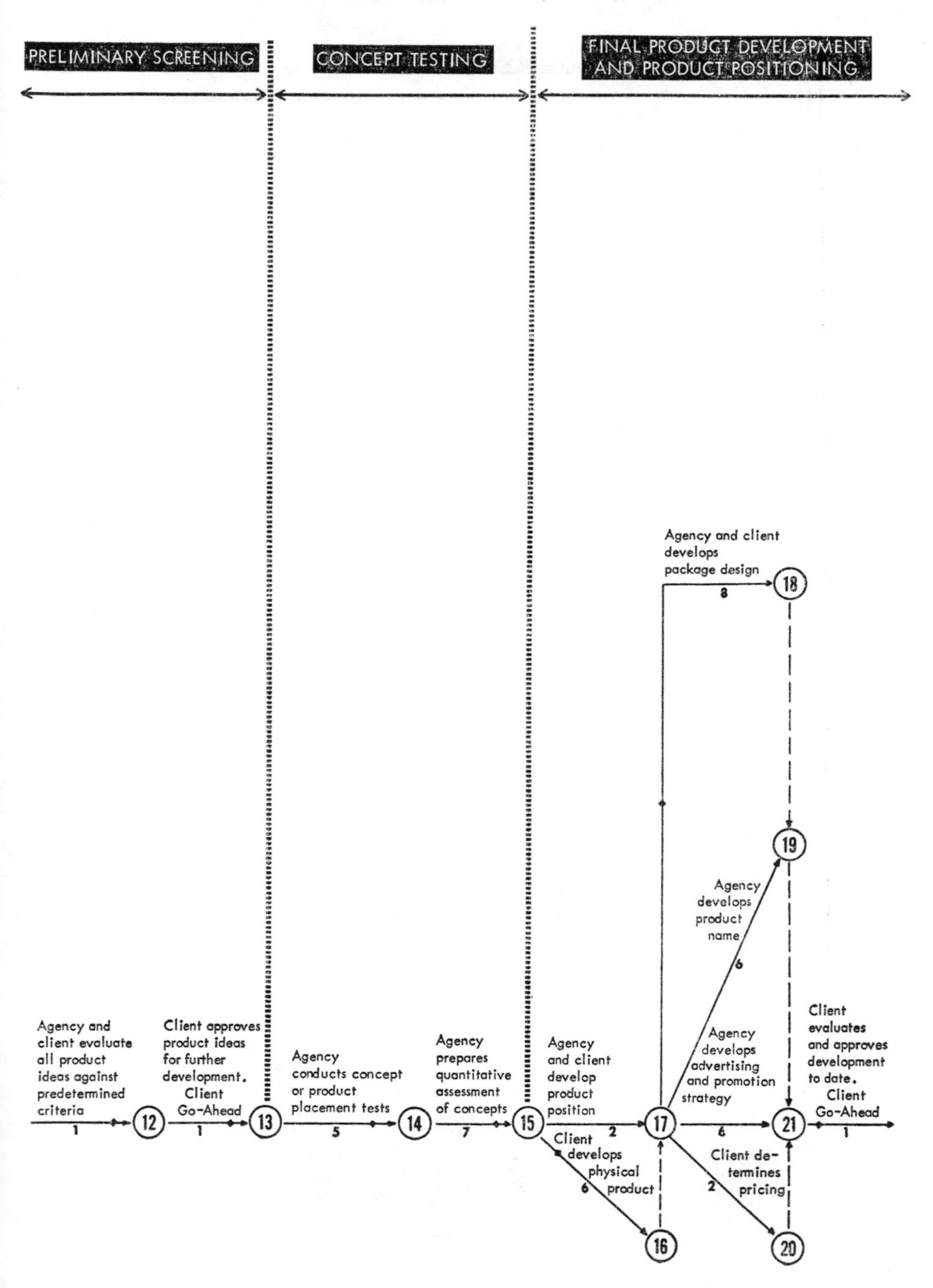

CRITICAL PATH ANALYSIS (CONTINUED)

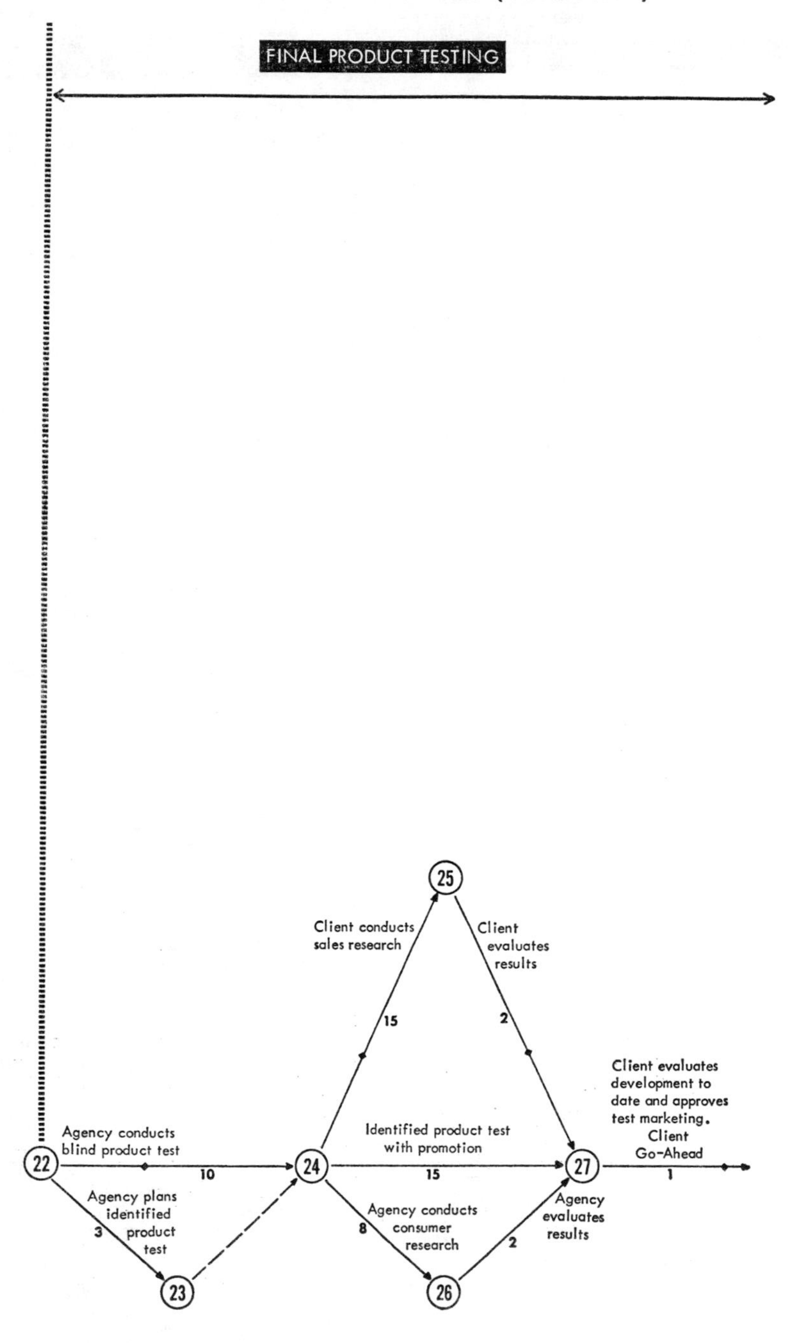

CRITICAL PATH ANALYSIS (CONCLUDED)

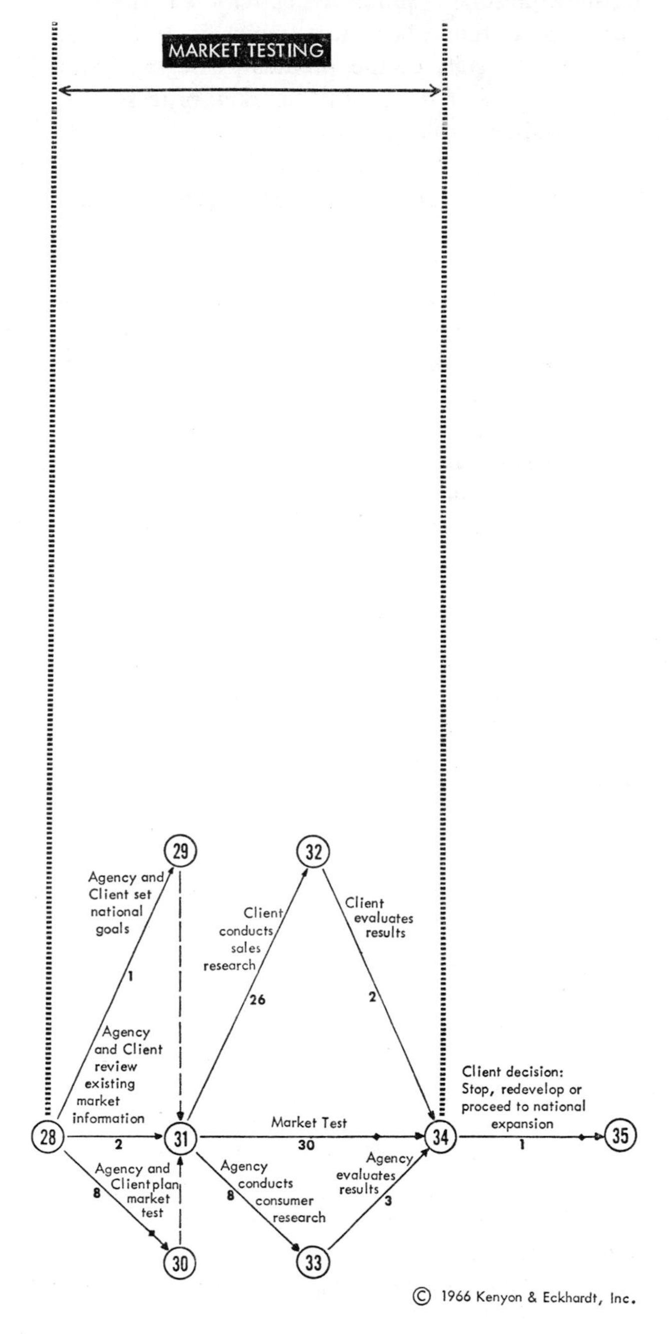

5, and 6 together, the time required for activity 4 is the critical path, and the sum of the critical time allowances, which is 108 weeks, is the total time allowed from the start of the process—category evaluation—to its conclusion, the completion of the test market process.

This process requires a total of two years, almost a year and a half of which precedes actual market testing. Obviously, many factors can change this timetable, but, if anything, it represents somewhat more speed than can normally be expected.

By following the chart from activity 1 through 35, it will be seen that opportunities for marketing research are at numbers 3, 4, 8, 12, 14, 17, 18, 19, 23, 24, 25, 26, 27, 32, 33, and 34. Furthermore, the amount of time allowed for each step is apparent. If this chart is on the wall when the research people come in to talk about the research recommended in developing a new product in the snack food category, for example, the proposal can be weighed in terms of all the decisions it will be necessary to make and it can be evaluated in terms of:

1. Importance—the relative importance of the decision area.
2. Cost—the cost in time and dollars of the project.
3. Validity of technique—what the chances are that the technique being used will yield valid information.

While most packaged-goods marketers place greatest stress on product concept and placement tests and on advertising concept and execution tests, the relative importance of each decision area must be treated as an individual problem in most cases, varying with the product category and, most particularly, the amount at risk.

Evaluating time demands is not too difficult. Research jobs in relatively unimportant areas requiring 12 weeks when only 6 weeks are programmed for the decision area are easily eliminated. But if research in important areas requires one more week than allotted, adjustments can be made at other points on the schedule.

Costs are not so easily evaluated. The best approach to cost control is to budget a total amount for an activity area—for a new product introduction, for example, where an adequate program can range in cost from $50,000 to $100,000. Whatever the budget for the activity, it is given to projects in the order of their estimated importance, and in this way the manager exercises financial control. Admittedly, this is not a satisfactory answer for any one program, because the budget may have been set too high or too low. The only final answer is experience, including mistakes, over a number of programs.

The answer to the quantity problem, then, is the judgmental balancing of time, cost, and importance of alternatives against a program and a budget—and learning from experience through systematic programming and evaluation.

Also, the first step toward solving the quality problem has been taken. For by continuing to operate the same program through time in a number of product introductions, the productivity of research in each of the decision areas can be assessed. Learning which techniques work in a product area and which do not leads to constant discarding of old techniques and trying new ones. The quality problem is solved by a continuing practical testing program.

Good research programs, like good advertising programs, must be tailored specifically to product needs. Many techniques or services that are available simply have little or no value in some situations. For example, one company in the toiletries industry tests television commercials for a new product before it makes the product and doesn't introduce a product until it has a high-scoring commercial. But a cigarette company can find little or no relationship between commercial pretesting results and sales results in the marketplace.

By fitting marketing research projects into a system, the manager has gone a long way toward solving his problems of how much research to do and what techniques to use. And he has the framework for securing constant improvement.

He can also help to overcome his communication problems with the research professionals, because with this approach both he and the researchers are focusing on the results he desires. This means he can put the burden of technique selection on them, where it properly belongs. They must then assume responsibility for the satisfactory performance of the technique selected.

OBSTACLES TO MARKETING RESEARCH EFFECTIVENESS

But while the systematic approach to marketing research is a basic necessity to the productive use of research, by itself it will not guarantee results. Two other ingredients must be added: the right input and the right interpretation.

The input problem has two aspects. The first can be stated by saying that research cannot test something that doesn't exist. So if the purpose in testing products is to develop a marketable product, and if the products being tested are all bad products, all research can do is to prevent one's making a mistake. A corollary is that the better one's business judgment and intuition in selecting alternatives for testing, the more productive the research will be.

The second aspect of the input problem is that the narrower the differences between alternatives, the higher the cost and the lower the probability of finding meaningful distinctions between the alternatives tested. The rule is that the greater the differences between alternatives, the more productive the research dollar becomes.

The problem of interpretation of results is even more critical. One case history will illustrate the point. Macleans toothpaste, introduced in this country in 1962, quickly attained a major market position with advertising promising the benefit of white teeth and emphasizing the tingling taste of Macleans. A competitive dentifrice manufacturer is reported to have asked his research department to use its current techniques and standards to blind-test Macleans and report back to him. The report came back, "Under our procedures we would never introduce this product." Why not? Because Macleans lost the blind test in numbers—more people preferring their current product. But what this company's procedures didn't allow for (and the Beecham Company's procedures did) was the strength of the preference among the smaller number who liked Macleans. There were enough people who liked Macleans very much to justify introducing it and to enable it to build a very satisfactory market position.

It is, therefore, of the utmost importance that research information be properly interpreted and that its interpretation be the responsibility of senior members of the organization. For errors of interpretation can nullify the finest research and can even, as in the case cited above, turn research into a negative influence.

There are several points that are worth remembering when dealing with this problem of interpretation. The first is the all-too-common belief that a bigger number is always better than a smaller one. This is not necessarily so, for there are many cases in marketing where the smaller number points to the opportunity, as in the case of the Macleans blind test. Do not overlook profitable opportunities to sell smaller segments of the market whose needs and desires are quite different from majority needs. Volkswagen and Sara Lee are other cases in point.

Another commonly accepted interpretation is that negative numbers are always bad. Taking as an illustration a hypothetical piece of copy research, the copy research determines that ad *A* is preferable to ad *B* because in some instances ad *B* has a negative effect—it is rejected by some of the prospects for the brand. At this point most advertising managers will reject ad *B;* the numbers clearly show why. And here is the burial ground of some very good advertising campaigns, because it is with advertising as it is with people—if the advertising has a sharp, meaningful, and strong message, it is likely that some people are going to disagree with it violently. If it is a me-too message which has no new content and is full of glittering generalities, it is unlikely that there will be any negative effect on anybody, nor will there be a positive effect. If a negative number in a copy test is registered, it uncovers an area which should be of great interest for further examination and analysis. What is behind the negative should be analyzed before throwing out the idea. Negative numbers can be, in fact, signposts along the road to discovery.

A third barrier to good interpretation is the belief that all differences in numbers are meaningful. This is the area of statistical significance which is little understood and less used. Table after table in audience ratings and in research studies of all kinds show differences in numbers which are not statistically significant. The failure of the people who prepared the reports to state clearly the differences which are significant and of readers of these reports to demand and use this information means that in many cases decisions are made on the basis of meaningless differences, comforted by the support of numbers.

Finally, anyone interpreting a research finding must remember that the information derived was a fact only at a single point of time in the past and that even as he is reading the report the situation is changing. The shift in the marketplace to smaller cars and the long lead time involved in planning a new car were surely major factors in the Edsel failure.

ACHIEVING OPTIMAL RESULTS

It would appear that the basic problem of marketing research is that its techniques and services have expanded more rapidly than management's capacity for harnessing research findings to its decision-making process.

The solution to the problem is no mystery. It is simply the patient application of sound management methods which have solved even more difficult problems. It requires, first, the substitution of the systematic approach for the *ad hoc*—the establishment of a systematic marketing research program tied in to the realities of the decision-making processes. It requires, second, much greater attention to the quality and diversity of the input into the program, for research cannot measure something that doesn't exist, nor can it create good alternatives when only bad ones are tested. And it requires, third, that the interpretation of research findings be placed at a sufficiently high level to assure that the interpreter will have the background and knowledge to make valid interpretations and to command the respect of the line decision makers.

One additional measure is recommended—a periodic audit in which management reviews with the research technicians each research project conducted during the period—its cost, its results, and the decisions based on it. For it is this kind of frequent examination of research programs which will ultimately improve their real productivity.

It seems very clear that learning to use marketing research productively and efficiently can be an even greater competitive weapon in the future than it has been in the past. In fact, the ability to learn the lessons of this book may in some instances make the difference between survival and disappearance in the next decade, a decade which is sure to be noted for both the ferocity and the sophistication of its competition.

The Advertising Research Foundation: Why, How, and for Whom? •

ALCUIN W. LEHMAN

THE ADVERTISING RESEARCH FOUNDATION WAS CREATED in 1936 by the Association of National Advertisers in cooperation with the American Association of Advertising Agencies. Its founders visualized an organization which would be dedicated to increasing the effectiveness of advertising through objective and impartial research. It has not deviated from its original aim to increase the effectiveness of advertising, but has refined its procedure for executing this general objective and has modified its organization to fit the changes that have taken place in the advertising industry since 1936.

A few years after ARF's creation, media organizations began turning to it for help in the conduct of studies that would be impartial but would still reveal the relative values of the media which financed the various studies. From 1938 on, one media group after another sought its help, until by the early 1950's nearly 200 media research surveys costing over $1.5 million had been conducted under ARF's supervision. These surveys supplied research data about newspapers, farm publications, car cards in the United States and Canada, business papers, weekly newspapers, leading Canadian magazines, and executive management publications. (The ensuing reports were published for the benefit of the industry as a whole.)

In addition to those 200 media studies, the Foundation, in its early days, obtained underwriting for *Economic Effects of Advertising,* frequently referred to as the Borden or Harvard study; a report, *Copy Testing,* which was prepared by ARF; a study, *Traffic and Trade;* and *Public Opinion Poll on Certain Phases of Advertising Distribution and the Consumer Movement,* a study designed and conducted under the supervision of Dr. George Gallup.

During that period the Foundation was governed by a bipartite board. The directors were appointed by the AAAA and the ANA. Because of the great interest expressed by media both in having the cooperation of an impartial body representing the buyers of advertising and also in being included in its councils, ARF was converted, late in 1951, into a tripartite organization composed of advertisers, agencies, and media. It was to be governed by a board which would have an equal number of directors drawn from each of the three groups.

Since 1952 over 500 research items pertaining to advertising and marketing problems have been published by or in cooperation with ARF.

With its reconstitution as a tripartite organization, the single general function of the Foundation underwent a process of refinement. Today the objectives of the Foundation are:

1. To further, through the fostering of research, scientific practices in advertising and marketing.
2. To make consultation and advisory facilities available to the industry.
3. To establish research standards, criteria, and reporting methods.
4. To offer consultative and professional guidance in the conduct of research studies of general interest to regular members in cooperation with interested groups.
5. To review and appraise published research.
6. To analyze and evaluate existing research methods and techniques and to define their proper applications and limits of usefulness.
7. To help develop new research techniques.
8. To collect and disseminate advertising and marketing research data and information.

As the ARF program has been broadened on the one hand and made more specific on the other, it has continued to expand the availability of information related not only to basic research problems but also to current day-to-day problems.

To carry out the eight objectives, ARF currently provides its members and the industry with five specific facilities:

1. Consultations.
2. Appraisals.
3. Analyses of syndicated services.

4. Supervised studies.
5. Commentaries on methodological research.

THE ARF CRITERIA

Industry self-regulation almost invariably involves a set of standards. To help accomplish this self-regulation, ARF in 1953 published its *Criteria for Marketing and Advertising Research.* It still serves as the standard for all ARF technical activities. These criteria serve to set standards by which existing research studies may be evaluated and by which future research may be planned. The criteria asked the following questions:

1. Under what conditions was the study made?
2. Has the questionnaire been well designed?
3. Has the interviewing been adequately and reliably done?
4. Has the best sampling plan been followed?
5. Has the sampling plan been fully executed?
6. Is the sample large enough?
7. Was there systematic control of editing, coding, and tabulating?
8. Is the interpretation forthright and logical?

While each question is followed by several specific suggestions, the criteria are still sufficiently general to require interpretation. They are standards which avoid the pitfalls of standardization. Naturally, these interpretations have changed with time and will continue to change with learning.

The criteria are administered by ARF's Technical Committee, which is composed of leading research executives from advertiser, agency, and media firms. The committee is divided into working panels, the number of which varies from time to time, each designed to perform a specific function.

The Technical Committee is ARF's most active body of volunteers. In administering the criteria, it has made its influence felt on many millions of dollars worth of research done in the United States since the criteria booklet was first published. Though only a fraction of all media studies have passed through ARF, most media research expenditures are ARF-influenced. The larger the study, the more likely is the sponsor to seek ARF guidance.

Members of the Technical Committee are not paid for the time and effort they devote to ARF technical services. Their rewards come instead in whatever satisfaction they derive from knowing that a particular study was done better than it would otherwise have been. They also know that as a result of their continuing effort standards for research gradually rise, creating assurance that the advertising dollars are being allocated more rationally today than ever before.

FOUNDATION ACTIVITIES

As mentioned above, ARF offers five principal services. Let us consider each of these functions in some detail.

Consultations. The purpose of ARF's consultation facility is to advance standards in advertising research by helping research sponsors develop more accurate and useful data from their research expenditures. The consulting members of the ARF Technical Committee help to fulfill this purpose by rendering advice emphasizing the viewpoints and needs of users of research data.

Any organization planning a research project may consult with ARF. Media concerns, however, in seeking greater acceptance and use of their research findings, have been the most frequent users of this facility.

During the course of a consultation, before the study is undertaken, the committee advises the study sponsor and the research organization. ARF consultation insures that the study design, questioning technique, sampling plan, and reporting procedures meet established standards. Hence the service helps develop more dependable data from research expenditures.

When a study is completed in accordance with the advice and suggestions of the committee, a statement regarding ARF's participation in the study is issued to the sponsor for inclusion in the printed report. All ARF members automatically receive copies of the report, and the sponsor may distribute them to whomever he wishes.

Appraisals. Appraisals are *post-factum* analyses designed to help members judge the adequacy of research techniques employed in a particular study and determine the dependability of the data collected. These "public" studies are usually sponsored by media. To avoid conflicts of interest, only advertiser and agency members of the Technical Committee serve on the appraisal panel. ARF's *Criteria for Marketing and Advertising Research* serves as the basic guide in the formulation of the panel's opinion about the study.

Any member may request an appraisal, but each request must be approved by the panel and the board before the evaluation is undertaken. This decision is generally based on the study's recency and importance.

In making an appraisal, the panel examines and evaluates the research method and the contents of the published report, together with any additional materials supplied by the sponsor or research firm. An appraisal generally contains a summary of opinion and a description of the study and points out in some detail any instances where the research deviates from the criteria.

Upon completion of an appraisal draft, the committee sends it to the sponsor, who is invited to comment on it. These comments are published in the completed appraisal if the sponsor so desires. With the concurrence of the board, the completed appraisal is published and offered to members for their confidential use.

Analysis of syndicated services. The objective of ARF's analysis of syndicated services is to produce reliable information that will facilitate intelligent decisions on the proper use of such services. A syndicated report or service is one which gathers data or information simultaneously for several or many clients. Any research company may request the Foundation to review its operations, methods, and procedures as related to a report or series of reports which it syndicates.

Because syndicated services differ so markedly from one another in their method of operation as well as in the nature of information they undertake to report, the Foundation does not consider it feasible completely to standardize its procedures for analyzing and reporting upon such services. The general method of operation is to obtain, through the means best suited to the purpose, reliable information about the service's techniques. This includes a review of the survey design and method, an examination of survey materials, a sample check of the data processing, and a review of reporting procedures. Inspection of field work may be included for those services which are being analyzed for the first time; however, an inspection must be made when a service is analyzed for the second time.

This information is analyzed and reported to members together with appropriate comments. To avoid any misunderstanding of the analysis report, ARF also points out those areas in which it has been unable to obtain adequate information to permit the formulation of satisfactory conclusions, the significance of these gaps in information, and, where it seems called for, the reasons why the information was not available.

An analysis need not necessarily contain a single overall evaluation or make any general recommendation for or against use of the service. Rather, it will aim to provide descriptive and analytical information so as to aid members in reaching their own determination concerning the suitability of the service to their own individual purposes.

Since an analysis is undertaken entirely at the volition of a service, the nonexistence of a report on any particular service has neither positive nor negative implications.

The analysis report is copyrighted by ARF. No use of or reference to it may be made without ARF's prior specific approval in writing, other than by distributing it in its entirety and without any change in wording or emphasis. In addition to sending the report to members, ARF makes copies available to the sponsoring service, which has the privilege of distributing complete copies of the report as it sees fit.

Supervised studies. In furthering its stated objectives of promoting greater effectiveness in advertising and marketing through objective and impartial research, ARF is interested in exploring the possibility of supervising any research project which may increase the industry's knowledge of how to make advertising more effective. In a supervised study the Foundation assumes responsibility for the study design, selecting a qualified research organization to conduct any necessary field work, supervising field work, checking tabulations, and publishing the results.

The proposal for supervision of a research project may originate from any source: from an individual, from an organization, or even internally from one of ARF's committees. However, before it is begun, each proposal is approved by the board on the basis of its importance to the industry.

A supervised study may be financed by ARF, by one or more underwriters, or jointly by ARF and others. In the case of total or partial underwriting, charges may be based on either a predetermined price quotation or expenses as incurred. These charges include services contracted for outside ARF and the staff time devoted to the project.

With the approval of the board, ARF appoints a committee to oversee the study. Under the direction of this supervising group, ARF staff is responsible for each step from field work through preparation of tabulations. Generally, the report is drafted by staff members and reviewed by the committee in charge. The report normally includes a description of the problem or problems investigated, a summary of results, supporting data, and a technical appendix containing a full description of the study methodology.

When the draft of the report is approved by the de facto committee supervising the study, it is presented to the board for authorization to publish. It is sent to all ARF members and may, at the discretion of ARF, be made available to interested nonmember parties. All rights in and to the report belong to ARF.

Commentary on methodological research. ARF believes that progress in advertising research can best be made by the development of better research techniques. This development can be aided by the conduct of specific and limited methodological studies, each designed to explore a particular methodological problem. Therefore, ARF is concentrating part of its activity on advising and commenting on methodological studies which are designed to improve techniques and advance the standards of research.

The request for assistance in the conduct of methodological studies may come from any individual or organization planning such research. Each request must be approved by the directors.

In noncompetitive methodological studies it is desirable, but not necessary, that the sponsor comply with ARF's published criteria as they are applied in consultations, appraisals, and supervised studies. However, the commentaries point out those areas where the studies do not comply with the criteria and may express opinions concerning the possible effects of this on the findings. ARF participation does not constitute an endorsement of the techniques utilized.

If a sponsor decides to seek ARF guidance in the conduct of the study, he submits a formal proposal to ARF headquarters, which in turn sends it to the Committee on Improving the Measurements of Advertising (CIMA). The material submitted usually includes a comprehensive review of the study design, including questionnaires, sampling design and procedures, and the proposed method of reporting study results.

For each commentary the extent and nature of the observation of interviewers and field work are determined by the committee. However, such participation is not designed, as it is in a supervised study, to provide detailed supervision or certification of the field work.

After the survey is completed, or parts of it are, the working group in charge reviews the report and prepares the commentary. A statement regarding ARF participation in the study expresses the extent to which ARF participated, points out those areas where the study does not comply with ARF standards, and may express an opinion concerning the result of any deviations.

While this new ARF activity is carried on under the supervision of CIMA, the committee has adopted the policy of appointing working groups to oversee each project. These groups are composed of individuals who are associated with ARF members and who have deep interest or expertise in the area being studied.

General publications. ARF has issued a large number of publications relating to many advertising problems and subjects. The following examples are cited to indicate the catholicity of ARF activities:

The Application of Subliminal Perception in Advertising.

Tachistoscope Tests and Recall and Recognition Techniques in the Study of Memory.

Toward Better Media Comparisons.

The Intelligent Man's Guide to Broadcast Ratings, by Martin Mayer.

The Intelligent Man's Guide to Sales Measures of Advertising, by Martin Mayer.

From time to time the Foundation publishes bibliographies and directories, and it has sponsored the publication of books such as *The Use of Survey Research Findings as Legal Evidence,* by Hiram C. Barksdale (Printers' Ink Books).

These general publications are designed to provide members and others with pertinent reference material in advertising research—authoritative information on the application of different research techniques—and to aid in establishing standards for the conduct of advertising research projects.

Annual conferences. The ARF conference has been held annually in the fall of each year since 1955. Generally a one-day affair, it is a forum open to all. It has become the industry's most important meeting place for the discussion of new advertising research ideas. Each year 12 to 20 papers are given by outstanding experts on a wide variety of subjects. The proceedings are published and sent to members and to those who attended; they are available to others on request.

The Journal of Advertising Research. The *Journal* is edited for the benefit of the users of advertising research as well as for the practitioners. In general, it aspires to provide members and subscribers with more useful research information per unit cost than could be provided by any other procedure or device. It especially seeks to unearth and disseminate information not generally available.

It solicits original papers and prefers to report actual findings whenever possible, although it does from time to time publish theoretical articles. Broadly dedicated to making the measurement of advertising more scientific, it has discussed a wide variety of research methods and topics, such as copy testing, media analysis, experiments in advertising allocation, and the use of Federal statistics in advertising. Not only does the *Journal* have a worldwide circulation, but it regularly receives contributions from many experts located outside the United States. In fact 21 percent of the published articles were written by individuals residing in ten countries: England, France, Germany, Denmark, Norway, Sweden, Italy, Australia, Japan, and India.

The *Journal* is published quarterly. Since its establishment in 1960, each issue has contained about eight articles and from 20 to 25 reviews of books and reports pertaining to advertising research. It is sent free to any individual associated with a member company and is sent to nonmembers who subscribe to it.

SUMMARY AND CONCLUSION

When ARF was created by the two leading advertiser and agency associations, its founders, while feeling the need to learn, through research, how to make their advertising dollars produce more, did approach the task in a rather parochial manner. The sponsoring bodies decided what studies should be undertaken and weighed each project solely from the viewpoint of the needs of advertisers and agencies. They also assumed responsibility for defraying such costs as were not covered by project underwritings or grants.

When ARF was reconstituted in 1951-1952, its board became tripartite, and since that time potential projects have been evaluated in terms of the needs of the advertising industry as a whole. At that time, too, it was decided that basic operating costs should be defrayed by its then 80 dues-paying members, rather than by the founder associations as during the first 15 years of its existence.

Today ARF is supported by about 360 members who pay annual dues of about $250,000. In addition, cooperating organizations pay the Foundation from $100,000 to $175,000 each year to defray the actual cost of such projects as consultations, analyses, supervised studies, and commentaries.

While ARF has a broad program, what activity it engages in is determined primarily by the needs of its members and the industry, rather than by the type of research project that it can "sell." It aims to undertake any type of project that can best be carried on by industry cooperation rather than as a commercial venture. A distinctive feature of ARF is that it is one of the few advertising research organizations that operates on a purely voluntary basis. In that aspect it differs substantially from commercial research companies.

ARF is governed by a board of directors of 26 in all: eight representatives each from advertisers, agencies, and media concerns; and two *ex officio* members, the president and the immediate past chairman. The policies and procedures of the Foundation are established by the board, with the assistance of a large number of volunteers who are members of the following committees: Executive, Policy, Finance, Technical (and several panels thereof), the Committee on Improving the Measurements of Advertising (with a sizable number of working groups), and *ad hoc* committees appointed from time to time. These volunteers are assisted by the technical staff, which serves as the catalyst for all ARF activities. A good portion of staff work is directed toward assisting the committees to enable them to develop projects readily and serve members and the industry efficiently.

Today the ARF horizon is expanding. Its concern with printed media studies will maintain, but new efforts are now being organized into such areas as general field-work audits, available to all suppliers; a new publication designed to communicate significant research developments to marketing and sales management; and new methodological studies designed to throw light on improved copy and media measurements. The Foundation enjoys improved relations with the academic community, which has increased its participation in ARF programs. Significant steps are planned and projects are at all times under way to improve our understanding of how advertising works.

BIOGRAPHIES OF THE CONTRIBUTORS

JOSEPH C. BEVIS, chairman of the board and president of Opinion Research Corporation, Princeton, New Jersey, has devoted his professional life to research. He is currently concerned with projects to aid business executives in making decisions in the fields of marketing, sales, advertising, public relations, and employee relations. Formerly, he did work on population surveys for the Federal Government. In the course of his graduate work, at Northwestern University, Mr. Bevis directed one of the first telephone surveys of radio listening habits ever made.

EMANUEL H. DEMBY and LOUIS COHEN are president and vice president, respectively, of Motivational Programmers, Inc. (MPI), New York, New York. Dr. Demby is senior research consultant to the College of Business Administration, Fairleigh Dickinson University, and director of the college research center. Since 1947 Dr. Demby has participated in well over 1,000 studies, both in the United States and abroad. He was one of the first practitioners in motivational research. Mr. Cohen is instructor in statistics and research on both the graduate and undergraduate levels at Fairleigh Dickinson University. He has participated in and directed over 250 research studies both in the United States and abroad. He has developed a number of research techniques and has pioneered in the application of mathematical marketing models to the solution of business problems.

GEORGE W. DICK is chairman of the board of the American Research Bureau, New York, New York, a subsidiary of C-E-I-R, Inc., a position he has held since May 1966. Prior to that, as president of the Bureau (1964-66), Mr. Dick organized two important advisory panels—one a methodology panel, consisting of some of the world's foremost statisticians and sampling experts, and the other a broadcast industry group, which serves as a two-way communications force in providing proper guidance in the role that audience research plays in the industry.

STEPHENS DIETZ is executive vice president and director of communications services of Kenyon & Eckhardt Inc., New York, New York. He is in charge of the media, research, TV-radio, and merchandising services for all Kenyon & Eckhardt offices and is a member of the executive committee of the agency's board of directors. Mr. Dietz has had broad experience in advertising, as both agency and client executive. He is a member of the A.A.A.A. Committee on Government Relations.

THOMAS A. EHRHART and LOUIS J. BABIC, JR. are partners and founders (in 1958) of Ehrhart-Babic Associates, Inc., New York, New York. The company is now a leading marketing research organization specializing in market sales testing. Together Mr. Ehrhart and Mr. Babic have written an article, "The Use of Latin Square Techniques," for the American Marketing Association and a booklet called "The Prerequisites of Controlled Sales Tests"; they have contributed to articles in *Printers' Ink* and *Advertising Age*. Mr. Ehrhart is active as a guest lecturer at leading universities.

ROD ERICKSON is with Kenyon & Eckhardt Inc., New York, New York, as head of the agency's radio-TV department, a post he has held since April 1966. Prior to that he was executive vice president and member of the board of directors of the American Research Bureau. He was formerly senior vice president in charge of marketing services for Maxon, Inc. (1963-1965); president of Filmways, Inc. (1960-1962); and vice president and general manager of the television department of Young & Rubicam, Inc. (1948-1958).

GEORGE GALLUP, founder and director of the American Institute of Public Opinion, is vice president of Gallup & Robinson, Inc., in Princeton, New Jersey; chairman of the board of The Gallup Organization, Inc.; and president of the International Association of Public Opinion Institutes. He has taught courses in journalism and psychology at several leading universities. Dr. Gallup has received many awards, among them nomination to the Hall of Fame in Distribution (1962), the Advertising Gold Medal sponsored by *Printers' Ink* (1964), the American Marketing Association Parlin Award (1965), and the Wisdom Award (1965). He is the author of many articles on public opinion and advertising research and has published books on widely varied topics.

NORTON GARFINKLE is founder and president of the Brand Rating Research Corporation, New York, New York. Formerly, Mr. Garfinkle was assistant director of research at Doyle, Dane, Bernbach, Inc., and, prior to that, he was a market research group supervisor at Benton & Bowles. Before joining the business community, Mr. Garfinkle taught economics and economic history for four years at Amherst College, and during his teaching years he served as an editor of the *Journal of Economic History*. He has written articles for a number of scholarly journals and has edited a college textbook which is used in universities throughout the country.

EVELYN KONRAD is head of Evelyn Konrad Public Relations, a firm specializing in corporate public relations for service industry. Over the past eight years this firm has represented a broad variety of companies whose services contribute to the marketing mix. Included among the clients have been an industrial design company, innovator of corporate identity programs, new product development, and design efforts and creator of packaging for advertisers in most consumer industries; international and domestic advertisers; major advertising agencies serving blue-chip packaged-goods clients as well as industrial accounts; a media trade association; major media such as TV station group operators and national magazines; station representatives; marketing research firms; and diverse computer service companies.

PETER LANGHOFF is president and chief executive officer of the American Research Bureau, New York, New York (a subsidiary of C-E-I-R, Inc.), a position he has held since May 1966. Prior to that he was with Young & Rubicam, Inc., first as director of research, then as vice president, and finally as senior vice president. Dr. Langhoff is director and chairman of the Advertising Research Foundation. He is former chairman of the A.A.A.A. Committee on Research, past president of the Market Research Council, a former national director of the American Marketing Association, and a former member of the Intensive Review Committee on the Census of the Department of Commerce. He serves as consultant to the Secretary of Defense, the Secretary of the Army, and the Hoover Commission.

ALCUIN W. LEHMAN, retiring president of the Advertising Research Foundation, New York, New York, has been connected with the Foundation for 25 years. He served as technical director for 4 years, as managing director for 16 years, and as president from 1960 to 1966. Following his retirement in May 1966, he was appointed, by unanimous vote of the Foundation's board of directors, as adviser to the president. Mr. Lehman has served as assistant managing director of A.N.A., as technical director and consultant for the Traffic Audit Bureau, and as general manager and president of the Cooperative Analysis of Broadcasting. He was a guest lecturer at the American Press Institute of Columbia University's School of Journalism for five years and is the author of a number of articles on advertising research.

WALTER P. MARGULIES is president of Lippincott & Margulies, Inc., New York, New York. For more than 20 years Mr. Margulies has pioneered new concepts in marketing communications and guided their implementation by a distinguished cross section of corporations, institutions, and government agencies. He has authored numerous articles on the evolution and practices of design/research/marketing techniques. As an industrial designer he is noted for his insistence on total, unified marketing concepts and his frequent disavowals of "design for design's sake" awards.

ARTHUR C. NIELSEN, JR. is president of A. C. Nielsen Company, Chicago, Illinois. Mr. Nielsen has conceived and developed a number of new business services, including the Nielsen Clearing House, which has streamlined the handling of billions of merchandise coupons and other types of consumer promotions. During the past few years, Mr. Nielsen has made a number of trips to Europe, India, the Middle East, and Japan, as a marketing consultant to the United States Government. He has served as a director and officer of the American Marketing Association and the Chicago Association of Commerce and Industry, and he is a director and officer of the U.S. Management Executives Society.

ALFRED POLITZ is chairman of the board, Alfred Politz Research, Inc., New York, New York. Mr. Politz has lectured on consumer research techniques at several leading universities, and he established the first course in probability sampling at New York University. In addition to his academic lectures, Mr. Politz frequently addresses professional groups and is the author of numerous articles. For his contributions to the field of marketing and advertising research, Mr. Politz has received many awards. He was named in 1953 to the Marketing Hall of Fame by the Boston Conference on Distribution, and in 1960 *Media/scope* awarded him its annual award for creativeness. He received the 1963 Annual *Media/scope* Award for Creative Media Research. In 1961 the Syracuse University School of Journalism awarded to "Alfred Politz, Researcher, Author, Scientist" its annual award for Distinguished Service in Advertising.

HERBERT W. ROBINSON is president and chairman of the board of the Council for Economic and Industry Research, Inc. (C-E-I-R, Inc.), New York, New York. He has been senior lecturer in mathematical statistics, economic theory, trade cycle theory, and industrial organization at University College in England and was personal scientific adviser to Prime Minister Churchill. He served as assistant director of programs and planning for the British Ministry of Production; as British staff member of the Combined Production and Resources Board; and as chief of economic analysis for the U.S. Veterans Administration. He was also chief of the Operational Analysis Division of the UNRRA Mission to Poland; staff member, Loan and Economics Department of the International Bank for Reconstruction and Development; and deputy division director, Office of Program and Requirements, Defense Production and Administration. Dr. Robinson has written numerous books and papers on statistics and economics.

He is a fellow of the Association of Incorporated Statisticians and the Royal Statistical Society as well as being an active member of American professional associations.

HORACE S. SCHWERIN is board chairman of Schwerin Research Corporation, New York, New York. The company, which pioneered and is a leader in the testing of broadcast commercials and programs, has become increasingly active in measuring the effectiveness of print advertising and has also entered the field of outdoor advertising research. SRC was founded in 1946, but Mr. Schwerin's own research career dates back prior to World War II, when he was among the first, along with Dr. Paul Lazarsfeld and Dr. Frank Stanton, to study audience reactions to radio. While he was in the Army, his food conservation studies led to savings of $100 million annually and earned him the Legion of Merit with Oak Leaf Cluster.

DANIEL STARCH is founder and chairman of Daniel Starch and Staff, Mamaroneck, New York. His research activities in marketing and advertising go back more than 50 years. Dr. Starch has taught psychology at the University of Wisconsin and at the Harvard University Graduate School of Business Administration. In 1922 he devised the method now widely used for measuring the readership of advertisements and in 1932 inaugurated the continuing project for currently measuring and reporting readership studies. Dr. Starch has written numerous articles for professional and trade periodicals and has authored several widely used books. Among his many honors and awards are the Certificate of Achievement awarded to 100 living graduates of the University of Iowa (1947), the Converse Award in Marketing of the University of Illinois (1951), and nomination to the Boston Distribution Hall of Fame (1954).

RUSSELL S. TATE, JR. is president and chief executive officer of Market Research Corporation of America. He understands the meaning and application of research from the practical standpoint of sales executive, product manager, information analyst, and economist—because he has held each of those positions himself. Before joining MRCA in 1952, Mr. Tate was vice president for sales of the Continental Milk Company. Prior to that he was with Armour & Company. Mr. Tate served on the Board of Economic Warfare and the War Production Board.

ELMO C. WILSON has been president of International Research Associates, Inc. (INRA), since 1948. Prior to that he was director of research of the Columbia Broadcasting System. He was O.W.I. chief of surveys in the European Theater of Operations and also served in the same capacity with the Psychological Warfare Division of SHAEF. Earlier, he taught current history and formation of public opinion at the University of Minnesota. He is past president of the Market Research Council of New York, the American Association for Public Opinion Research, and the International Advertising Association. He is a board member of The Americas Foundation, a trustee of the Institute for American Universities (Aix-en-Provence, France), and a board member of the American Research Bureau and The Roper Public Opinion Research Center. Mr. Wilson is the author of many articles on opinion and marketing research and has collaborated in the writing of two books.